Walking with God in the Classroom

Christian Approaches to Teaching and Learning

Third Edition

Harro Van Brummelen

Walking with God
in the Classroom

Christian Approaches to Teaching and Learning

Harro Van Brummelen

Third Edition

purposeful design®
PUBLICATIONS

Purposeful Design Publications is the publishing division of the Association of Christian Schools International (ACSI) and is committed to the ministry of Christian school education, to enable Christian educators and schools worldwide to effectively prepare students for life. As the publisher of textbooks, trade books, and other educational resources within ACSI, Purposeful Design Publications strives to produce biblically sound materials that reflect Christian scholarship and stewardship and that address the identified needs of Christian schools around the world.

The views expressed in this publication are those of the author, and they may not necessarily represent the position of the Association of Christian Schools International.

Unless otherwise identified, all Scripture quotations are taken from the Holy Bible, NEW INTERNATIONAL VERSION® (NIV®), © 1973, 1978, 1984 by International Bible Society. All rights reserved worldwide.

Printed in the United States of America
14 13 12 11 10 09   2 3 4 5 6 7

Van Brummelen, Harro
Walking with God in the classroom: Christian approaches to teaching and learning

Third edition
ISBN 978-1-58331-098-4 Catalog #6605

Design team: Mike Riester, Julia Evans, Lindsey Shearer
Editorial team: Mary Endres, John Conaway

Purposeful Design Publications
A Division of ACSI
PO Box 65130 • Colorado Springs, CO 80962-5130
Customer Service: 800-367-0798 • www.acsi.org

Contents

Preface

This book deals with Christian approaches to teaching and learning. The Bible has much to say about our view of persons and their relationship to God, to each other, and to God's created reality. It also gives guidelines for nurturing children, guidelines that have implications for the classroom. Yet the Bible is not a sourcebook for specific teaching strategies or discipline procedures, and we should not use it as such. Nevertheless, the Bible, as God's revealed Word, does provide an overall framework for teaching and learning. This book shows how Scripture informs the aims and practices of contemporary schools and teachers.

I do not claim to present *the* Christian approach to teaching and learning. God has created humans in such wondrous ways that no one individual can begin to exhaust the complexities of human learning and classroom teaching. God's Spirit graciously continues to deepen my own understanding, often as a result of the perception of others into the wisdom of Scripture or the wisdom of practice. Besides, students and teachers all differ in personality, learning style, range of abilities, community context, and even tolerance for noise, open-endedness, and tiredness. All these factors influence learning situations.

This book is intended for a fourfold audience. First, it serves as a textbook for courses that introduce teaching and learning to Christian college and university students. Second, prospective and current Christian school teachers can use it to think about what it means to walk with God in their classrooms. I have been gratified that many Christian school staffs have used the first two editions as a discussion guide. Third, the book encourages Christians teaching in public schools to consider how and to what extent they can teach Christianly. Finally, board members and supportive parents may read the book to gain further insight into Christian schooling.

After ten years, a third edition of *Walking with God in the Classroom* was needed. The principles on which I based previous editions have not changed. However, we face new social and educational trends and issues. In this edition, the most significant additions include a much more extensive biblical foundation for student assessment, a new chapter on student diversity, and additional promising practices for Christian teachers in public schools. Most chapters can be read independently. Instructors using the book with university students could, for instance, begin a course with the consideration of chapter 2.

This book would never have become a reality if I had not been part of an encouraging and perceptive Christian education community for many years. The discernment and expertise of numerous leaders and pre-service and in-service teachers deepened and extended my insights. I also owe thanks to many Christian educators throughout the world for giving counsel and advice for previous editions of this book. A few of these I want to mention by name. John Vanderhoek coauthored the original version of chapter 6. Elaine Brouwer, codirector of Alta Vista in Seattle, has made both direct and indirect contributions to improve the manuscript. Students in Christina Belcher's, Steve Bailey's, and Stuart Williams' classes completed a survey about the second edition of the book. I incorporated many of their suggestions. Jill Horsman and Shane Coutlee provided helpful comments about sections relating to Canada's native people. And over the years, my wife, Wilma, has kept me aware of the realities of life in the classroom as she shared her experiences as a superb, sensitive, kindergarten teacher.

I dedicated the first edition of this book to the late Geraldine Steensma. In 1972, as a young teacher unexpectedly thrust into taking on a high school principalship, I was inspired by her incisive little book *To Those Who Teach*. A few years later, we coedited *Shaping School Curriculum: A Biblical View* (1977). I benefited a great deal from her vision, a vision that so obviously stemmed from her love of the Lord and for children. My work continues to reflect some of her basic insights.

Harro Van Brummelen
Trinity Western University
Langley, British Columbia
March, 2008

Part One

The Contours of Schooling and Teaching

Chapters 1 and 2 will help you understand why we have schools and how they function in their communities. You will consider the aims of Christian schooling and then look in more detail at how the Bible informs teaching and learning. You will also examine issues such as these: What personal characteristics do you need to have for successful teaching? How do you set a positive tone for learning in a classroom? What are some ethical and legal aspects of teaching that you need to consider? Teaching is a rewarding calling, especially when your teaching is rooted in love for God and for the students He entrusts to you. These chapters will help you think about the context and purposes of schooling and teaching—understandings that will make you more effective as you guide students in God's truth.

What Is the Nature and Purpose of Schools?

1

Chapter 1 guiding questions

- Why do we have schools?
- What are the aims of teaching and learning?
- How do schools function in their communities?

Ms. Jones starts her eleventh-grade world history class when the bell rings. After quickly reviewing the concepts of the previous day, she continues to present a clear, detailed outline of the causes of World War II using computer slides. The students take careful notes, realizing that they have to "know their stuff" for the weekly quiz. Ms. Jones welcomes questions for clarification. However, little discussion of underlying issues takes place. The students implicitly accept Ms. Jones' interpretations as objective and correct.

Across the hall, in Mr. Wong's classroom, students in the same course rearrange desks into groups representing Germany, Poland, France, England, Russia, and the United States. Final group strategy sessions take place. Students review their research notes. Do they know their assigned roles for the simulation session that will focus on the causes of World War II? They realize that Mr. Wong will evaluate them on clarity and accuracy, the thoroughness of their research, and the force of their arguments, as well as on the contribution each person has made to the group.

Next door, Mrs. Jensen's students come to class well prepared. They have read the textbook section on the causes of World War II. They respect Mrs. Jensen's ability to ask penetrating, thought-provoking questions. They don't want to be embarrassed by not knowing the concepts that form the basis for class discussion. Mrs. Jensen makes students think. She constantly elicits ideas, poses challenges, gives counterexamples, and presents different points of view for them to consider. She forces them to look behind the facts at the motives, the root causes, and the consequences of the actions and decisions of leaders.

Ms. Jones, Mr. Wong, and Mrs. Jensen all believe they are implementing their school's mission statement, its aims, and its social studies goals. They use the same curriculum guide. Yet, if these lessons are typical ones—and always be cautious about drawing such a conclusion!—then each teacher has different implicit beliefs about the nature and purpose of schooling, teaching, and learning. Students in each class experience learning quite differently. They consider the same topics but learn different content. They practice different cognitive skills. They acquire diverse views on how to interpret history. The different classroom structures lead them to develop distinct views about what kind of knowledge is important.

Reflect and respond 1-1

The differences among the three classrooms described raise important questions: What should a history course accomplish? How should we implement it? Assuming that the lessons described are representative ones, outline how Ms. Jones, Mr. Wong, and Mrs. Jensen differ in their views about teaching and learning. Before reading the rest of the chapter, write down what you believe to be the key purposes of schooling and how teachers can attain them.

This chapter presents one possible view of the nature and purpose of teaching and learning in schools. As you read, jot down points that indicate your own view. Doing so will help you develop a statement of your own approach to schooling, teaching, and learning. Remember that this book's aim is to help you walk with God as a classroom teacher in new, responsive, and deeper ways.

Before you read on, you may also want to consider why you are or want to be a teacher. Is it because you enjoy working with children or young people? Is it because you want to make a difference in young people's lives? If it is the latter, what kind of difference? Is it because you enjoy giving leadership to groups of people? Is it because you love a particular school subject and feel that it is important for students? Is it because you are fond of learning and want to share that liking? Is it because you'll have steady work with long vacations? Or is it a combination of these? Be honest with yourself! Then ask, Why should I be a teacher?

I believe that, as much as possible, Christian school teachers should educate children and young adults for a life of responsive discipleship in Jesus Christ. However, like any compact statement, this one leads to many questions. Isn't that true of parental nurture and church education as well? If so, how does the educational role of the school differ from that of the home and the church? What do we mean by "responsive discipleship"? Is this phrase just a platitude, or can it truly enhance what happens in classrooms? Is it meaningful to talk about responsive discipleship when we teach mathematics or Spanish? This chapter begins to discuss these questions. While I focus on Christian schools, I also consider how Christian teachers in public schools can modify this aim.

As a practicing or prospective teacher, you need to define and refine what you believe about the nature and purpose of schooling and about your role as a teacher. Doing this does not guarantee that your teaching will perfectly reflect your views. The interaction between theory and practice is complex. Circumstances sometimes prevent you from fully implementing your views. But having an explicit conception helps you reflect on what happens in your classroom. You can then plan and implement appropriate changes. That process, in turn, will deepen your insight into how you view learning and teaching.

> ### Word alert
>
> A *disciple* is both a student and a follower. So *discipleship* means that a person accepts the way of life that has been taught and demonstrates and applies it in all aspects of her or his life.

Reflect and respond 1-2

Some years ago, I participated in writing *A Vision with a Task* (Stronks and Blomberg 1993). There we described *disciples* of Jesus Christ as persons who acknowledge and trust Christ's trailblazing. They use His power and directives to nurture the potential in themselves, in others, and in the rest of God's creation. They respond to God's calling with wisdom and knowledge, with discernment and creativity, with playfulness and perseverance, and above all with love and compassion.

We also listed three basic characteristics of responsive discipleship. First, we said, it means that schools help to *unwrap students' gifts* so that they use their God-given talents to develop their unique potential (Matthew 25:14–30). Second, students learn to *share one another's joys and burdens*, developing their individuality in order to offer their unique gifts to their neighbors and to society (Romans 12:3–8, 15). Third, schools *promote shalom*, the biblical peace and justice that heals brokenness and restores relationships (Luke 1:50–53). In all these ways, students learn to respond to God's call in obedient and responsible ways.

Consider once again the classrooms of Ms. Jones, Mr. Wong, and Mrs. Jensen. In what ways do they bear out these three characteristics? Can you think of other important elements of *responsive discipleship*? Think of examples of how you could include each component of responsive discipleship in your classroom.

In the first edition of this book, I used the term *responsible discipleship*. Which adjective do you prefer? Or should we use both? Why?

Agencies of Christian nurture and education

The nurture and education of students involve many institutions. The traditional ones are the home, the church, and the school. Today, the media, businesses, community agencies, and sports leagues also play important roles. Neil Postman, for one, has shown how television's emphasis on immediate gratification and quick emotional response can undermine listening and writing skills as well as logical thought. He adds that computers foster self-centeredness and a lack of commitment. Today, Internet-based activities and computer games aggravate those effects. Therefore schools, he claims, must give youth a sense of coherence and meaning (Postman 1993).

As Christians, we rightfully oppose television's superficial hedonism and technology's underlying faith in its ability to provide happiness for all. However, our starting point for thinking about Christian approaches to education must not be reactionary fear. Our positive point of departure is that the key agencies of nurture ought to help children live and become committed to bringing glory to God's name.

The basic agency of Christian nurture is the family. God directs injunctions to nurture children first of all to parents (Deuteronomy 6:6–9, 11:18–21). Paul adds that parents must bring children up "in the training and instruction of the Lord" (Ephesians 6:4). Ideally, children experience and develop their ability to live the Christian life within a secure family environment based on a Christian atmosphere of love, support, and discipline.

How parents or guardians model their convictions and lifestyle is crucial for children. More than anyone else, parents can communicate to their children how the insights gained from an obedient listening to God's Word should govern the Christian life. Most of the home's education is informal. It takes place through daily interaction and discussion, devotions, provision of toys and games and books, sharing chores, going out together, and so on. Children learn most from parental modeling and from the way parents structure everyday family life.

The second agency of Christian nurture is the church. The book of Acts emphasizes the teaching ministry of the church. Both Peter and Paul taught how God works through history and has fulfilled history with the Good News of Jesus Christ. In Corinth and Ephesus, Paul stayed for lengthy periods, teaching people the Word of God (Acts 18:11, 19:10, 20:31). Similarly today, the church must teach young people the Good News and how to take up full responsibility in the fellowship of believers. The teaching function of the church does not stop after conversion or profession of faith. Rather, the church continues to guide people from the more elementary truths of God's Word to its more in-depth implications

(Hebrews 5:12–14). The church's educational programs emphasize what we believe, how we apply our beliefs to life, and how we function as part of God's church.

The injunction to nurture children in the Lord goes beyond the family and the church, however. Both Deuteronomy 6 and Psalm 78 also address the people of Israel collectively. Telling "the next generation the praiseworthy deeds of the Lord, his power, and the wonders he has done" (Psalm 78:4) is a responsibility shared by the whole Christian community. In biblical times, schooling took place within the extended family and, later, in synagogue schools.

Today, society has become so complex that few homes and no regular church education program can provide adequate general education. Besides, society provides few meaningful full-time roles for adolescents and young adults outside formal education. Schools and colleges therefore have become necessary and influential. Indeed, with widespread family breakdown and low church attendance, schools at times take on some roles that used to belong to the family or church.

I am personally convinced that Deuteronomy 6 and Psalm 78 imply that in today's society distinctly Christian schools are desirable, whether they be nonpublic or, as in some Canadian provinces, alternative public schools. The Christian ethos that at one time undergirded North American society has all but disappeared. Yet children must develop thoroughly Christian minds if they are to be ambassadors of Christ in a secular society. That is difficult for the family and the church to accomplish by themselves with so many counteracting influences in society. We shortchange children's nurture in the Lord if their schooling does not openly proclaim that "the heavens declare the glory of God" and that "the precepts of the Lord are right, giving joy to the heart" (Psalm 19:1, 8). At the same time, we need Christian teachers to be salt and light in public schools. If you are or plan to be a public school teacher, you will still, by God's grace, be able to implement much of what this book says about learning and teaching.

The home, the church, and the school ideally form an educational tripod standing firm on the base of the Word of God and the flame of Christ's Spirit. All three need to work together to prepare children for the Christian life. If the school "leg" of the tripod rests on a different base, children will have difficulty staying

> ## Word alert
>
> *Nurturing* children means bringing them up and cultivating their capacities in supportive, encouraging, and compassionate ways. Biblical nurture directs and redirects people to follow God's path of integrity, righteousness, justice, and mercy.
>
> *Educating* students involves deliberately stimulating and developing their perceptions, insights, and abilities. *Schooling* refers to educating students in a formal institution set up for that purpose. Ideally, education and schooling both embrace nurture based on the Great Commandment to love God above all and others as oneself.

in balance as they respond as Christians to the secular world around them. At the same time, the school can replace neither the family nor the church. The home in particular provides an essential base for the school's more formal education task.

Reflect and respond 1-3

Debate the pros and cons of Christian schools. Do so in terms of potential benefits and drawbacks for students and for the Christian community. Under what circumstances would you favor Christian schools? public ones?

The United Nations Universal Declaration of Human Rights says, "Parents have a prior right to choose the kind of education that shall be given to their children" (Article 26.3). Some parents argue that this declaration is meaningless unless all schools receive equal funding from the taxes governments collect from their citizens. Do you agree? Why or why not?

Promoting a vision of the kingdom of God

Almost no schools today function without a mission statement. Such mission statements summarize their central purpose and the type of learning community they want to be.

It is easier to design a mission statement than to ensure that it guides a school's overall program. Nevertheless, mission statements underscore the fact that education is never neutral. Schools give form to concepts and ideas. They shape attitudes, values, and dispositions. They teach about the past, attend to the present, and consider possibilities for the future, both on a personal level and for society (Groome 1980). Schools use basic beliefs about the purpose and meaning of life to set out an overall educational direction. Education is always religious in the sense that it must go forward on the basis of faith commitments and ideals.

As you read the following sample mission statements for a public school and a Christian school, ask yourself in what ways each is grounded in basic beliefs about life:

- *The school will help students acquire knowledge, skills, and attitudes needed to function as respectful and self-directed citizens who contribute to a sustainable economy.*
- *The school will be an encouraging learning community that stimulates its students to be and become followers of Jesus Christ by developing and using their gifts and God-given resources responsibly and creatively to serve God and their neighbors.*

The public school statement emphasizes the importance of preparing students for employment in the marketplace. This is a worthy but limited purpose. The

Christian school statement looks at life much more broadly. Unless you are familiar with the Christian faith, however, you may not understand the meaning of phrases like "followers of Jesus Christ" or "to serve God and their neighbors." Mission statements need to be fleshed out.

An important theme that is central in the teachings of Jesus Christ and that is implicit in the Christian school mission statement is the kingdom of God (which we can think of as the mission of God). The vision of the kingdom of God points Christians not only to the redemption of God's people, but also to the realization of God's intents and promises for His whole creation and for His people (Ridderbos 1962). The kingdom of God is a symbol of God's liberating or re-creating action. The whole of life and reality are to be transformed by God's grace and power. As Brian McLaren puts it,

> His kingdom, then, is a kingdom not of oppressive control but of dreamed-of freedom, not of coercive dominance but of liberating love, not of top-down domination but of bottom-up service, not of a clenched iron fist but of open, wounded hands extended in a welcoming embrace of kindness, gentleness, forgiveness, and grace. (2004, 83)

The fulfillment of the kingdom of God began with the death and resurrection of Jesus Christ. Its final significance will be revealed at Christ's return. The great gift of God is that, despite our shortcomings and sinfulness, the seed of the kingdom is already here. Christian schools may therefore challenge and prepare children to be and become citizens of the kingdom of God. On the one hand, Christ has already established that kingdom. On the other hand, it will not find its ultimate fulfillment in this present life (Luke 4:18–21, 17:20–21; Revelation 21–22).

Helping children become kingdom citizens has a number of educational implications. First, to be part of the kingdom calls for conversion (Matthew 3:2). A school has a much broader educational task than the church. Nevertheless, the Christian school's instruction must proclaim the necessity of heeding God's call to repentance, conversion, and obedience. Personal submission to Jesus Christ as Savior and Lord of creation is a prerequisite for being co-heirs with Christ. Our commitment affects our whole way of life, including our academic endeavors. Christian school attendance can benefit children who are not Christians. However, only those who devote their lives fully to Jesus as Lord will personally grasp the fullness and joy of the responsive discipleship that the school fosters.

Second, kingdom citizens are not only individual imitators of God (Ephesians 5:1) but also members of the Body of Christ (Ephesians 4:1–16). God calls us to use our unique talents in service to the whole Body. Christian schools must be training grounds for such communal action. They must help children be "fellow citizens with God's people and members of God's household ... being built together to become a dwelling in which God lives by his Spirit" (Ephesians 2:19, 22).

Third, kingdom citizens have a mandate: "Go and make disciples of all nations ... teaching them to obey everything I have commanded you" (Matthew 28:19–20). Significantly, this injunction comes at the end of Matthew, the Gospel of the kingdom of God. Christian teachers must study and understand Christ's teachings so that they can apply them in the school situation. They need to develop the implications for various areas of life with their students. They must encourage their students to take up their calling, not just for the future, but for here and now. They must help them to reach out to others whom God similarly calls to obedience. The classroom must be a laboratory for practicing the central love command. Here students learn to accept and use God's gifts of life on earth while at the same time not setting their hearts on earthly treasures. Here students learn what it means to live a life of surrender to God and of love for others. Christ had much concern for the widow and the orphan, the disadvantaged and the oppressed, the hurting and the sick. Promoting righteousness and justice is part of obeying Christ's commands and must be an integral part of schooling.

In the fourth place, kingdom citizens live the fruit of love, service, and truth in response to God's mandate. "All over the world," says Paul, "this gospel is bearing fruit and growing, just as it has been doing among you since the day you heard it and understood God's grace in all its truth" (Colossians 1:6). Being citizens of God's kingdom leads us to doing good and creative works, always striving to be wholly good again (2 Timothy 3:17). The school's educational programs must provide constant opportunities for students to put their faith, their service, their kindness, and their outreach into practice. Furthermore, discipline unto discipleship, also in the school, "produces a harvest of righteousness and peace for those who have been trained by it" (Hebrews 12:11).

Finally, a Christian school itself must be a signpost of God's kingdom to the world. By existing in a secular society and by actively promoting a vision of God's coming kingdom through its programs, the school is a witness to the fact that God is sovereign and that Christ is Redeemer and Lord. A Christian school stands in the community as a monument to the fact that Christ claims *all* of life, including education in the school.

Christian schools and Christian teachers are far from perfect. Sin captures all people to a lesser or greater degree. That is also true in institutions that take hold of God's promises and proclaim a vision of God's kingdom. Yet, God will work in Christian teachers "to will and to act according to his good purpose" so that they may "shine like stars in the universe as [they] hold out the word of life" (Philippians 2:13, 15–16).

Reflect and respond 1-4

Some educators urge Christians not to try to answer whether a school is Christian or not, but rather to find out to what extent it is Christian. In view of God's calling for kingdom citizens, do you agree? Why or why not? Can you see characteristics of public schools that might be termed "Christian"? characteristics of Christian schools that are "secular"?

In the Canadian provinces of Alberta and Saskatchewan, many Christian schools operate as public alternative schools. This means that most costs are paid from general taxation. Fees for parents are low, and therefore many more students can attend. However, some Christian school supporters fear that because these schools have to meet government regulations and conditions, eventually they will no longer be distinctively "Christian." At the same time, public school critics claim that such schools will ghettoize and fragment society. What do you think?

Two classroom examples

Perhaps the last section seemed theologically sound but left you wondering how the concepts would affect what happens in classrooms. Here are two classroom examples:

- *Ms. Kovacs begins her kindergarten year with a unit about creation. On one wall she outlines a large circle divided into four equal parts. She labels the four parts* things, plants, animals, *and* people. *She discusses these four "realms" with her students and asks them to draw pictures for each category. She helps the students paste their pictures in the right quadrants.*

  Ms. Kovacs also has a picture of a huge hand above the circle. "Who looks after our world?" she asks. She elicits from the students that God created and sustains the world, and that God's hand is in control. She stresses that God made people special. They form a separate realm and are not just part of the animal realm. God gave them a special task—to care for the earth and to praise God. The students trace their own hands, cut out the shapes, and paste them between the people "quadrant" and God's hand to symbolize that God has given them, too, a special calling.

  Then Ms. Kovacs asks her students how we can praise God (sing, go to church, pray to God, love others). How can we care for the earth? (look after animals and plants, don't waste food). She explores how God has given us a beautiful creation but that people often mess it up. She then asks the students how they can serve God and neighbor inside the classroom (clean up, obey the teacher, be kind to others). In this way, Ms. Kovacs helps students realize, young as they are, that they can already take up their calling as disciples of Christ in a responsible and responsive way—and thus participate in God's kingdom.

- *Now let's look again at the World War II example at the beginning of this chapter. If we are to promote a vision of the kingdom of God as we teach this topic, we will first ask, "What is God's creation intent for society?" God wants civilization to flourish in a stewardly and peaceful way as humans unfold the possibilities of His creation.*

  We then ask, "What went wrong before and during World War II?" So we explore the motives of the decision makers leading up to and during that war. We trace the sinfulness that led to the incredible destructiveness of the war. We explore how the war affected politicians, soldiers, and innocent bystanders. We are truthful about the inhumanity committed on all sides: the atrocities of the Holocaust, but also, for instance, the forced internment of Japanese Canadians. We review how and why many Christians passively accepted Nazism.

  Next we consider, How can we help to restore, at least in part, God's intent for the world? We see how the theologian Bonhoeffer answered this by considering and writing about the cost of discipleship. He voluntarily returned to Germany to oppose the Nazis—and forfeited his life as a result of an unsuccessful plot to assassinate Hitler. We see how many Dutch Christians risked—and lost—their lives to save Jews from the gas chambers.

  The unit's focus then becomes a responsible Christian attitude to war. Should Christians be pacifists, as is true of the Quakers and Mennonites? If not, when is a war "justifiable"? To ensure that students do not just think that the issues of World War II are only of the distant past, we also discuss questions such as, What role should Western and other nations play in fostering peace around the world? Is it right for Western nations to profit from supplying armaments all over the globe? How can Christians be agents of reconciliation and hope in today's violent society? What do the beatitudes say about our response to conflict? What are some of the biblical principles that guide our actions in conflict situations, whether in school, among friends, in society, or in a war?

Our pedagogy—our teaching and learning strategies—also affects whether or not we promote a vision of the kingdom of God. The Bible does not prescribe specific teaching methods. Indeed, the Bible itself uses a range of strategies. It does emphasize, however, that learners must respond to what they learn in a personal way.

At the start of this chapter, Ms. Jones was well organized. Her students likely did well on their exams. However, did they learn to understand and take up their calling as agents of reconciliation and peace? Mr. Wong's students learned a great deal about positive interaction and cooperation. However, did they apply such learning to the underlying issues we face when dealing with human conflict? Mrs. Jensen's students learned to think clearly and evaluate different perspectives. However, did they grasp what it means to apply the Great Commandment to issues of war and peace?

Given the brief descriptions at the beginning of this chapter, we can only guess at the answers. What is clear, however, is that teachers can use not only choice of content but also teaching and learning strategies to affirm or to detract from promoting a vision for the kingdom of God.

Reflect and respond 1-5

With two or three other persons, brainstorm some ways in which you could promote a vision for the kingdom of God as you present a topic regularly taught in school. How would your ideas affect the way you teach the topic?

The aims of teaching and learning

Schools are for learning. Teaching intends to promote learning, but learning also takes place through experience and individual study. This book deals with the processes of teaching and learning based on biblical views of persons and of knowledge.

Learning and teaching must take place in humble dependence on God: "Trust in the Lord with all your heart and lean not on your own understanding" (Proverbs 3:5). The Christian's starting point is that "the fear of the Lord is a fountain of life" (Proverbs 14:27) as well as the beginning of wisdom and knowledge (Psalm 111:10, Proverbs 1:7). The latter verse adds that all who follow God's precepts have good understanding. Conversely, if we allow God to give us understanding, we will be able to keep His law and obey it with all our heart (Psalm 119:34).

A major aim of Christian teaching and learning is to discover God's laws and apply them in obedient response to God. That may involve using the laws of gravity and wind resistance in building a model airplane. It may mean applying the laws of language creatively in composing a story. Students may investigate how God's laws of justice and righteousness apply to economic life, or what God's law of love and faithfulness implies for personal relationships and for marriage. The key point is that teaching and learning points to God as the Creator and Sustainer of all of reality, including the norms of human life (Job 38–41, Proverbs 3:19–20).

As the sample Christian school mission statement implies, the overall aim of Christian education is to help and guide students be and become responsible and responsive disciples of Jesus Christ. Disciples are followers who grasp the vision of their leader and then apply that vision in their everyday lives. Becoming disciples of Jesus Christ, therefore, involves understanding and committing oneself to Christ and Christ's vision of God's kingdom. Disciples who are responsible begin to carry out the mandate of the kingdom in their lives. For instance, they begin to live as peacemakers and agents of reconciliation. They love the disadvantaged and look for ways to help them. They take joy in practicing moral purity. They eschew love of material possessions and oppose societal structures that exploit. Disciples use their God-given authority to serve others in humility, and they maximize their God-given abilities to serve Him and other people (Matthew 5:8–9, 44; 19:21; 20:1–16, 26–28; 21:12–13; 23:8–12; 25:14–30; 2 Corinthians 5:16–21). In short, disciples learn to walk with God both in their personal lives and in their societal callings.

Word alert

Aims are generally considered broader than *goals*, and goals broader than *objectives*. However, the phrase *intended learning outcomes (ILOs)* has generally replaced *objectives*. Learning outcomes describe what we expect students to learn—and what they can demonstrate they have learned. ILOs are small pieces that contribute to the more general aims.

Our society is selfishly individualistic and ethically relativistic. In that context, responsive discipleship is a radical challenge! It takes a life of personal faith in Christ. It calls for a willingness to build Christian relationships in the community. And it needs pertinent insights, abilities, and dispositions that enable our students to participate in and influence our culture in a God-glorifying way.

Christian schooling intends that students become committed to Christ and to a Christian way of life, willing to serve God and their neighbors. There are at least three parts to this general aim. First, students learn to unfold the basis, framework, and implications of a Christian vision of life. Second, they learn about God's world and how humans have responded to God's mandate to take care of the earth. Third, they develop and responsibly apply the concepts, abilities, values, and creative gifts that enable them to contribute positively to God's kingdom and to society.

Note that these aims include but go well beyond what people often think of as the "basics." Students' fundamental commitments—how they interact with others, what values they put into practice, and how they are disposed to use their God-given abilities—deeply affect the purpose and meaning of their lives. Whether intentionally or not, schools do much more than teach basics. Therefore, we need to consider carefully the aims and related outcomes of schooling.

On the next two pages, I ask you to reflect on and respond to desirable outcomes of Christian schooling. This is an important activity in that it will help you develop a framework for the learning you want to foster in your classroom. If you are or intend to be a teacher in a public school, change the statements so that they are suitable for teaching in that context. As you do so, remember that by law public schools may not promote any particular religion.

Reflect and respond 1-6

Christian schools can advance Christian nurture by implementing one overall aim and three related (but still broad) goals. For each of the latter, I have indicated a number of outcomes that contribute to the broader goal. Assign a numerical value to each outcome from 1 (unimportant) to 10 (essential). You may want to add some other subgoals yourself.

When you have completed the chart, discuss your results with one or two others. After your discussion, you may want to modify your chart. Then use your completed chart as a reference point for developing a set of your own goals and outcomes. Feel free to change the broad aims as well! (If you teach or intend to teach in a public school, revise the statements accordingly.)

I suggest that you keep your set of goals and outcomes, and review it once you have finished reading this book—and perhaps every year or two thereafter. We gain further insights as we journey!

OVERALL AIM: To become committed to Christ and to a Christian way of life, willing to serve God and their neighbors.	SIGNIFICANCE (1–10)
1. To unfold the basis, framework, and implications of a Christian vision of life.	
• Acquire knowledge of the Bible and its basic themes.	
• Understand the Christian faith and its implications.	
• Formulate a Christian worldview as a guide for thought and action.	
• Compare and contrast a biblical worldview with others in order to understand the motivating ideas and spirit of the times and their effects on life in society and on cultural formation.	
• Understand, experience, and exercise biblical mandates such as the Creation Mandate, the Great Commandment, and the Great Commission.	
• Grow spiritually by committing oneself to God, appreciating and applying the essentials of the Christian faith.	
• Discern the influence of Judeo-Christian morals and values on our cultural heritage.	
• Grow in a lifestyle of being conformed to the image of Jesus Christ, becoming disposed (1) to act on the basis of biblical principles for ethical, social, and economic responsibility and (2) to serve others willingly and unselfishly.	
• Understand how sin results in problems such as injustice and violence, and strive for reconciliation with God, self, others, and the world.	
• Realize the vital role of the family, church, community, and nation, and know and exercise the privileges and responsibilities of belonging to them.	
•	
•	
2. To learn about God's world and how humans have responded to God's mandate to take care of the earth.	
• Understand the concepts of number and space, and the orderly laws governing them, and use those concepts and laws to solve everyday problems.	
• Understand and apply the fundamental concepts, structures, and theories of physical things, both living and nonliving, and recognize the impact of science and technology on life in society.	
• Understand the interrelations between people and their environment and how to use and enjoy resources prudently.	

• Know the practices that constitute a healthy lifestyle.	
• Become aware of and experience various forms of aesthetic expression.	
• Use language to clarify thought, to develop perception and insight, and to serve God and others through edifying and creative communication.	
• Appreciate the role of humans in shaping culture, including social, economic, and political structures.	
• Recognize how Christians can be involved in humanitarian service regardless of ethnic, cultural, social, or religious background.	
• Value the essential role of government and law in human affairs, and learn what it means to be a responsible citizen.	
• Clarify basic moral and value precepts and their role in human life.	
•	
•	
3. To develop and apply the concepts, abilities, and creative gifts that enable humans to contribute positively to God's kingdom and to society.	
• Become proficient in using the concepts, processes, and skills of language and literacy, science, mathematics, physical movement, and aesthetics.	
• Extend analytic thinking skills: reflective and critical reasoning; decision making; synthesis, analysis, and evaluation; etc.	
• Develop sound research skills.	
• Acquire social and emotional skills and attitudes for participating responsibly in group situations.	
• Unfold special talents and learn to cope with weaknesses.	
• Share knowledge and gifts with others.	
•	
•	

A biblical worldview and knowledge

A basic question for Christian educators is, What is God's way for today? In school, students need to encounter the contours of a biblical worldview and to understand in a deeper way each year its relevance for living in today's society. Teachers help students extend their awareness that the whole world is God's creation. Then they help students explore how sin often undermines God's intent for the world.

Teachers also help students recognize that they have a special task in God's reality, a task made possible through Christ's redemption. Christian teachers need to be honest about the fact that Christians often disagree about how to apply biblical norms—to politics and economics, for instance. At higher grade levels, teachers must also ensure that their students learn to see truth more clearly as they become familiar with views that differ from Christian ones. Christians often learn much from persons who are not Christians.

In all this, Scripture gives us many clear directives, and Scripture must be our final point of reference. Kindergarten children can already understand that God created them as beings with the special calling to give Him glory through all of life. Primary pupils can see how God ordained families with mothers, fathers, and children to be the basic building blocks of society, even if our families often fall short of that ideal. In science, students can learn how they can care for God's marvelous creation in trustworthy ways. They can explore a Christian vision of life and reality, and a biblical lifestyle based on the mandates of God's Word.

Schools are academic institutions; they are concerned with "knowledge-that" (concepts and cognitive content) and "knowledge-how" (abilities and skills). But we as Christians must choose concepts and skills as means to an end, not as ends in themselves. Does our content point to the marvelous deeds and power of the Lord and His grace in Jesus Christ? Does it show how God has created a world that we may care for? Does it help students see how God calls them to service—both personally and as part of Christ's Body—in social relationships, in the world of commerce and industry, in political life, in cultural pursuits? Do our schools develop our students' abilities to enjoy, use, and shape God's world?

As we plan for learning, we develop "knowledge-that" and "knowledge-how" outcomes. But we also include related "knowledge-why" and "knowledge-with" outcomes that are rooted in biblical mandates. God's Creation Mandate (Genesis 1:28, 2:15) bids us to take care of the earth in stewardly ways as we unfold its potential. His Great Commandment (Matthew 22:37–40) directs us to love God and all His creatures who stand in relationship to us. Christ's Great Commission (Matthew 28:18–29) enjoins us to teach our students everything Jesus commanded us. Jesus calls us blessed, for instance, if we are meek, merciful, pure in heart, or peacemakers (Matthew 5:1–12). So "knowledge-why" teaches about our ultimate purpose and values. "Knowledge-with" enables us to relate to others in community.

Ultimately, all knowledge, including knowledge of a biblical worldview, is in vain unless through the Holy Spirit our students accept Christ's grace. Therefore, teachers invite students to commit their whole lives—their thoughts, words, and deeds—to Christ as their personal Redeemer and Lord of life. They encourage students to make a personal commitment to God and to a Christian way of life.

To encourage such a commitment, schools need to do more than proclaim a Christian vision of life. Christ modeled what He taught, and He called for meaningful response. For instance, He modeled Christian service and humility by washing His disciples' feet. He sent out His twelve disciples long before we would have considered them ready. He told the rich young man to sell his possessions and give to the poor if he was truly interested in following Jesus—and lived with few possessions Himself. Fostering biblical dispositions and attitudes requires more than formal teaching. It requires teachers to model a Christian vision of life and requires students to experience that vision in all aspects of the learning situation. Students need to practice values and dispositions in harmony with biblical guidelines.

Word alert

Knowledge-that depicts what we grasp and understand. *Knowledge-how* consists of our skills and abilities. *Knowledge-why* refers to the beliefs and values that guide our attitudes, dispositions, and actions. *Knowledge-with* helps us form healthy relationships. A balanced curriculum takes all four into consideration.

Knowledge, in other words, involves much more than intellectual comprehension and analysis. It must result in committed response and action. Teachers strive to be servant leaders and models. They help students use their unique gifts to complete products that are personally meaningful. They encourage students to make judgments and decisions within a biblical framework. They give students space to become responsible and to learn from failures. They help students to show love for God and neighbor through community-oriented activities both within the school and outside. Their students not only see but also experience what it means to walk with God in all their activities.

Reflect and respond 1-7

A paragraph in this section claims that schools are academic institutions. However, don't the questions in that paragraph also apply to the education of children in the home, in the church, and in some community organizations? If so, can you distinguish among their respective educational roles? What are the specific educational tasks of each? Under what circumstances, if any, can parents adequately attain the tasks usually assigned to the school by homeschooling their children?

Realizing the aims: Learning about First Nations people

Many sets of goals exist for both Christian and public schooling. It is one thing to write an inspiring set of goals. It is quite another, however, to design and implement a set of learning experiences likely to attain those goals. Below is an example of a classroom unit that tries to do so (with thanks to Wilma Hettinga, Judy Newland, and Jill Horsman):

Mrs. Neufeld teaches a unit about First Nations people to her fourth-grade class. She wants to instill an appreciation of North American aboriginal cultures. More than that, she wants her students to see, in concrete ways, that worldviews affect cultures and their ways of life. Her class will explore characteristics of First Nations cultures. They will study mythology and religion, family composition, resource stewardship, aesthetic expression, and interaction for learning and work. Her students will also investigate how the relations between First Nations and Europeans have affected the First Nations way of life, often in detrimental ways. Her students will consider how diverse cultures can live and interact responsibly in our world, enriching one another. What does it mean to show Christian justice and compassion? How do all cultures benefit from repentance and faith?

In the section on the Haida First Nations on Gwaii Haanas (Queen Charlotte Islands), Mrs. Neufeld's students explore Haida culture both before and after the arrival of Europeans. She bases the first activities on her students' experiential knowledge of British Columbia's rain forests: the climate, the vegetation, the types of animals—the resources the Haidas could use. Each child draws a map and makes a brief, illustrated report that contributes to a mural on the Haida rain forest. Next, Mrs. Neufeld has her class study Haida village and family life, the nature and reasons for the potlatch, and Haida religion and legends. She discusses how the Haida's societal and political structures rivaled those of other highly developed cultures. The students read and discuss, and then they write stories, poems, and legends for their Haida "book." The class builds a model Haida village and creates some Haida-style artwork. The students examine masks and totem poles, view a video of an elder describing a potlatch, simulate an extended family as well as a chief-and-council meeting, and prepare Haida food. Mrs. Neufeld then charts the changes in Haida culture after the arrival of Europeans, including recent efforts to restore the culture.

The students learn many concepts and develop many abilities in this unit. They learn to appreciate how the Haidas used the diverse God-given resources to develop a unified way of life. As they hone their insights, they also develop further skills in reading, writing, drawing inferences, map reading, research, art, and so on.

Mrs. Neufeld does not include an activity just because it happens to be interesting. Rather, each activity contributes to the overall goal of understanding how beliefs structure a way of life. Some activities are highly structured and teacher-centered. Others allow for a great deal of latitude and personal response in creating unique products. Still others require students to plan and work together in groups.

Mrs. Neufeld carefully leads the activities in this section to a concluding one. The class develops a large chart contrasting the materialistic Western way of life with the Haida one. The students suggest competition for the first column, cooperation for the second. Becoming rich is contrasted with sharing, as is the nuclear family with the extended one. Mrs. Neufeld elicits from the students that First Nations cultures often reflect a more biblical worldview than Western cultures. For instance, the First Nations cultures are collaborative and relational rather than individualistic and materialistic. She then asks students to complete a third column: a Christian way of life. What does a Christian lifestyle entail?

After completing the chart, Mrs. Neufeld discusses how the Haidas recognized some important values that God put into the creation order. However, she also points out that the knowledge of Christ as Savior and Lord had not yet been revealed to them. She also discusses how people in European communities, although they may have a Christian background, often show little love for God and neighbor.

Mrs. Neufeld feels, however, that the Haidas are still too much of a "foreign" culture. None of her students have visited Gwaii Haanas or met any Haidas. The next part of her unit, therefore, is the study of a local First Nations band. She stresses how aspects of European culture have influenced the band: the fur trade, the establishment of reserves, outbreaks of diseases such as smallpox, the influence of missionaries, and schooling for First Nations children. Her students pretend to be among the first European people having contact with the band, and they discuss how they might have done certain things differently and shown godly respect for people who are also created in the image of God.

Mrs. Neufeld then takes her class to visit the band reserve. The students have prepared questions for the chief. What are some of the projects your band has initiated? What are your schools like? What changes would you like to see in your community? How does your cultural background make your community distinctive? Why are treaties important to you? How would you like to govern yourselves, and why?

After the students write a report on their visit, Mrs. Neufeld concludes the unit by asking the students, How is the cultural background of these First Nations people both the same as and different from yours? What can you learn from these First Nations cultures? What things do they display and value that should be part of our own way of life? What does it mean to love our neighbors as ourselves when we interact with different cultures?

Reflect and respond 1-8

Discuss in what ways Mrs. Neufeld has met this chapter's aims of schooling. Are there any ways in which she falls short? Then look at the personal set of aims you are developing. How would you change Mrs. Neufeld's unit in order to attain your aims? What are some specific intended learning outcomes of this unit in each of the cognitive, ability, and value categories? How would a teacher assess whether students have attained those outcomes?

Schools as social institutions

Schools are educational institutions that, in the first place, focus on attaining educational aims. Some activities are better done by families or other agencies. Schools need to avoid spreading themselves so thin that they fail to accomplish their educational goals. Teachers and parents should cooperate but should recognize their respective, distinct tasks in nurturing children. Schools educate students by planning and implementing structured learning activities.

Nevertheless, society does implicitly assign roles other than strictly academic ones to schools. Schools are prime agencies of socialization. For twelve or thirteen years, students spend one quarter of their waking hours in school. There, they learn to interact with others according to certain behavior standards and patterns. Students see schools as places for social activities that range from forming friendships to being bullied. Parents know intuitively that schools have a big impact on their children's social and emotional growth.

Therefore, schools attempt to be supportive learning communities in which all students are able to contribute and to feel accepted. Schools appreciate all students for their unique gifts and contributions. Students learn to cooperate, not just to compete, with a goal of "beating" someone else. A balance of individual, small-group, and large-group activities helps students use their talents to contribute to the community in different ways. Students learn to serve one another. Schools may engage them, for instance, in peer tutoring or in planning projects and assemblies.

In effective schools—Christian and public alike—the school board, the principal and teachers, and the parents and students cooperate to implement a common mission and vision. Effective schools maintain close contact between teachers and parents. They involve parents as volunteers. They establish new policies and programs collaboratively. Schools need to exist and work within a supportive community in order to attain their goals.

Within a few months of opening, a public school in my neighborhood had gained a reputation for being an excellent school. My neighbors soon tried to transfer their children into that school. How had this come about? First, the principal was able to choose a team of teachers with similar views on education, willing to work together in a united and positive way. Next, he involved parents on advisory committees to develop policies and recommend programs. He held a number of public meetings in which he solicited input on how the school could best serve the community. He also required the teachers to hand in unit plans for every topic—and to discuss those plans with him before teaching the unit. His leadership was servant leadership. He had clear goals for the school, but he involved the teachers, parents, and students in ways that made a difference in how the school implemented its programs. He served the community by providing excellent programs for the type of schooling that the school and the community had jointly planned.

Reflect and respond 1-9

Many students coming to school today have dysfunctional backgrounds and do not function well in social settings. Research suggests that kindergarten and the first two grades are crucial in turning this situation around. It's in those early years that children need help in feeling accepted, in relating positively to their classmates and teacher, and in learning to contribute to the classroom community. In kindergarten, they learn much of this kind of knowledge through structured play activities. Yet the trend today is toward more individual student work on the "basics" in kindergarten. What is more important at this level, social/emotional development or academic achievement? Is it possible to combine the two? If so, how?

Christian schools and their communities

Christian schools are organized in different ways. Some are operated by transdenominational organizations of parents. Within this structure, parents themselves make key decisions through an elected board and an appointed education committee. The parents are directly involved with the educational environment of their children. However, within this structure it may be difficult to maintain a clear sense of direction, despite well-defined statements of mission and aims. To sustain the school's purpose, many schools that are organized in this way hold orientation meetings that parents new to the community are required to attend before they can become involved in governing the school.

Other Christian schools are ministries of particular churches. Such schools often have a clear theological basis and educational direction. However, tensions may arise between the church and school administrations, especially about ultimate responsibility and finances. Further, some church members may wrongly assume that the Christian school is an extension of the church's educational program. Yet the school's education, while biblically based, plunges students into a broad study of all aspects of God's world.

Still other Christian schools have self-perpetuating governing boards. These maintain a clear direction but limit the role and involvement of parents in governing the school. Parents can exercise their responsibility by choosing the particular school for their children. They may serve on advisory committees, but they do not have the final say in setting the school's direction and policies.

The Bible does not specify any particular form of organization for Christian schools. However, it does indicate that parents have the primary responsibility for their children's education. Therefore, any organizational structure should allow for meaningful parental input into school policies and practices.

Christian schools in my surroundings attract all but the highest and lowest social classes—those with mean family incomes close to their public school counterparts. Family life is somewhat more stable than in society in general, even though the number of single parents has increased substantially over the past decades. Of course, the prevailing mindset of society influences Christians. Individualism and hedonism also affect Christian school students, and Christian schools are far from perfect communities. Also, some parents send children to Christian schools because they have not done well in other schools. Nevertheless, overall, Christian schools have a relatively united and supportive parent community.

This milieu helps Christian schools focus on their educational goals. There is a danger, however, that such schools might become hothouse shelters for the middle class. This is especially true since Christians in the Western world all too often are at ease with today's materialism. Therefore, schools may need to plan socialization experiences that help students relate to the poor and underprivileged in society in the way Christ commands. They must also help students reject the values and patterns of secular culture. The extent to which Christian schools prepare their students to raise signposts and to be signposts for the coming of God's kingdom remains an open question. There is no question, however, that God calls them to do so.

Reflect and respond 1-10

Find out how parents in the schools in your community are involved in the schools. What roles do parents take on in Christian schools operated by parent organizations? by churches? by self-perpetuating boards? by public school boards? Do parents play an important part in setting school aims and policies?

As children's primary caregivers, parents have the right and the responsibility to choose where and how their children are schooled (until students reach a certain age of discretion). Schooling, however, is a shared commitment. Teachers make many professional judgments. Society legitimately expects schools to empower students to function effectively in their communities. Governments set appropriate basic standards. Describe and give examples of how each of these stakeholders affects schooling. How could each overstep its role and infringe on the responsibilities of other stakeholders?

Public schools and their communities

In most jurisdictions, citizens elect school board members to operate public schools. While the powers of such school boards vary considerably, there has been a trend to involve parents more meaningfully in local schools. Often, parent advisory councils advise the principal and staff on school policies and programs.

Public schools serve all sectors of the community. Most often, they serve a local geographical community. However, many communities also have publicly funded special and charter schools that implement particular programs. My local community has schools emphasizing the fine arts and immersion in French and Japanese, for instance. The local neighborhood school often serves a fairly homogeneous socioeconomic group, but the values and beliefs of parents usually differ considerably. The strength of such a school is also its weakness. It helps people of many different religious and ethnic backgrounds learn from and about one another. However, this diversity also makes it difficult to establish and implement a common vision that goes beyond educational platitudes.

By law, public schools may not favor any particular religion or worldview. At the same time, it is impossible for education to be neutral. Education always advances certain values. The question for public schools therefore becomes, Which values do we promote? Answers will continue to be debated. Even teachers who studiously try to avoid teaching values cannot escape doing so. First, they teach the value that all persons are autonomous moral agents, free to choose their own values. Second, by implication they often teach that the only universal absolute is that there are no universal absolutes. In practice, of course, almost all schools teach commonly held values such as honesty, respect, and equality under the law. A democratic society cannot function effectively for long unless its citizens uphold such values.

On the one hand, it is inappropriate for public schools to promote a biblical vision of the kingdom of God. The overarching aim for schooling in this chapter's chart is "To become committed to Christ and to a Christian way of life, willing to serve God and their neighbors." That aim is not suitable for public education. On the other hand, many of this chapter's aims for Christian schools also pertain to public schools. With a few minor revisions, that is true for the subgoals listed under numbers 2 and 3 in the chart. In a public school, you can, for instance, choose content and teach it in such a way that students marvel at reality and at how it functions. You can help students to live responsibly, using their gifts within a framework of generally accepted values. I suggest that you reread the description of Mrs. Neufeld's unit and decide how you could adapt her approach in a public school setting.

For the goals listed under number 1, it is appropriate for public school students to discern the influence of Judeo-Christian morals and values on our cultural heritage, as long other influential values and morals are not neglected. Teachers can discuss how basic values such as integrity and compassion pervade almost all cultures. They can also ask students to compare different worldviews embedded in literary works and in social and political decisions. They can point out and discuss the religious roots of cultures and the religious motives that drive people. They can emphasize that everyone holds to personal beliefs and values, whether or not their beliefs and values are religiously based.

When I taught in a public high school, some of my most vigorous discussions took place with tenth-grade students about the meaning and purpose of life. While I was careful to discuss different points of view, I did not hide my own basic beliefs and motives. In fact, the students soon asked me, "What makes you tick?" I remember a number of parents thanking me for being more than just a mathematics teacher for their adolescents. However, I did at times feel caught between what I felt was best for my students and what the school administration required.

> ### Word alert
>
> *Indoctrination* is instruction aimed at inculcating a certain point of view or behavior. The word is usually used negatively to denote one-sided or biased teaching. As students grow older, they need to explore different points of view about issues and develop their own thinking. But in order to mature as confident and responsible persons, children need to grow up with a well-founded faith and value foundation. It is unwise and indeed impossible to teach youngsters without some indoctrination (e.g., a first-grade teacher reading a story in which respect for others is encouraged). So indoctrination is not necessarily negative, particularly with young children. Can you give some examples of both legitimate and unacceptable indoctrination in Christian and public schools?

Western culture is rooted in Christianity. It is important that students, no matter what their background, understand those roots and their implications. Moreover, a Christian voice has as much right to be heard in the public sphere as any other voice. However, in our increasingly pluralistic society, it is more difficult than it once was to give voice to Christian beliefs and values without appearing to favor a Christian worldview over other ones. How teachers can do so will no doubt continue to be the focus of much debate. I will explore this issue further in chapter 9.

Chapter 1 enduring understandings

- Traditionally, the three main agencies of Christian nurture and education have been the home, the school, and the church. Today, the media also play an increasingly significant role.
- Education is a shared responsibility of parents, teachers, schools, and society as represented by the government. Parents have the responsibility of choosing a school suitable for their children. Teachers make professional decisions about teaching and learning within parental, school, and school system guidelines.
- The overall aim of Christian schooling is to help students be and become responsive disciples of Jesus Christ. Students learn concepts, abilities, and forms of creative expression that enable them to serve God and their fellow human beings with mercy, justice, and integrity.
- Public schools prepare students for responsible citizenship. They are not value-neutral. Since they may not favor any particular religious view, they often implicitly promote the view that faith and religion are inconsequential.

References

Groome, T. 1980. *Christian religious education: Sharing our story and vision.* San Francisco: Harper and Row.

McLaren, B. 2004. *A generous orthodoxy.* Grand Rapids, MI: Zondervan.

Postman, N. 1993. *Technopoly: The surrender of culture to technology.* New York: Vintage.

Ridderbos, H. 1962. *The coming of the kingdom.* Phillipsburg, NJ: Presbyterian and Reformed Publishing.

Stronks, G., and D. Blomberg, eds. 1993. *A vision with a task: Christian schooling for responsive discipleship.* Grand Rapids, MI: Baker.

What Does It Mean to Teach Christianly?

2

Chapter 2 guiding questions

- How can the Bible inform teaching and learning?
- Which metaphors affect and enrich our practice of teaching?
- How can Christian teachers foster a positive classroom tone?
- How do we deal with ethical and legal concerns in teaching?

Ms. Spark thinks of herself as an artist. For her, teaching is like painting a picture or directing an orchestra. "Students are not like machines that you can program," she says. *"Rather, I use artistry and drama and surprise. I plan my lessons carefully so that, as much as possible, there's a sense of excitement as my students learn. I want them to be motivated to explore, to imagine, to create. At least once a day, I try to do something special, something that brings out the aesthetic side of teaching. I want my students to appreciate the beauty around them, not only physical beauty but also how we as people can structure situations creatively." During a science unit on weather and climate, Ms. Spark's room becomes a symphony of colorful student-made posters and displays. Ms. Spark shows video clips of tornadoes, blizzards, and thunderstorms. The students act out how different types of weather affect people, in their local area and in different parts of the world. In their notebooks they sketch the types of clouds they observed during the first two weeks of the unit. The students read and write stories in which severe weather plays an important part. One day, the class imagines that the classroom is an igloo in the far North; on another day, that it is an island in the tropical Pacific Ocean. At the end of the unit, the students apply what they have learned as they produce video-recorded weather forecasts. They either produce forecasts for the next week or create imaginary ones for fifty years from now, taking into account the effects of global warming. Ms. Spark looks at teaching as an art.*

Ms. Sharp, by contrast, tries to be a master technician. She structures her lessons very carefully, outlining specific learning outcomes beforehand. In class, she proceeds at a brisk pace but in small steps. She gives detailed instructions and explanations. To ensure that her students grasp the material, she gives many examples. She anticipates and reviews concepts constantly, asking many specific questions. Ms. Sharp gives frequent small seatwork assignments that she constantly monitors. She arranges the work so that students have an initial success rate of at least 80 percent on such assignments, and 90 percent on follow-up ones.

In her weather and climate unit, Ms. Sharp first teaches well-structured lessons on the layers and composition of the atmosphere, the effects of the sun and the water cycle, and the motions of the earth's air and water currents. She then instructs students on the factors influencing weather, such as cloud types and weather fronts, and she explains how weather is predicted. The students make careful notes. Ms. Sharp frequently asks them to read short passages and answer questions both orally and in writing. Using her laptop computer, she carefully selects and projects images that clarify and expand the points she wants her students to know. She gives a quiz every third or fourth day, both to keep her students on their toes and to give her feedback on the quality of her teaching. Students who get less than 80 percent on a quiz must take another one the next day. Ms. Sharp considers teaching to be a science.

Mr. Helps uses yet another approach. Before he starts the unit on weather, he sets up six learning centers in his classroom. The students explore various topics related to weather. Each center offers many optional activities. On the first day, he asks his students what they know about weather and climate, and what they would like to learn. The students classify this information and display it on big charts. He then describes how some of what they would like to learn relates to learning-center activities, and he suggests other possible activities. He tells his students that they must keep a log of their daily and weekly goals, as well as of the work they do each day. He will meet with each student at least once a week to discuss the student's goals and portfolio of products. Mr. Helps considers teaching to be a process of facilitating learning.

Reflect and respond 2-1

Ms. Spark, Ms. Sharp, and Mr. Helps think of themselves, respectively, as teacher-artist, teacher-technician, and teacher-facilitator. These are three of eight metaphors discussed in this chapter. The other metaphors view teachers as storytellers, craftspersons, stewards, priests, and guides. Before continuing, jot down some classroom strategies for teachers who uphold each metaphor. Can you suggest some strengths and weaknesses for each metaphor? If possible, do this with two or three other persons.

Ways in which the Bible informs teaching and learning

David Smith has written a helpful article describing six different ways in which we can use the Bible to inform what takes place in schools (Smith 2001). His six suggested ways are not easy-to-follow recipes. Rather, it takes discernment to decide which ones to employ, and when and how to employ them. A teacher's personality and the dynamics of a classroom also come into play. Even so, Smith's categories are helpful, and I use or suggest the use of each at some points in this book.

The first way we use the Bible is to *teach it as educational content*. Particularly in Christian schools, the Bible functions as an object and field of study. It differs from other texts in that, as we study, we also submit and commit ourselves to its content as the authoritative Word of God. Nevertheless, studying the historical and cultural backgrounds of the Bible and analyzing the meaning of its text helps our students understand and respond to God's story of creation, sin, and redemption in Jesus Christ. It enriches their insight into God's purpose and meaning for their lives.

Second, *the Bible's values and ethical norms provide a framework for the Christian teacher's character and actions*. Smith calls this the Bible's "incarnational emphasis." For instance, by prayerfully contemplating biblical passages, teachers can nurture kindness, patience, self-control, humility, and love in their own lives and in the lives of their students (Galatians 5:22–26). A danger here is that we reduce the richness of the Bible to a number of personal moral injunctions. However, in the passage referred to above, Paul emphasizes that, as we live by "the fruit of the Spirit," we keep in step with the Holy Spirit. Later in this chapter I will come back to such embodiment of the traits that Jesus lived and taught.

In the third place, *there are biblical principles that lead to truth claims about life in the world and about life in schools and classrooms*. Again, we have to be careful here in how we interpret and apply biblical principles. The Bible does not specifically mention schools. We cannot transfer some guidelines directly to today's classrooms because of cultural differences (e.g., "I do not permit a woman to teach," 1 Timothy 2:12). Moreover, the principles often do not tell us what to do in specific situations. Even if we can apply Paul's advice to "Correct, rebuke and encourage—with great patience and careful instruction" (2 Timothy 4:2) to teaching and learning in schools, the Bible still doesn't tell us how to construct and mark a test.

The Bible is not a pedagogical textbook. Yet its standards clearly require, encourage, and permit—as well as forbid—certain classroom approaches. For instance, the text in the last paragraph requires that as teachers we support our students and teach conscientiously. Paul also tells us to think about whatever is true, noble, right, pure, lovely, and admirable (Philippians 4:8). That verse, in my view, encourages us to teach art. Such an interpretation is also supported by the fact that the reason Bezalel was filled with the Spirit of God was to engage in all kinds of artistic craftsmanship in order to decorate God's tabernacle (Exodus 31:1–5). On the other hand, the Bible forbids giving false testimony (Exodus 20:16). That means that as teachers we must present historical situations fairly, including, for instance, how at times Christian leaders have exploited people under their care. (Examples include *apartheid* in South Africa and the abuse of aboriginal children in Canadian residential schools.)

I have applied biblical principles throughout this text. I expect, however, that some of you will disagree with how I have done so in some cases. Often God does not give specific formulas. He has created us to work out His norms for specific instances in principled and thoughtful ways. But disagreements will arise. All Christian teachers want to uphold the biblical principles of justice and grace, for instance. But there is a diversity of views on how those principles are to be applied in grading students for report cards.

The fourth way David Smith suggests that the Bible can be used in education is that *the "stories" or narratives we tell in our curriculum reflect a biblical worldview.* Every teacher tells stories. For some it may be the story that science and technology will overcome all obstacles to progress. It may be that personal autonomy leads to a satisfying and successful life. It may be that humans create their own destiny. When you teach probability in mathematics, you can teach it as the story that life is full of unpredictable chances, and that you have to take advantage when things go your way. Or you can tell the story that while individual happenings are unpredictable, probability deals with consistent patterns in God's reality by which He upholds quantum mechanics as well as genetic regeneration.

The biblical "grand story," or metanarrative, comprises at least four acts. First, God created the world. Second, humans fell into sin, disrupting all of life. Third, God sent Christ Jesus to redeem the world, giving hope and enabling humans to obey God's call and begin to restore the earth to what He intended. Finally, Jesus will fully restore God's kingdom when He returns to establish a new heaven and a new earth. In chapter 1, I described how we can tell the story of World War II according to this biblical schema, and I will give several more examples in chapter 3. What is important here is that students begin to recognize that they are "actors," or participants, in Act 3 of this biblical story.

For the fifth category, David Smith uses the work of theologian Walter Brueggemann (1982), who showed how the Bible itself uses at least three different broad types of pedagogical or instructional strategies. Brueggemann suggests an implication for us—that *we should use a similar diversity of strategies as we teach.*

The Bible uses a direct method of instruction when it teaches the Torah, the Law of God. Here children are taught, "This is God-given truth. Here are absolute standards by which you must live." Then there are the prophets, who say that things have gone wrong but that they could be different. Their words suggest that teachers and students need to seek to apply God-given truths to current contexts. This effort calls for discussion and deliberation. Brueggemann then points to the wisdom literature in the Old Testament. Here, he says, the writers say, "Go and wonder. Think about the cause and effect. Draw conclusions as to whether and when these generalizations apply. Investigate and explore how God wants you to live." I am inclined to add several more pedagogical strategies found in Scripture to these three. For instance, telling stories and narratives is another biblical

> ## Word alert
>
> A *metanarrative* is a "master story" that gives a comprehensive explanation of human life and culture and how it came to be. The biblical metanarrative is the story of God's redemption and the coming of His kingdom on earth. Postmodern thinkers reject the concept of the existence of metanarratives, believing that persons create their own individual stories.

teaching method that we can use effectively in our classrooms. Through vicarious experiences in stories, students learn a great deal about having values, making personal decisions, and adopting a responsible way of life. In addition, Jesus often taught through metaphors (e.g., parables, such as the story of the withered fig tree).

It's not important how many groups of strategies we bring to light from Scripture. Rather, the point is that, as we find in the Bible, if we use a combination of direct instruction, discussion of issues, experiential learning, and teaching through storytelling and metaphors, our students will learn more effectively than if we use only one or two approaches. Further, there are times when we need to say, "This is the truth," but there are also times when we explore with our students how we interpret and apply such truth.

The sixth and final way Smith proposes to relate the Bible and education is to *use and apply biblically informed metaphors.* Metaphors shed beams of light on concepts in enriching and often surprising ways. For instance, in education we can look at students as blank slates (as John Locke did), as organisms to be conditioned (B. F. Skinner), or as image-bearers of God (the Bible). These three metaphors lead to very different approaches to education. I expand on these and other metaphors for humans in chapter 4. I describe some biblically based metaphors for teaching in this chapter. Further, in chapter 6, I will use other biblical metaphors to explore a biblical approach to student assessment.

In short, throughout this book you will find me using the foregoing ways of having the Bible shed light on the tasks of teaching and learning. But even though the Bible is God's Word, my extrapolations are human ones and therefore fallible. So read critically!

Reflect and respond 2-2

Choose a curriculum topic at a grade level that you teach or intend to teach. Complete the table below for the categories that are applicable. It may help to brainstorm with one or two other persons and to discuss the completed chart with several others.

WAYS TO USE THE BIBLE IN TEACHING	EXAMPLE FOR A CURRICULUM TOPIC
Teaching the Bible as content	
Modeling biblical qualities	
Applying biblical principles	
Using the biblical metanarrative	
Using biblically based learning methods	
Using biblically informed metaphors	

Do you consider each of these six categories valid ways to relate the Bible and teaching? Can you suggest any other ways besides these six?

Metaphors of teaching

In this chapter, we discuss the contours of Christian approaches to teaching. Teaching can refer to the profession of someone who teaches. However, here I am using teaching as an act: the deliberate attempt to bring about learning. This is a proper but rather sterile definition. Indeed, metaphors used in thinking about teaching affect practice more than this definition does. Sometimes teachers name and use various metaphors explicitly, but more often, they illustrate them tacitly. Such metaphors reveal valuable insights about teaching and about how teachers view themselves. However, it is difficult for any one metaphor to capture the full complexity and richness of the concept of teaching. Metaphors often are one-sided or limited in scope. They may overlap. In addition, their interpretations are rooted in specific worldviews, including some that may be incompatible with a biblically based worldview.

For the metaphors that follow, ask yourself which are biblically informed. Moreover, think about which metaphor or combination of metaphors best portrays your outlook on teaching, or choose or develop one that is not included here. In this chapter, we will consider the teacher as an artist, a technician, a facilitator, a storyteller, a craftsperson, a steward, a priest, and a shepherd-guide.

The teacher as artist and as technician

Two common but very different metaphors see *the teacher as an artist* and *the teacher as a scientist* or *technician*. Teacher-artists bring out the importance of creative teaching strategies and student response. They do not treat students as objects to be processed in assembly-line fashion. Instead, their teaching benefits from artistry and spontaneity. They help students use content and abilities in original and inventive ways (Highet 1950; Rubin 1985).

The excitement generated by original and well-crafted strategies stimulates learning. Teaching, however, is more than an art. An important focus in teaching is the understanding, insight, and wisdom we want students to acquire. The apostle Paul was known for his long sermons and difficult writings. Yet the content of his message is so powerful that he continues to influence Christians today. Looking at teaching as just an art can make us lose sight of the goal of enculturating students to their heritage.

Teacher-technicians, on the other hand, emphasize efficiency and precision learning. They use a structured approach to teach precise concepts and abilities. They also apply specific steps to prevent or correct classroom management problems. Examples include Rosenshine's seven steps of direct instruction and Bloom's mastery learning. These prescribe well-defined goals, structured skill instruction, high expectations for student achievement, and frequent positive reinforcement (Hunter 1984; Rosenshine and Stevens 1986).

However, viewing the teacher as a technician falsely assumes that prediction and complete control of human behavior are desirable and possible, and fails to recognize that students and teachers bring their own personality and background to learning situations. Both teachers and students are active agents, but individuals do not react to stimuli in the same way. Their motives and personalities affect learning in complex ways. Further, persons favoring this metaphor often focus on the means of attaining sequential, measurable learning outcomes. As they do, they often neglect long-term outcomes as well as the environment within which learning takes place. Even for learning specific skills and concepts, the long-term benefits of scientific instruction are uncertain.

The teacher as facilitator

Another metaphor that pervades the thinking and practice of many is *teacher as facilitator*. The teacher's main role is to *facilitate* learning. Teachers provide the right environment and motivation for learning. They pose problems and encourage students to set personal goals, and often to choose their own activities. Students are to create their own understandings and interpretations. Teachers may ask questions about whether student work is coherent and useful, but their primary focus is to enable students to generate and explore concepts and theories and to resolve discrepancies. They are "guides on the side." Many who favor this metaphor consider themselves *constructivists.* That is, they believe that students do not discover knowledge but rather that they *construct* it, either individually or through social interaction. Learning should help students create their own world of meaning as they construct concepts, schemas, interpretations, and values.

Again, there are positive aspects to this metaphor. In the long run, learning will attain the aims described in chapter 1 only if teachers involve students in their learning in meaningful ways and encourage them to respond personally. Teachers who see themselves as facilitators recognize that imparting information for regurgitation on tests is an unacceptably narrow approach to teaching. They see the need for students to reflect on important issues, both personally and in group situations. They stimulate curiosity and wonder. They give students a serious voice in their learning. There is no doubt that a key role of teachers is to facilitate learning.

Yet this metaphor, too, falls short. Teachers must do more than facilitate. Jesus facilitated learning in a number of ways. He asked pointed questions, often in response to questions His listeners asked. He told stories whose meanings became clear only after personal reflection. He modeled an unusual lifestyle that led people to consider how they should live. But He did much more than that. He gave guidelines for everyday living in the Sermon on the Mount. He worked closely with a small band of disciples, explaining what the kingdom of God was all about. He sent them out with detailed and clear instructions in response to what He had taught. He condemned the Pharisees for their legalism and hypocrisy.

In other words, Jesus did more than facilitate. He also clearly enunciated a way of life and called people to follow it. He referred to the Scripture as a guide. Similarly, God calls teachers to make clear that there is truth embedded both in the Bible and in the reality around us, even if our understanding is limited. God has given us an orderly world. There are right and wrong ways to do things, as well as efficient and inefficient ones. Moreover, there are universal, God-given guidelines and values that direct our personal lives and our society. Of course, we develop personal interpretations, some of which are more valid than others because they are closer to God's laws and His intentions for creation. Those laws include both the physical laws of nature and the precepts He has established for human life (Psalm 19).

Teachers, therefore, are much more than facilitators. They are guides who at times instruct directly, who at times share and discuss insights, who at times allow students to explore and create, and who constantly stimulate students to use their insights and abilities in responsive and responsible ways. Teachers guide not only from the side, but also from the front and back!

The teacher as storyteller

Artists, technicians, and facilitators—these are three of the most common metaphors for teachers. They are not the only ones, however. Another one worth considering is *teacher as storyteller*. Kieran Egan (1986) promotes this metaphor, particularly for teaching at the elementary grades. Piaget, Egan says, looked too narrowly at rational or cognitive skills for his theories to be useful for classroom application. Children understand profoundly abstract concepts very early, Egan points out, as long as we present them in concrete story settings. That is especially true for those that can be expressed in terms of binary opposites such as good and evil, or courage and fear. Therefore, especially at the primary level, Egan says we should set up a sense of conflict or dramatic tension at the beginning of *any* unit or set of lessons.

Egan continues that teachers should design classroom units that tell a "story." Each unit would end with the resolution of the tension between the two opposites. A unit on nutrition, for instance, might focus on scarcity versus plenty. It might trace how people have succeeded but also failed at providing adequate and healthy diets. Throughout the main "story" of the unit, shorter stories contributing to the theme could be told or read. John Bolt (1993) develops this concept more specifically for Christian schools, noting that we must pass on our Christian and cultural "story" so that students appropriate their heritage and vision.

In Christian schools the "story" that is told can consider basic worldview questions. For a unit on cities, for instance, we can investigate why and how cities developed; how they provide centers of services and cultural development; how they are affected by pollution, poverty, and crime; and how Christians can help make cities more livable places. Exactly what and how teachers will plan for their unit depends on their students' age level, of course. But at all levels students should learn that God intends cities to be attractive and habitable places where people's basic needs are met so that they can fulfill their calling. They should also consider how human sin has undermined God's intent and consider their role in cities as followers of Jesus who look with hope to the future. As Egan points out, when units are developed in narrative form, students also examine and learn about transcendent values. Children can deal meaningfully with abstract concepts and themes if teachers present them within a specific story context. So, in addition to units organized as "stories," children also benefit from considering the underlying themes of biblical and other stories, even if not on a purely analytical level. They can consider story themes in the context of human intentions and emotions, often in spontaneous, creative ways.

All teachers are storytellers. Many are very good ones, either telling their stories directly or organizing their units in a storytelling way. Yet to cast all learning into a storytelling mode can become one-sided and artificial. Jesus saw the power and value of stories and parables in His teaching, but He also taught through modeling, demonstration, and direct instruction. This metaphor, like the previous one, contains useful insights but does not give a complete view of teaching.

The teacher as craftsperson

Teachers are *craftspersons* insofar as they use reflective, diligent, and skillful approaches (Tom 1984). Some persons have more of a natural bent for teaching than others. Yet all prospective teachers benefit from learning various teaching strategies and ways of structuring the classroom. However, they do not become skilled teachers simply by listening and reformulating—or by reading this book. Rather, as in any craft, they must practice teaching in a real classroom setting.

Teachers who become master craftspersons are ones who continue to do so diligently, reflectively, and perceptively. They systematically analyze and reflect on their teaching and its effects, constantly learning from practice. They use this knowledge to make specific decisions about their day-to-day teaching. They keep their goals in mind as they teach, but they do not unthinkingly follow the steps suggested in a teachers' guide. Gradually, they develop a versatile repertoire of teaching approaches. They show their mastery by using some approaches intuitively, but they always continue to look for ways to improve their expertise and proficiency. They use a conscientiously deliberative approach to teaching, and they are courageously self-critical as they react to what they perceive. They revise their teaching accordingly. This metaphor includes but goes beyond another common one: the teacher as a *reflective practitioner*.

Effective teachers hone teaching as a craft. But being a craftsperson is not enough. Carpenters can be craftspersons by skillfully building according to plans that someone else designed. The moral and religious aspect of their trade is limited to doing an honest job well. In teaching, however, we set out a direction for our students and thus influence their lives. We affect the way they view life and how they act on what they hold to be important. We help to forge their personalities. We set the stage for interaction and relationships in the classroom.

We decide not only what content to teach but also what strategies and activities will enable students to learn. We do all this on the basis of the explicit and implicit beliefs that frame our worldview and our preferred classroom approaches. Teaching has strong moral and religious components that go well beyond its being simply a craft.

> **Word alert**
>
> Teachers are often reminded that they should be *reflective practitioners*. That is, they should thoughtfully, carefully, and consistently reflect on the teaching and learning in their classrooms in order to improve their practice.

Tom (1984) therefore develops the metaphor that teaching is a *moral* craft. I believe we should go one step further. If we define religion in its broad sense as a system of ardently held beliefs that guide practice, then teaching can be said to be a religiously based act. The Bible itself makes clear that teaching is a religious act. Scripture usually discusses the concept of teaching in one of two contexts. First, teaching must lead to walking in the paths of the Lord or the "the way you should go" (Psalm 32:8; see Deuteronomy 11:19, 1 Samuel 12:23). Second, teaching must point to the "marvelous deeds" of the Lord (Psalms 71:17; see 78:4 and the "teaching psalms," 104–106). In both cases we teach the law of the Lord, His law of life. That law includes both the wonderful physical, life-sustaining laws embodied in God's physical creation (Psalm 19:1–4) and His laws that shed light on endeavors involving human relationships (Psalm 19:7–11). Consequently, if teaching is a craft, it is a *religious craft*.

Reflect and respond 2-3

Discuss the classroom implications of using the metaphor of teaching as a religious craft. In what ways does this metaphor contain aspects of each of the other metaphors discussed thus far? In what ways does it differ?

The teacher as steward

The next three metaphors differ from the previous ones. The ones up to this point are not directly mandated by Scripture, although they do not necessarily contradict it. But the next three metaphors refer to biblical injunctions for Christians in general, and therefore also for Christian teachers. None of the metaphors is complete in itself. Each, however, describes an important dimension of what it means to teach Christianly. The three I will discuss, along with what I believe are some biblical implications, are the teacher as steward, as priest, and as shepherd or guide.

Jonathan Parker develops the metaphor of *the teacher as steward*. His starting point is the biblical parable of the talents (Matthew 25:14–30). This parable "portrays stewards as people who are assigned responsibility for the growth and development of someone else's assets" (1995, 179). He then describes how teachers are stewards of knowledge, of student characteristics, of the school environment, and of instruction.

All four of these components are necessary for good teaching; none is sufficient in and of itself. Good teachers have broad general knowledge, professional knowledge, and knowledge of their specialties. They also must honor and be able to work effectively with students who have a broad spectrum of characteristics. Being stewards of the school environment includes being able to provide positive classroom structures and discipline, and to work well with colleagues and parents in fostering affirming surroundings for learning. Stewardship of instruction involves managing strategies and activities to bring about optimal learning.

Jesus Himself compared teachers of the law (and all Christian teachers teach God's laws!) with householders or stewards who bring both old and new treasures out of their storeroom (Matthew 13:52). Jesus' parables made clear that teachers have "talents" entrusted to them for use in serving their students. As the apostle Peter put it, "Each one should use whatever gifts he has received to serve others, faithfully administering God's grace in its various forms" (1 Peter 4:10). While Jesus thus calls teachers to be stewards, not all stewards are teachers. As such, stewardship itself is a necessary facet of teaching, but it does not encompass the totality of teaching.

The teacher as priest

That teaching has a religious basis and focus becomes clear when we recognize that it is a calling or ministry with the purpose of preparing students for works of service (Ephesians 4:12). As teachers, we work at this calling with all our heart, as working for the Lord, not just for our school board or even for our students (Colossians 3:23). We are "a chosen people, a royal priesthood, a holy nation" that declares God's praises (1 Peter 2:9). We exercise godly authority worthy of our calling only to the extent, however, that we possess and continue to deepen our pedagogical insight. Such insight grows as a result of our studying Scripture, reading about and discussing educational issues, and especially teaching in perceptive and reflective ways.

First Peter 2:9 makes clear that God calls teachers, like all believers, to be *priests*. As such, we foster a loving and caring learning community in our classrooms. We accept all students for who they are (not that we always condone what they do!). Prayerfully, we try to heal broken relationships. Our own repentance and surrender to Christ enable us to intercede in broken situations. We listen carefully to the students involved and confront them in order to bring about healing. We ourselves and our students may face periods of tension and frustration before God grants victory over sin. We help students develop specific skills to deal with frustration and conflict. Sometimes we may have to confess our own mistakes to the class, asking forgiveness and forgiving those who have offended us. As priests, we are ambassadors of Christ. We experience and demonstrate His reconciling love.

Note that Peter speaks of a *royal* priesthood. Sovereigns in Scripture were to rule wisely in justice, fairness, and righteousness (Proverbs 29:14, Isaiah 9:7, Jeremiah 23:5). They were to administer or manage affairs so that they served people unselfishly. Moreover, they were to "testify to the truth" (John 18:37). In the classroom, you therefore determine and implement structures that help students perform their tasks in loving, just, and righteous ways (see chapter 6).

Another important "royal" task of teachers is to plan a curriculum that testifies to the truth and declares the glory of God. We choose topics that help students grow in their understanding of God's world and their place in it. Does the material help students to be "hearers and doers" of the Word (see James 1:22) in their situation? Do they experience the relationship of concepts and skills to real situations? Are the interpretations balanced and fair? Do the methods contribute to students' understanding and personhood? Chapters 3, 4, and 5 will discuss how you can exercise such responsibilities.

Finally, Peter adds that our priesthood is a *holy* one (1 Peter 2:5). God calls His people to be holy, separated from the evils of the world. Yet God places teachers and students in the middle of life, to be agents of healing in a broken world. We encourage our students to commit their hearts to the Lord. We model biblical piety. We give evidence in our own lives of wanting to listen to the Word of God, and of taking our concerns to our Father. We bring students into frequent contact with the Bible and encourage them to search the Scriptures and apply the Scriptures to everyday situations. We show how God concerns Himself with the details of daily living. We deal with our students in a Christlike attitude of love, and we expect them to reciprocate. In these ways, we sow the seeds for holy living. We may then depend on the Holy Spirit to give the increase and to lead our students into a holy life.

Reflect and respond 2-4

The metaphors of the teacher as steward and as priest are unusual. In what ways are they powerful? In what ways does each fall short? Look up biblical passages about stewardship (e.g., Matthew 13:52, 1 Corinthians 4:2, Titus 1:7, 1 Peter 4:10) and discuss how these pertain to the role of a teacher. Also read 1 Peter 1 and 2. How is the concept "royal priesthood" relevant when we are thinking about teaching? Give some specific examples.

The teacher as shepherd or guide

Christian teachers are knowledgeable stewards of their own God-given talents and of those of the students God entrusts to them. They are loving priests who bring encouragement and compassion to their classrooms. Yet we all know persons who have these characteristics and who serve the Christian community in notable ways but who cannot teach students effectively. Teaching also requires diverse competencies as well as a sense of direction and purpose that enables a person to be an effective *shepherd* (to use the biblical metaphor) or *guide*.

God calls Christian teachers to guide young persons into the knowledge and discernment that lead to service for God and their fellow human beings. It is in Christ, Paul says, that all the treasures of wisdom and knowledge are hidden. He adds that we must shun hollow and deceptive philosophies based on human tradition (Colossians 2:3, 8). Instead, "let the word of Christ dwell in you richly as you teach and admonish ..." (Colossians 3:16). That is the basis of our guidance—our shepherding—as we walk with God in the classroom.

The Bible calls Jesus "that great Shepherd of the sheep" (Hebrews 13:20). A shepherd guides his sheep, using his rod and staff to nudge them in the right direction. The intent of such guidance is that the sheep go where they have food and are safe from danger. In other words, they are then able to fulfill their intended role. Today, just as the Spirit of truth guides us into all truth (John 16:13), God calls teachers to guide their students in the way of wisdom (Proverbs 4:11). We are shepherds: pathfinders, mentors, coaches, and counselors. We guide students to develop their gifts in order to take on life's calling in an ever deeper and fuller way. We guide them into becoming competent, discerning, responsive disciples. Such guidance requires unfolding content and structuring our classrooms in such a way that we enable students to take on their life's calling. Van Dyk (1986–1987) originated a similar model without the structuring dimension.

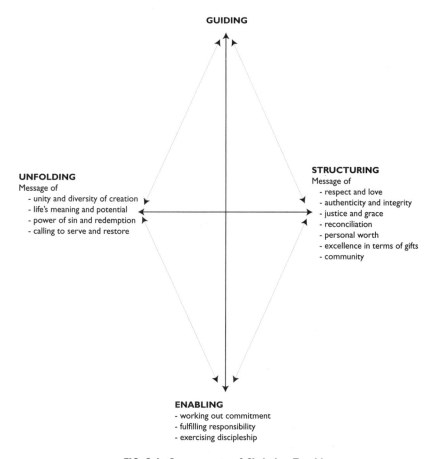

FIG. 2.1. Components of Christian Teaching

To guide students into paths of wisdom requires much more than disclosing content. As teachers we need to provide classroom structures that let students experience what it means to live out of a biblical worldview. We permeate classroom structures with righteousness, justice, compassion, and respect. Without these, teaching reaches the minds but not the hearts of students. Then it is relatively ineffective in guiding students to become persons who understand and do the will of the Lord. Teachers need to set high but realistic expectations. Their strategies must consider the diverse learning styles and modes of knowing, and each individual must be treated as a bearer of God's image. Chapters 6, 7, and 8 will suggest how teachers may implement a pedagogically and biblically responsible framework for structuring their classrooms.

Failing to structure a classroom according to such biblical guidelines has been the downfall of many teachers. Teachers may teach and interpret content from a biblical perspective. They thwart their intentions, however, when they do not want or are not able to create Christian learning communities in their classrooms. Then the students' intellectual knowledge of Christian principles may have little effect on their lives. In some cases, students have become bitter about their school experience because of a teacher's inability to provide a stable structure that encourages learning.

Effective guidance also calls teachers to unfold the basis, contours, and implications of a biblical vision of life. As Christian teachers, we are prophets in that our teaching proclaims God's handiwork in creation, the effects of sin, and the possibilities of reconciliation and restoration (Luke 1:76–79). This requires us to have a thorough knowledge of what we teach, the ability to interpret such knowledge authentically, and the skill to communicate effectively. Presentations should be well prepared. They relate information new to students' experience, emphasizing key points and regularly monitoring understanding. They are useful when students need an organized overview or interpretation of a topic that is not available in suitable form in other resources.

Unfolding requires more than just telling or presenting, however. We use a range of strategies to unfold knowledge. We use incisive questioning and case studies for discussions that stimulate higher order thinking about topics and issues. We use brainstorming activities, field trips, and simulations. We give students perplexing problems to solve. We ask them to pose problems for other students to solve. We have them unfold and reformulate knowledge through independent reading and study, interactive computer programs, and group and individual activities and projects. Sometimes students become "unfolders" by tutoring a peer or a small group in a collaborative setting, by a class presentation, or by role-playing. What is important here is that we use various unfolding strategies that suit both the topic and the class dynamics.

Unfolding deepens students' insight into God's world and their place in it. It leads them to take delight in God's creation as well as to feel hurt by the effects of human sinfulness. Unfolding demands far more than the imparting of factual information. Students must evaluate concepts, theories, and issues. They must think critically about them, solve problems, and consciously develop related value systems.

An obstacle that we as Christian teacher-guides must overcome is the pervasive influence of our secular society on ourselves and our students. God calls us to help students develop the insights, abilities, and dispositions necessary to serve God in all aspects of their lives in society. But Jesus also warns of the grave risk of leading children astray (Matthew 18:6). Teaching is a responsible and rewarding profession but, as James points out, also a potentially dangerous one (James 3:1). We must guide our students into the truth. Therefore, we must search out the will of God for what content we teach and how we go about teaching it.

Let me give some examples. When our unfolding teaches that applying the scientific method or using the most up-to-date technology can solve humankind's problems, we are leading our students astray. The same is true when we fail to counter the superficial humanism or the self-centered ethical relativism of some resources. When our classroom structure does not set out clear expectations, or we do not enforce rules lovingly but firmly, we hinder students from living as disciples. We do the same when we plan only one or two kinds of learning activities in a subject, day after day; by doing this, we fail to adequately nurture the abilities of those students with learning styles that are unsuitable for those types of learning. As Christian teachers we constantly consider how our unfolding and our classroom structures can foster discipleship.

Teachers guide their students in order to enable them to use their gifts in service to God and their fellow creatures. Enabling is a natural consequence of effective structuring and unfolding, and it overlaps with them. It embraces exercising abilities and developing dispositions on the basis of scriptural norms and principles. It starts in kindergarten when, for instance, children learn certain prereading and coordination skills. But enabling goes far beyond such basic skills. We also enable kindergartners by helping them relate to one another in positive ways and learn to deal with interpersonal problems themselves. We enable students when they learn mathematical problem solving as a tool to enrich their lives. We enable them when they learn to apply research and investigation skills in new situations. We enable them when they learn to produce poems, stories, videotapes, and works of art. We enable them when they learn to think through problems they face at home, in school, or in everyday life. We also enable them when they learn to exercise communication and cooperation skills that contribute positively to human relations. And, of course, we enable them when they learn to apply God's laws for morality, for family and social interaction, for leisure, and for economic life.

All four components of teaching—guiding, structuring, unfolding, and enabling—are closely intertwined. Each one affects the others. Our structuring and unfolding must lead to enabling our students, and the degree and scope of their enabling affect our further structuring and unfolding. We push pupils toward becoming responsible for their own enabling, and we gradually but consistently attempt to diminish our own structuring and unfolding and to encourage students to take charge of their own enabling. Our intent as teacher-guides is that eventually our students can function responsibly, independent of our guidance.

Reflect and respond 2-5

Make a chart with four columns headed *Guiding*, *Structuring*, *Unfolding*, and *Enabling*.
Then divide the chart into top and bottom halves. In the top half, give examples for all
four aspects that would advance your aims of schooling. In the bottom half, give examples
that would hinder your aims. From this chart, can you draw any general conclusions about
effective teaching?

Teaching responsibly and responsively

*Let's look in on a unit on work in Mr. Reid's tenth-grade Health and Career
Education course. (This unit is based in part on a unit taught by teachers Harry
Fritschy and Peter Reedyk.) Two Bible texts above the chalkboard set out the theme:
"If anyone serves, he should do it with the strength God provides, so that in all things
God may be praised through Jesus Christ" (1 Peter 4:11) and "Whatever you do, work
at it with all your heart, as working for the Lord, not for men" (Colossians 3:23).
Mr. Reid's unit emphasizes that while sin often distorts the meaning and results of
work, human work can be a calling in the service of God. Specifically, he wants his
students to become aware of and to experience Christlike attitudes toward work and
in the workplace. Work, Mr. Reid believes, can be joyful fulfillment rather than just
a means of personal gain, recognition, and power. He also intends that his students
consider how to choose a vocation in which they can work "for the Lord."*

*Mr. Reid starts the unit by asking his students about their notions of work. On an
overhead transparency he presents a list of everyday activities. He asks his students to
distinguish between leisure and work activities. He asks, How can both be enjoyable
as well as emotionally demanding? How can both be done in service to God and
our neighbors? Is all time God's time? Next, he helps students investigate how work
and jobs have changed throughout history and are still changing today. Mr. Reid
distributes lists of occupations. He has students make a list of points that could be
included in compositions about these careers. The students then research and write
short compositions about a historical career and a contemporary one. Later, students
form small groups in which they share and respond to one another's compositions.*

*Mr. Reid chooses several compositions as a starting point for analyzing how
technology is changing the workplace. The students complete charts indicating past
and possible future technological changes in offices, service industries, manufacturing
plants, resource industries, and so on. Mr. Reid completes the first chart with the whole
class, discussing both beneficial and adverse changes. Small groups complete the others
and then present them to the whole class.*

Next, Mr. Reid asks the students to read a number of case studies about daily work. He has the students arrange their desks in a U shape so that they can see one another as they answer and debate pointed questions about the cases. Mr. Reid then gives a presentation and discusses the meaning of work with the class, including such questions as these: To what extent may we choose a career because the pay or the working conditions are good? Do we take into account how we can use and develop our gifts in an occupation? In what ways can we serve (or fail to serve) God as a missionary? a carpenter? a dietitian? a computer analyst? a film producer? a lawyer? When can work become a deadening experience? How can we avoid that? Should the ultimate goal of business be to make a profit or to provide a useful service? How can we balance work with other parts of our lives? For homework, Mr. Reid has the students look up twenty Bible passages, asking them to reflect on how these passages affect their attitude toward work, and to relate them to work they do at school and in part-time jobs.

The students have kept daily time-chart journals since the beginning of the unit. They now discuss these in terms of the amount of time they spend on "work," including schoolwork, chores at home, and part-time work opportunities. What motivates students to take part-time work? What has been positive in their experience? What problems have they faced? What about pay and its relationship to responsibility? What is the place of management and unions in the workplace?

Mr. Reid asks the students to respond to his view that all persons have gifts and that therefore all have responsibilities, contributions to make, or "work" to do at home, in school, in church, and in the community. He asks his students to complete an interest inventory as well as a chart of their abilities and how they could use them in various settings. The students use these to plan their community service projects. These projects form an integral part of the unit. All students must complete a certain number of hours of volunteer work in a work setting. As much as possible, Mr. Reid plans these projects to capitalize on students' abilities and interests. At the end of their service project, the students write a short report about their experiences. They include a description of what it is like to work in that setting. Mr. Reid uses part of his lunch hours to discuss personal issues and questions with students who want to do so.

Mr. Reid then has three concluding activities. First, his students plan the school's annual career day. Second, Mr. Reid brings in a person from the local employment office to discuss the changing nature of the workplace and how technology, the global economy, and global warming are affecting jobs. The students prepare questions beforehand: How can we attain the education and training we need for what we would like to do? Will there be suitable jobs when we graduate? Will the careers we are interested in still exist twenty years from now? Third, the class investigates characteristics of exemplary workplaces and steps they could take to enhance a workplace environment for themselves and their fellow workers. They use these concluding activities to sum up the themes of the unit by developing and dramatizing, in small groups, discussions taking place among employees about their work in specific settings.

As you probably concluded, Mr. Reid's teaching is creative and yet carefully structured. He looks for innovative and motivating ways to stimulate learning. At the same time, he maintains time-on-task and has high expectations. He carefully designs, organizes, and implements his learning activities to attain his intended learning outcomes. He uses presentations, case studies with incisive questioning, student research, written assignments, debates, large- and small-group work, service work, and dramatizations, always giving students frequent formative feedback for encouragement and improvement. He is an expert teacher-craftsperson who reflects constantly on the effectiveness of his strategies. Mr. Reid realizes that his plans do not always succeed. But he tries to be perceptive and considers how he can improve learning the next time, even when some factors remain beyond his control.

But Mr. Reid is much more than a teacher-artist, a teacher-technician, a facilitator, a storyteller, or even a craftsperson. He is also a steward. He faithfully administers the content he believes to be important, the gifts he wants students to develop, and the classroom environment so students can work and learn in a positive learning environment. Further, he is a priest in the sense of encouraging and supporting his students to develop their various gifts. More than half of them work part-time outside school hours. He therefore also tries to help them contribute positively to their work environment and overcome problems they may face in their part-time jobs. He becomes a personal mentor to some of his students.

Above all, Mr. Reid is a guide. Throughout the unit, he models a Christian approach to his own work. He plans conscientiously, making sure that his units have a clear Christian focus. He takes joy in his teaching, and shows genuine interest in the views and progress of each student. For each class, he develops varied activities intended to stimulate student thought and learning. He keeps in mind his main themes as he guides class and group discussions as well as individual work. He does not just "deposit" information in students' minds, but designs his lessons and assignments to enable his students to internalize concepts and apply them in personally meaningful ways.

For Mr. Reid, teaching is a rewarding calling in and through which he serves his Lord. He sees his task in the context of helping his students become responsive disciples of Jesus Christ. He leads students to the truth but avoids forcing them into accepting it. He gives direction but does not put his students into a straitjacket. He knows he cannot *insist* on commitment. That, after all, is the work of the Holy Spirit. He guides response but allows his students to discuss conflicting views and forge their own responses. He determines an instructional and disciplinary framework within which his students have to make choices and gradually take on more responsibility. He regularly lets them choose among alternative assignments. He gives them responsible tasks in the classroom and the school (such as planning the school's career day).

Mr. Reid also holds his students accountable for their choices and tasks. Generally, they respond well to being given such responsibility, although sometimes they fail. For the few who show that they cannot be responsible, Mr. Reid lays down strict guidelines and enforces them firmly and consistently. In all these ways, Mr. Reid guides his students into responsive discipleship.

Reflect and respond 2-6

List ways in which Mr. Reid guides, structures, unfolds, and enables. Can you suggest ways to improve his unit? Some schools may be reluctant to teach such a unit, saying it is not sufficiently "academic." Do you agree? Why or why not? How does this unit help prepare students for the workplace? How would you change the unit if you were to teach it in a public school?

Reflect and respond 2-7

Read over your personal statement of aims for schooling. In view of those aims and what you have read in this chapter, are there one or two metaphors that would mostly guide your teaching? Are there metaphors not discussed in this chapter that are also relevant to your teaching? With several persons, act out a skit of a classroom lesson or situation that demonstrates your preferred metaphor(s).

Personal characteristics of Christian teachers

We cannot guide pupils in the truth in authentic and effective ways unless we possess certain personal characteristics. In the first place, we must be committed personally to Jesus Christ. Being new creatures in Christ changes our perspective and our purpose. Jesus saved us from sin so that we would consecrate ourselves to serve God and our students in and through our teaching. We see our authority as servant authority. We seek His guidance for our guiding. Our personal commitment to Jesus Christ is the basis for teaching our students to walk in God's ways and delight in His faithfulness. Modeling a Christian way of life is effective only if we are committed to it ourselves and if we show this commitment in our dealings with our students.

Our commitment to Jesus Christ leads us to being Spirit-filled. Becoming Spirit-filled can take place momentarily, as with Paul, or it can be a gradual process that takes place through prayer, searching the Scriptures, interaction with other believers, worship, meditation, and service. Whatever ways God uses, the Holy Spirit produces in our lives, both outside and inside our classrooms, the qualities that Scripture calls the fruit of the Spirit: love, joy, peace, patience, kindness, goodness, faithfulness, gentleness, and self-control (Galatians 5:22–23) as well as the spirit of truth (John 14:16–17). The Spirit empowers us to teach with wisdom and responsibility. These are biblical principles that provide a framework for our calling as teachers.

Note that *love* is mentioned first. Love is the undergirding characteristic that all teachers must possess. Biblical love is not wishy-washy sentimentality. Rather, it seeks to understand students and what is best for them. Such understanding calls for empathy and patience, but also for firm action. True love is compassionate, but it demands obedience. We try to see situations through the eyes of our students, discovering their motives. We see students not just as objects to be trained, but as unique persons, created in the image of God with their own characteristics, abilities, shortcomings, and pedagogical and emotional needs. Such insight helps us guide them in what is "right and just and fair—every good path" (Proverbs 2:9).

We use loving nurture, for instance, when we patiently help students write with a pen or when we teach them to patiently wait their turn when they want to gain our attention or to work at a particular learning center. We fail to love, however, when we punish a student who still lacks the fine motor coordination needed for skillful handwriting. Similarly, we do not love when we value students for superficially conforming to the "rules" when their behavior does not reflect a genuine attitude and disposition. Loving nurture, at the same time, involves calling students to commit themselves to definite responsibilities—and enforcing consequences when they do not live up to such responsibilities.

Christian teachers also *model* the fruit of the Spirit. Not surprisingly, research shows that students not only preach as their role models preach but act as they act. Also, they tend to adopt the beliefs and values of a community in which they find love and acceptance. Teachers have beneficial formative influence by being positive role models and by fostering supportive classroom learning communities. Sometimes I ask university students which teachers they admired most and why. They usually point to the ones who affected them personally. The list includes those who cared about them, those who inspired them through their love of people and love of learning, those who were fair, those who went out of their way to be helpful, and those who cultivated classroom cultures of trust, grace, and redemption. Such personal characteristics yield more long-term effects than the content taught. Students may experience countermodels—of selfishness and violence, for instance—in other parts of their lives, on television, and through computer games. Yet, by God's grace, schools and teachers that model the fruit of the Spirit still have positive effects. Those effects happen, however, only when love sustains the practices of the school.

We all fall short as teachers as well as in our personal qualities. We need not hide that fact from our students. They need to see in us, however, that we humbly and prayerfully let Christ's Spirit rule our lives as we make daily decisions while we teach.

Reflect and respond 2-8

Make a list of personal characteristics that enable a teacher to "walk with God in the classroom." Which of those you listed are essential? desirable? What personal characteristics can undermine a teacher's effectiveness? Now reflect on how your personal characteristics may influence your teaching both positively and negatively. How can you work at building on your strengths and overcoming your weaknesses as a person?

The tone of teaching

The metaphor of teacher as priest that I described earlier does not, of course, refer to being in charge of religious rituals as the Old Testament priests were. What the term "teacher as priest" refers to is that we represent God to our students, model a holy lifestyle, intercede for them with God, and prevent and heal broken situations. All these as well as a teacher's personal characteristics relate to the tone of teaching that teachers set and maintain in their classrooms. That tone affects not only interpersonal relationships in the classroom but also the emotional and social well-being of our students. Here are two personal examples:

I vividly remember my first elementary school experience. Because my literacy and numeracy skills were already at the second-grade level in my kindergarten year, I was placed directly into Miss Sweet's second-grade class. Miss Sweet disapproved. When my mother brought me to school, the first words I heard from my new teacher were, "Boys with big heads like that can never learn well." I sensed she was out to prove her point.

On the very first day she forced me to switch from left-handed to right-handed writing. I aroused and feared her wrath when my lack of right-hand coordination resulted in writing she considered to be inexcusably poor. I even committed the unpardonable sin of somehow producing a large, smudged inkblot on my paper. My dislike for Miss Sweet never lessened. We remained antagonists throughout the year. I found it ironic (without knowing the word!) that her name was "Sweet." I looked out the window at times, fervently hoping that I would see Jesus return on the clouds right there and then. Generally, I was a good student. For children with less ability, Miss Sweet's class must have been an especially sour experience—even though, today, I have no doubt that Miss Sweet meant well.

I also have vivid memories of my sixth-grade teacher, Miss Milligan. As a recent immigrant boy who knew no English, I was confronted for the first time in my life with schoolwork that I couldn't do. On a spelling test three or four weeks into the year, I cheated. Miss Milligan saw me. She said nothing then, but at recess time, on my way out, called me and asked whether I had anything to say. I tried to explain things away, in broken English. It didn't work; it wouldn't have worked in any language. I just saw her sad but penetrating gray eyes look into mine, not accusingly, but deeply disappointed. I sensed I had hurt Miss Milligan profoundly. She had loved me, encouraged me, challenged me, supported me—and I had let her down. The silence between us spoke volumes. I had failed much more miserably than if I had just done poorly on a spelling test. After a while she just asked, "It won't happen again, will it?" I shook my head, fighting back tears. Miss Milligan had gained a student who set out to prove that he wouldn't let her down again.

Each classroom has a mood, a certain atmosphere that sets the stage for learning. A good tone is fragile, subtle, yet all-important. The mood of a classroom is set by how we are present and how we interact with our students, and how they in turn are present and how they interact with us and one another (Van Manen 2002). Miss Sweet projected to her children that she wanted to process them uniformly, as objects, with as little bother to herself as possible. Woe to those who didn't fit her predetermined mold! The tone of Miss Milligan's class, on the other hand, was one of respect and compassion. Her pupils felt secure and wanted to work together on learning, while being motivated individually to strive for excellence.

Perhaps Miss Sweet's explanations were clearer than Miss Milligan's. Perhaps her students even did better on standardized tests of basic skills. But Miss Milligan's students learned a great deal more about living as children of light (Ephesians 4). They not only gained intellectual knowledge but also stretched their creative and social gifts. They became excited rather than fearful about learning. They experienced what it meant to live as a Christian community. Both Miss Sweet and Miss Milligan were Christians. Sad to say, Miss Sweet taught in a Christian school; Miss Milligan, in a public one.

The atmosphere of a classroom can easily become alien, threatening, tension-filled. As teachers we may not understand what motivates students. Our failure to get to know them personally may create misunderstanding or apathy. Without intending to do so or even realizing it, we may be impersonal, abrupt, or unnecessarily sharp. Our students, in turn, become fearful or resentful. As teachers we can be too demanding—or not demanding enough. If too demanding, frustration or resignation sets in. Students may develop a dislike for us that reveals itself in behavior problems and friction. If we are not demanding enough, students will express boredom through noise, mischief, and idle chatter. We need to take stock frequently and make adjustments when we realize that we have inappropriate expectations.

What we need to do as teachers is to set a tone that encourages acceptance and security. Then we understand our students and deal with them as persons with their own feelings, beliefs, interests, and goals. We recognize that we teach for the sake of our students. We try to understand their motives, especially when things go wrong. We try to see how things appear through their eyes. We listen and respond. We receive before we send messages. We communicate with our students at their level. We establish trust by allowing them to express their thoughts and feelings. We regularly give them personal attention and recognition. We allow them to fail when they meet new challenges; we allow them to learn from failure and try again. We don't expect students to do things for which they don't have the prerequisite skills. We encourage all positive efforts.

Of course, sin affects all classrooms. Sometimes we have a class in which, no matter how much we try to set a positive tone, some students undermine our best efforts. They may always insist on having their way. They may refuse to abide by basic classroom rules involving respect and responsibility. Fostering a positive tone can be a yearlong effort. It may require immense patience, steadfastness, and stamina. Yet even under arduous circumstances, we have the responsibility to set and continually reset the tone. We also hold students responsible and accountable for following our leading. Our goal is to foster a mutually supportive attitude, which is essential for a healthy emotional classroom tone.

As teacher-priests, we demonstrate compassion and forgiveness. At the same time, we set a tone that directs and redirects students and ourselves into walking in God's way of truth and uprightness. Within such a context we can support our students in their efforts to meet suitably high learning standards in terms of their personal aptitudes.

Reflect and respond 2-9

List four or five ingredients that you consider important for a classroom tone that encourages meaningful learning. Compare your list with that of several other people. How did your own personality and your personal beliefs about schooling influence your list?

Teachers can also negatively affect the tone of a classroom and students' learning achievement by demanding too much or too little of their students. Give some examples. How can teachers set high but realistic expectations so that students feel supported? How can student assessment affect the tone of a classroom?

Ethical concerns in teaching

Alan had good academic ability except for one thing: he could not spell. His father, a respected and well-educated community leader, had a similar disability. In fact, Alan's family would regularly get up early in the morning to practice spelling. But it was to no avail. Alan averaged 35 percent on his French tests no matter how much effort he put forth. At the end of twelfth grade, he did very well in all subjects in which spelling did not count as part of the assessment, but he failed French.

For Alan, twelfth-grade French was a requirement for university entrance. With a foreign language, he would be accepted. Without it, he would be rejected. Explaining his situation to a prospective university, the school counselor found out, made no difference.

The teachers were divided about what to do. "Let's give Alan the 50 percent minimum pass mark that he needs to get into a university," some said. "He'll do well in the science program he wants to take, and he'll never again take another language. The 50 percent will indicate, particularly when compared with his other grades, that he is weak in that subject. If we fail him, we are denying him the possibility to develop his potential. Alan is someone who will likely contribute a great deal to society with a university education. The system, regrettably, just does not take special cases into account." But other teachers argued, "No, our grades must mean something. The integrity of our school is at stake. Alan failed the course. Granting him a pass would not be honest. Besides, how could we justify this decision to parents of children who did better than Alan but were given a failing grade? We feel bad for Alan. Universities have reasons for demanding success in a foreign language, however. We're not being up front by pretending he passed the course. Whether or not Alan will do well is beside the point."

Alan's case was a real one, with both ethical and legal implications. The teachers, after much debate and prayer, eventually reached a consensus to grant him the pass he needed. Today, Alan is a successful professional who applies his

Christian beliefs in his work. As a result, the teachers probably feel justified in the decision they made.

However, a number of questions arise. Should Alan's potential have influenced the decision? Indeed, is it possible to evaluate potential fairly? Does this decision imply that the end justifies the means? Can agreed-upon standards simply be set aside if such a step is deemed fitting? Are parents who object to this action right to accuse the staff of favoritism? What are the legal ramifications? On the other hand, shouldn't teachers take into consideration the special effort Alan put forth? Shouldn't they be somewhat flexible in their evaluation decisions, depending on the circumstances? What is the ethically and legally proper decision to make? What side would you have taken?

Teachers regularly need to make difficult decisions when the norm, such as fairness or honesty, is clear but the application of the norm poses a dilemma. "Love God above all and your neighbor as yourself," said Jesus Christ. That norm, as well as others in Scripture, is easy to understand. However, it is not always as clear how to apply such principles to specific cases.

Many ethical norms that guide teachers are obvious ones. We expect teachers to treat students with respect and dignity. They should unfold knowledge in up-to-date, representative, honest, and appropriate ways. They structure their classes to optimize learning for as many students as possible. They deal with sensitive and controversial issues in open, honest, and positive ways. They avoid discriminating against or exploiting students, or putting themselves in positions of actual or perceived favoritism. They treat information about students confidentially, releasing it only for legitimate academic or legal reasons, or with the students' consent. They work cooperatively with colleagues in the interest of fostering student development. They assess students fairly and openly, on the basis of stated goals. They respect the mission and goals of their school and uphold generally accepted community moral standards. They uphold their colleagues' reputation and go to them directly with any concerns or criticism. If that does not resolve the dispute, they involve the principal (British Columbia Teachers' Federation 2007; Murray et al. 1996).

Let's look at two of these principles more closely. First, *they unfold subject matter in a truthful and fair way.* Damon (1993) points out that "truth shading" is a common problem, though it is sometimes done with the best intentions. A teacher may exaggerate the risks of smoking and drinking in order to keep students from starting such habits. She may gloss over the faults of a historic figure that she admires. Another may downplay the cruelty that occurred between aboriginal tribes because of sensitivity to current political correctness. Both evolutionists and creationists have been known to present one-sided evidence to promote their own point of view. Some teachers emphasize only one side of certain political or social issues, sometimes deliberately or, at other times, because the textbooks they use are unbalanced. Many textbooks, for instance, minimize the place of religious motifs and motives in the past and present.

Such shading of truth is dishonest. It will also immediately or eventually undermine the trust relationship between teachers and students. And a relationship of trust is essential if students are to accept their teacher's guidance. Furthermore, dishonest communication will undermine some of the aims of education described in chapter 1.

Of course, no teacher is objective. All of us have certain explicit and implicit worldview beliefs. But that does not mean we cannot present content and issues fairly. Fair presentations provide a base for meaningful and engaging dialogues. Students may express their own beliefs, feelings, and views even if we disagree with them. We ask them to consider and weigh evidence. They analyze and advance arguments. They apply to the situation the basic principles they hold. But we may then also give our own view, with reasons, in ways that our students can understand. In this way, we show respect for our students' views and values, while they learn to respect ours (Damon 1993).

A second principle is that *teachers may not play favorites or discriminate against individuals or groups of students.* Research shows that unless we as teachers consciously analyze our own actions, we may not always recognize our own favoritism. We may, for instance, make implicit assumptions when we select students for reading or other ability groups. Also, remember that we may not use our relationships with students for private advantage. Most upsetting here are cases of sexual or emotional abuse. However, it is also unacceptable for us to offer goods or services to our students for personal profit. Similarly, I remember a case where as a principal I had to turn down the offer of free learning resources. The condition was that I had to endorse the purchase of the resources to parents of my students. We must always treat all our students equally and fairly, no matter what their circumstances or backgrounds. We must ensure that our position of authority does not lead us to take advantage of any of them. Here we need to take to heart the warnings of Jesus and James (Luke 17:1–4, James 3:1–2).

Reflect and respond 2-10

Discuss what course of action you would take in each case below, giving reasons.

You invite a politician to speak to your class about her views on a bill involving anti-terrorism legislation that will be debated shortly. Several parents object when they hear about it. They claim that the politician will just spread "left-wing propaganda." If you don't withdraw the invitation, they say, "we will make life difficult for you."

You have recommended that Kevin stay in kindergarten one more year. He is younger than most children in the class. Late in May, he knows only five or six letters of the alphabet and does not recognize all numbers up to ten. You feel that an extra year will help him develop academically as well as socially and will enable him to do much better in future grades. His parents, however, have obtained research reports that show that retention usually does not help children. They want Kevin to move to first grade with the others. You arrange a three-way meeting with your principal. The parents continue to insist on promotion, and the principal leaves it up to you.

As a Christian pacifist, you teach a unit on war and peace that emphasizes the horror of war. You hope that your own point of view will influence your students. Several parents, however, go to your principal demanding that the unit be dropped from the curriculum since it "distorts" the issues. Your principal comes to you stating that only a few parents share your personal views. Therefore he suggests that you revise your course and stress the benefits of "just war."

Juan comes to see you about receiving a C+ final grade. He complains that Rick received the same or slightly lower marks on his assignments and yet received a B-. You know that he is right. You gave Rick a B- because he usually struggles to get even a C and you wanted to reward the exceptional effort he put into the course. Juan also says that you must be racist since this shows that you favor white students over Hispanics. He says that he will ask his parents to discuss this with the principal.

Legal concerns in teaching

Upholding high ethical standards and following legal requirements are both necessary in your role as a teacher. Ethical and legal issues often overlap, of course. When we disclose information about a student to unauthorized persons, we are breaking both legal and ethical guidelines. Here we may face difficult decisions. If students ask to speak to us in confidence, point out to them that teachers have a legal duty to pass on information in cases of suspected sexual abuse or criminal activity.

As teachers we stand *in loco parentis* and are therefore responsible for our students' safety and health. We must guard against hazards and provide proper supervision before, during, and after school hours (unless the school uses other persons for such duties). We must not administer any drugs, including headache tablets, except with written permission from the parents and a doctor. We may administer necessary first aid, but we need to have students see a doctor or a nurse if there is any doubt about diagnosis or treatment.

For all activities involving potential danger, the courts expect us to teach and enforce specific safety procedures (for instance, the wearing of safety goggles during science experiments). We must always be present in situations where accidents may happen: the gymnasium; science, industrial arts, and home economics classrooms; and the playground. In one court case a kindergarten teacher and her school were held negligent because of an accident that resulted when a child wandered out of the room into the street while the teacher had gone to the washroom to bandage another child who had cut himself (Giles and Proudfoot 1984).

Learning activities outside the classroom can be a worthwhile and exciting part of the educational program. They promote different kinds of learning and build personal relationships. For these activities, teachers must take special precautions to minimize risks. Field trips require prior approval from the principal and the children's parents. Written consent slips from parents indicate that parents recognize and accept normal risks involved in such activities, and know their purpose and educational value. Signing permissions slips, however, cannot and does not prevent a person from taking legal action against teachers who do not exercise due care.

As Christian teachers, we must be sensitive to legal regulations, knowing and honoring our students' legal rights. In Canada students suspected of criminal activity must be told, for instance, that they may refuse to answer any questions except their identity and that of their parents, and that information obtained from them during an interview may be held against them. Similarly, we teachers need to know the copyright regulations in our jurisdictions. School choirs that use photocopied music are usually disqualified in competitions, and there are restrictions on how much may be copied from a book or magazine or recorded from television broadcasts for classroom use.

In all our teaching activities, the overriding principle must be "to act justly and to love mercy and to walk humbly with [our] God" (Micah 6:8). We must be fair, evenhanded, and aboveboard with students and parents. We must supervise and discipline our students much as a wise and careful parent would. Finally, we need to be willing to apologize if we have mishandled a situation, as we all will from time to time.

Reflect and respond 2-11

Discuss what course of action you would take in each case below, giving reasons:

Bill Jones, a senior colleague, teaches physical education to your class while you teach music to his. Your students tell you that often he leaves them in the gymnasium by themselves for five or ten minutes. You mention to him that for safety reasons you don't like this. He shrugs his shoulders and says that since he is also a coach he often has to make some arrangements for upcoming games. What do you do?

You have planned a simulation game dealing with world poverty. This year the copyrighted worksheets for the game were not available from the supplier. You wrote the publisher for permission to copy the old ones, but received no answer. The game has proved very popular and worthwhile in the past, but you can't do it without giving each student a copy of the worksheets. What do you do?

Teaching in a public school

Is it possible to teach Christianly in a public school? Obviously, it is easier to do so in a Christian school where it is expected that you do so and where you have the support of parents and fellow teachers. Public schools enroll children of parents of all faiths, including agnostics and atheists. The law is clear that teachers may not use their privileged position to proselytize or to promote particular beliefs.

Christian teachers in public schools face difficult challenges. Some of your colleagues, parents, and students may be skeptical regarding your Christian beliefs. Some may be antagonistic toward evangelical Christianity. Some may object to traditional carols being sung in a Christmas (or "Winter Festival") program. You may be frustrated by the confrontational attitude of your teachers' union and its views on moral issues. You may disagree with curriculum materials you must teach. You may feel confined in that you may not openly express in your classroom what is most dear to you in life.

Nevertheless, if you look back over this chapter, you will see that you can implement most of the suggested approaches. You are still a guide who enables students as you unfold content and provide structures that enhance learning. You set the tone of the classroom on the basis of your personal beliefs about the nature of human life in community. You are even a priest in that you model a biblical lifestyle and show respect and compassion toward your students. You can teach Mr. Reid's unit on work with just a few revisions. Instead of Bible texts, you might use a quote such as this: "Work is something made greater by ourselves and in turn that makes us greater" (Maya Angelou) and contrast that with "It is not real work unless you would rather be doing something else" (J. M. Barrie). The internet provides a wealth of materials that you and your students can use for exploring different attitudes about work and helping students develop their own points of view.

In short, in a public school classroom you can go beyond being a teacher-artist or a teacher-technician. There you can gradually develop a repertoire of approaches that enable you to teach responsibly and for responsibility.

Teaching for hope

We live in troubled times. We face seemingly unmanageable and irreversible environmental problems. The rapid advances of science and technology, while often improving our lives, have also led to distressing negative effects. We see, for instance, the perilous arming of unstable regimes and terrorists throughout the world. Moreover, a large proportion of the world's population has easy access to computer games that promote violence and to pornographic materials that undermine morality. Also, the gap between the rich and the poor is widening, both inside "rich" nations and between rich and poor countries, with prospects of increased hostility and conflict as a result.

Yet as Christians we have a source of hope. We know that Christ came to redeem not just individuals but also the world, and to establish God's kingdom. We know that the Spirit of God is active in our time. We know that while the grip of sin will remain strong and pervasive until Christ returns, God's grace is stronger and more pervasive.

Students today often have little hope for the future. They may despair and give up, perhaps using drugs as a way to escape. Or they may start living for a hedonistic today, not thinking about their personal future or the future of the planet. Christian teachers can take it upon themselves to give their students hope. They can point to the way individuals such as Mother Teresa and Nelson Mandela used their faith to make a difference. They can show how personal obedience to truth, stewardship, peace, and justice can affect their students' own lives and those of people around them. They can show how small steps of obedience to God by many individuals can change attitudes and decisions. They can encourage their students to make a transformational impact on culture.

Dutch Christian economist Bob Goudzwaard tells the story of thousands of people joining hands and encircling the building in Germany where the International Monetary Fund and the World Bank were meeting some years ago. That peaceful demonstration caused those agencies to make the decision to grant the poorest nations on earth relief from some of their debt and the ability to work toward greater self-sufficiency. Goudzwaard's book *Hope in Troubled Times*(2007) describes the ideologies that cause acute problems in today's world. However, he shows how God's intervening grace can cause individual and communal action to lead to a more peaceful and just world.

Perhaps I should add one more metaphor for teaching to conclude this chapter: *the teacher as prophet*. Prophets in the Bible dealt with the gap between what was possible and what was actually happening. They spoke a great deal about justice, especially for the marginalized and the exploited in society. God is described as an advocate for the poor and the oppressed, and as one who wants to see change. So the prophets called people to repentance and to a closer walk with God. Today's prophets state that restoration *is* possible because God will bless the actions of those who walk in His ways and who apply His truths to today's contexts (Brueggemann 1982).

For our classrooms, that means that as prophet-teachers we explore with our students how the truths of the Bible need to be interpreted and applied to today's cultural situations and conditions. We have to help students understand the need to create a more righteous, more just, more compassionate, and more inclusive society. But we also show, through both what we teach and how we teach, that there is hope for the future because God *will* establish His kingdom.

Chapter 2 enduring understandings

- Metaphors of teaching are rooted in worldviews, and they influence classroom practice. Teachers may see themselves as artists, technicians, facilitators, storytellers, religious craftspersons, stewards, priests, shepherds/guides—or as a combination of these or other metaphors.
- Teaching has four interrelated aspects: guiding, structuring, unfolding, and enabling. These must be implemented lovingly and responsibly.
- For optimal learning, teachers model and foster a welcoming and positive tone while maintaining high but realistic expectations.
- Teachers deal with ethical and legal concerns in their schools in ways that uphold the best interests of their students.

References

Bolt, J. 1993. *The Christian story and the Christian school*. Grand Rapids, MI: Christian Schools International.

British Columbia Teachers' Federation. 2007. *Members' guide to the BC Teachers' Federation 2007–2008*. Vancouver, BC.

Brueggemann. W. 1982. *The creative word: Canon as a model for biblical education*. Philadelphia, PA: Fortress Press.

Damon, W. 1993. Teaching as a moral craft and developmental expedition. In *Effective and responsible teaching: The new synthesis*, edited by F. Oser, A. Dick, and J. Patry. San Francisco, CA: Jossey-Bass.

Egan, K. 1986. *Teaching as story telling*. London, ON: Althouse.

Giles, T., and A. Proudfoot. 1994. *Educational administration in Canada*. 5th ed. Calgary, AB: Detselig.

Goudzwaard, B., M. Vander Vennen, and D. Van Heemst. 2007. *Hope in troubled times: A new vision for confronting global crises*. Grand Rapids, MI: Baker.

Highet, G. 1950. *The art of teaching*. New York: Random House.

Hunter, M. 1984. Knowing, teaching and supervising. In *Using what we know about teaching*, edited by P. Hosford. Alexandria, VA: Association for Supervision and Curriculum Development.

Murray, H., E. Gillese, M. Lennon, P. Mercer, and M. Robinson. 1996. *Ethical principles in university teaching*. North York, ON: Society for Teaching and Learning in Higher Education.

Parker, J. 1995. Effective stewardship: A model for teacher education programs in Christian liberal arts colleges. *Faculty Dialogue* 23:177–183.

Rosenshine, B., and R. Stevens. 1986. Teaching functions. In *Handbook of research on teaching*, edited by M. C. Wittrock. 3rd ed. New York: Macmillan.

Rubin, L. 1985. *Artistry in teaching*. New York: Random House.

Smith, D. 2001. The Bible and education: Ways of constructing the relationship. *Themelios* 26, no. 2:29–42.

Tom, A. 1984. *Teaching as a moral craft*. New York: Longman.

Van Dyk, J. 1986–1987. Teaching Christianly: What is it? *Christian Educators' Journal* 26, numbers 1–4.

Van Manen, M. 2002. *The tone of teaching*. 2nd ed. London, ON: Althouse.

Part Two

Planning for Learning

The three chapters in part 2 suggest ways to implement the aims of education discussed in part 1. Chapter 3 looks at planning topics or units for your curriculum. Chapter 4 develops a model for meaningful learning, including planning daily lessons. Chapter 5 discusses an approach to student assessment that encourages learning. These three chapters form a unity. You plan your daily lessons within the context of the learning outcomes you have chosen for your topic or unit. Your overall aims frame the content, abilities, values, dispositions, and creative expressiveness that you want your students to learn. Your assessment monitors whether students are attaining your outcomes in ways intended to enhance rather than hinder learning. Planning is an essential task of teachers if they are to help their students be and become responsive and responsible disciples of Jesus Christ.

How Do We Shape the Curriculum? 3

Chapter 3 guiding questions
- What is the role of the teacher in planning the curriculum?
- What is the worldview basis for shaping the curriculum?
- How do we design and adapt unit plans for our classrooms?
- How do we select classroom resources?
- How do we implement curriculum change effectively?

High school social studies teacher Wilbur Kowalski spends several weeks each summer planning for the next school year. He updates his yearly overviews. He organizes the first unit of each course in detail. And he locates, assesses, and plans for the use of new resource materials. If he is dissatisfied with last year's outcomes of a unit, or if he feels that the same approach may result in tedium, he revises that unit as well. Most years, he also joins other teachers in preparing a multidisciplinary unit (such as the role of technology in culture), in sponsoring a field trip, and in planning a combined major assignment (such as a research paper on a topic for both social studies and English).

Wilbur's careful planning contributes to students' appreciating his teaching. Textbooks do not determine his program. Rather, he develops and selects intended learning outcomes that fit the school's aims as well as expected government standards. He then decides on learning activities, assessment strategies, and resources that are fitting. He tries to meet the needs of students with different abilities and learning styles. He uses a variety of resources: text and reference books, magazines and newspaper articles, CDs, DVDs, and Internet sources. He carefully plans to challenge his students to think critically and explore causal relationships, both in assignments and in his assessments of their learning.

It took Mr. Kowalski a number of years before he felt satisfied with his curriculum planning. During his first few years of teaching, he made extensive use of outlines and textbooks available in his school. He did not have enough time to do justice to long-term planning. He planned daily lessons conscientiously. Often, however, his courses and units did not fully attain his goals. Gradually he planned, adapted, and organized his thematic topics more systematically. He set out to develop or rework several units in his courses each year.

While he now feels he's on top of his teaching, his planning still takes many hours per week. He has developed a personal schedule that usually enables him to do his day-to-day planning and assessment of student learning before and after school and on Saturday mornings. It was not until he had several years of experience and had learned to use his time well before and after school, however, that he was able to leave most evenings free for his family and other responsibilities and interests. A text that he has often thought about over the years is "Those who hope in the Lord will renew their strength. They will soar on wings like eagles; they will run and not grow weary, they will walk and not be faint" (Isaiah 40:31).

The teacher as curriculum planner

Curriculum is a dynamic, ever-changing series of planned learning activities. Worldview beliefs, society's expectations, and government policies scaffold the classroom curriculum. Governments and school boards describe content and set standards for teaching particular concepts and skills at different grade levels. Also, schools usually set out aims and content maps that guide teachers' planning.

Most states and provinces publish curriculum guides for various subjects. They give you a framework for planning your program. You use them to organize, plan, and implement your instruction. But you may well disagree with their worldview perspective, their suggested approaches, or their content emphases. So you need to interpret, revise, and adapt guides and other published programs to suit the needs of your school and your students. You bear the final responsibility for your planning and curriculum choices. The most crucial planning takes place at the classroom level. You adjust your plans as you teach and assess student understanding and achievement—from month to month, from day to day, and even from one part of a lesson to another. That's what life in the classroom is like!

Jesus Himself holds you responsible for what you teach. He graphically warned us against causing little ones to sin (Luke 17:2). Teachers can do so, for instance, by teaching content that hinders children from knowing and doing the truth. Jesus said that teachers of the law are like stewards ("owner of a house") who bring out of their storerooms new treasures as well as old (Matthew 13:52). You are a "teacher of the law" since you teach God's laws that undergird His creation order and His precepts for life. Therefore you are a steward or guardian of knowledge and instruction, choosing content and strategies to enrich your students. You teach children time-honored eternal truths and enable them to discover, reorder, analyze, and refine new insights. You help them apply the old and the new to their lives in contemporary society.

In short, Jesus expects you to choose, design, and adapt knowledge with care. You depend, of course, on the work and insight of other educators. You cannot yourself develop or even analyze all curricula. Within the context of a biblical worldview, however, you choose content and strategies that lead students to consider what Paul calls "excellent or praiseworthy" things (Philippians 4:8). You refer regularly to your overall aims to see whether your more specific planning realizes those aims. You will not reach perfection, but you are able to improve your program each year.

In this chapter we will first consider how different worldviews lead to different approaches to curriculum. Next, we'll consider how to plan topics and units that you will use in chapter 4 to prepare your daily lessons. Finally, we'll briefly consider some key points to keep in mind as you teach different subjects. Throughout, I will give classroom examples for your consideration.

> ### Word alert
>
> The word *curriculum* has more than one possible meaning. It can refer to course content outlined in a formal government document. Some educators also use it to describe everything that actually takes place in a classroom. My use of the term is somewhere in between: curriculum is a plan for teaching and learning, but it is one that constantly changes as teachers work in their classrooms. Curriculum is like a vacation journey. You have an ultimate destination, but as you go along, you may make changes to increase the value and enjoyment of the trip.

The traditional approach to curriculum

Christian teachers, in both public and Christian schools, often accept common approaches to curriculum without reviewing their worldview roots. As a result, their teaching does not fully reflect biblical views of knowledge, persons, and values. I will first describe two common curriculum orientations from which we can learn, but whose basic assumptions we must reject. The first is the *traditional* orientation; the second is the *constructivist* one. Keep in mind that such orientations seldom occur in their pure form in classrooms. Teachers often use aspects of several orientations, depending on the subject matter, school and community expectations, and the nature of their class. Yet most teachers lean more toward one than the others.

In a fourth-grade unit on trees, Mr. Traditionalist asks his students to learn, reproduce, and apply knowledge about trees. He presents details about the parts of trees and their functions. He explains the process of photosynthesis and how humans have classified trees. He asks students to think critically about abstractions related to classification. He presents the properties of trees in diverse biomes and explains how each tree suits its environment. He regularly assesses whether his students have grasped the content by asking questions, checking student notes, and giving quizzes. He largely ignores how the study of trees relates to his students' own lives or to life in society. For him, personal commitment is not a part of learning. He ensures that he "covers" all concepts and skills of the government science curriculum. He wants his students to know everything that is in the prescribed curriculum guide.

What we think of as traditional education is, paradoxically, the result of what is often referred to as modernity. The underlying faith that sustains modernity is faith in the triumph of technology over nature and in continuous economic and social progress. Through rational and systematic application of scientific principles, humans can bring about a golden age. Schools exist to enable students to use their abilities to fit into this ever-improving society. Teachers work toward this goal by carefully sequencing learning concepts and skills, applying educational research results to classroom learning, using new technologies, and testing frequently to ensure content mastery.

Traditionalists therefore focus on the transmission of knowledge and skills. Students are to become familiar with basic concepts and are to use them to think clearly about reality. Therefore, teachers employ carefully structured, step-by-step strategies. Such strategies may improve test scores if those tests favor short answers and convergent thinking. Used by itself, this type of approach leads to difficulties, however. It often assumes, wrongly, that students learn passively and usually in linear fashion. Meaningful learning is a complex process and requires a variety of strategies. A traditionalist approach often keeps generalization and application at a low level. It also gives short shrift to the fine arts and creative projects. Moreover, it often fails to take into account long-term effects, or even to consider what ought to be the basic purpose and nature of schooling.

At a deeper level, traditional education seldom addresses the ecological, social, ethical, and spiritual problems that affect students and society. The ideology of modernity on which traditionalism is based has resulted in technological advances that have extensively improved the lives of those living in the West. However, it has neglected the fact that its faith commitment has also led to an immense gap between rich and poor in the world, an alarmingly increased level of violence, and a global environmental crisis. In schools, test preparation has taken precedence over preparing students for a life that contributes to mercy, compassion, integrity, and justice.

Students in traditional schools generally have a good grasp of basic literacy and numeracy skills. They gain a background in essential knowledge. Moreover, they recognize that knowledge can be determined to be valid or invalid through observation and reasoning. Students who do well on tightly structured tasks may thrive on traditional approaches. However, traditionalism frustrates many others who learn better in different ways. Worse, its restricted, convergent focus curtails the ability of all students to be and become responsive disciples of Jesus Christ, able to apply biblical principles to all areas of life and culture.

The constructivist approach to curriculum

Ms. Constructivist, in her unit on trees, holds that students' intellectual processes are all-important. Her students learn to construct knowledge themselves. Her role as a teacher is to facilitate inquiry and problem solving. What she teaches is not as important as how her students create personally meaningful knowledge, including their own values. She asks her students what they want to learn about trees. She then helps them develop strategies to answer their questions: How will you approach your topic? What materials will you use? What will be your responsibilities? The students decide on group and individual activities. The resulting activities and projects are diverse in design and execution. One group of students experiments to see how much a branch will bend when they hang various weights from it. They try to establish a relationship between bending and branch thickness. Another group tries to come up with a tree classification schema based on their observations of trees. A third group decides to investigate how trees and forests affect their personal lives. Ms. Constructivist encourages students to raise their own questions, to explore possibilities, and to reflect on discrepancies. She wants them to engage actively in diverse learning activities in which they construct knowledge. That is more important, she believes, than learning a common body of concepts about trees. She wants her students to become self-directed learners who choose their own meaning and values.

The most common alternative to a traditional approach to curriculum is *constructivism*. Constructivism uses pedagogical strategies that actively involve students. It gives them a considerable voice in their own learning. Students experience and participate in reflective and creative activities. Rather than supplying information, teachers facilitate independent learning. They coordinate and critique student constructions. They lead learners to dialogue and to generate many possibilities. They do so through challenging, open-ended investigations, especially of problems and contradictions. They encourage students to deal with important life issues. Students themselves play an active role in selecting and defining learning activities. Constructivism recognizes that students in the same classroom learn different things and interpret what they learn differently (Fosnot 2005; Van Brummelen 1997).

While this may sound attractive, few teachers who think of themselves as constructivists realize the pitfalls of constructivism. Here are some of the noteworthy ones:

- Radical constructivists do not believe that humans discover knowledge about a well-ordered world with universal values such as integrity, respect, compassion, responsibility, and stewardship. Rather, they hold that knowledge does not and cannot represent an independently existing reality (Fosnot 2005; Phillips 2000). For them, humans construct all knowledge, either individually or through social interaction, in order to cope with their experiences. So no ultimate knowledge exists that is true for everyone. The most that can be said is that some constructions may be more feasible than others in a particular time and context. Students can choose their own truth, their own meaning, and their own way of life. All personal choices are legitimate. What results is relativism, which easily leads to self-centered individualism.

- Constructivism neglects the fact that there are rights and wrongs rooted in God's creation order. In the classroom, according to constructivists, learning begins with children's own ideas and explorations. Teachers elicit and value learners' constructions, viewpoints, and solutions. They cherish meaningful activity over right answers. Indeed, there are no single right answers. There are only discrepancies that students may analyze and resolve in a variety of ways: "Right answers are not possible in a constructivist textbook. It goes against the philosophy" (Baker and Piburn 1997, xv; see also Steffe and Gale 1995). So when students discuss a poem, each person's interpretation is valid. Students create their own reality, their own answers, their own values. Constructivism contributes to the concern that many people today "seem to believe that there is no such thing as truth—that there is no basis for saying some things are more beautiful and authentic than others" (Todd 2007). Todd quotes Alexander Hamilton, who said that "those who stand for nothing will fall for anything."

- Despite the claim of constructivists, students do not always have to form their own "constructions" to be active learners. That process is both too complex and too time consuming (e.g., asking students to arrive at a suitable algorithm for long division). Teachers need to instruct students about basic concepts, skills, and values. They can do so using strategies of active learning that constructivists try to co-opt for themselves but that good teachers have used throughout history (including Jesus as described in the Gospels).

- Constructivists cannot develop a general curriculum model because the curriculum organizes itself from students' personal experiences and interests. Books and articles on constructivism usually limit themselves to examples of how teachers implement constructivist strategies. That is deliberate since specific content is not as important to a constructivist as the process. Yet student interests may well truncate the scope of the curriculum or make it lopsided.

Constructivists implement some worthwhile learning strategies. Further, humans do develop, both personally and communally, descriptions and interpretations of our physical and social surroundings as well as of values and beliefs. Constructivists are also right that human knowledge is open to revision since our understandings are often incomplete. However, some interpretations are more right than others—and some can be shown to be false. Indeed, many constructivists will admit that some student knowledge constructions are better than others. That means, however, that they apply certain standards. In that way they compromise their own basic tenets: they then no longer give students full freedom to construct their own meaning. Hence constructivists ultimately contradict themselves.

In short, both traditionalism and constructivism employ useful learning strategies. Students do at times have to learn basic concepts and skills in structured, sequential steps. On the other hand, students also need to explore and carefully construct interpretations and understandings, using their imagination as well as their reasoning. But by themselves both of these approaches fall short. Traditionalists often fail to have students unfold and interpret knowledge in ways that reflect the diversity of the unique students in their classrooms. And constructivists do not allow the curriculum to promote a common vision with a moral purpose that transcends a personal construction of knowledge.

A Christian approach to curriculum opens up God's revelation in His Word and His world. It upholds truth while encouraging students to apply it creatively to their personal lives and to their life in society. It helps them be and become disciples of Christ who erect signposts for the coming kingdom of God.

> ## Word alert
>
> Many teachers who think of themselves as *traditionalists* or *constructivists* are not so in the strict sense of the terms. Traditional teachers, while emphasizing literacy and numeracy skills, may also include creative explorations in their classrooms. Teachers who think of themselves as constructivists often do so because they use constructivist learning strategies. However, often they do not accept the lack of curriculum structure or the relativism of knowledge and value that is embedded in radical constructivism. In this chapter, I use the terms to describe educators who understand and practice the implications of the basic theories.

Reflect and respond 3-1

Complete the following chart by listing specific teaching and learning strategies:

	TRADITIONALISM	CONSTRUCTIVISM
Ways in which the orientation agrees with your preferred approach to teaching and learning		
Ways in which the orientation differs from your preferred approach to teaching and learning		

Share your conclusions with one or two others. Then discuss what a curriculum orientation based on a biblical worldview might entail.

How the Bible informs a Christian approach to curriculum

In a unit in trees, students first explore and learn to appreciate trees as an essential part of the whole of God's plan in creation. They observe the functions of trees in their own lives, as well as in the life of their communities. They investigate what products we obtain from trees and the role of trees in soil enrichment and conservation, water control, and oxygen replenishment. They also investigate how forests provide a home for wildlife and for other plants. They learn about ecosystems with different trees, tree classification, parts of trees and their functions, the growth and reproduction of trees, and tree diseases. The students then use this background knowledge to investigate how humans have used trees and forests. The teacher guides students in asking, How did God intend humans to use trees? What has gone wrong in many places in the world? What are our human and our personal responsibilities as stewards of trees in God's creation? What is our hope for the future? Using the norms found in texts such as Deuteronomy 20:19–20, the students seek Christian answers to social issues involving trees. They discuss how they can apply biblical values such as justice, gratitude, and responsible stewardship as they consider the preservation and use of trees in society. They write to some local politicians about the results of their investigation and reflection.

The foregoing unit illustrates how we can gainfully use the Bible to shape curriculum in several ways. By asking questions relating to the biblical metanarrative, the unit tells a "story" that reflects a biblical worldview. The unit also incorporates several general biblical principles that provide a basis for education. First, it reflects what the Bible says about knowledge. Second, it upholds some important values that God ordained in His Word and encourages students to adopt them. I expand on each of these points below.

A biblical view of knowledge and its implications

The Bible makes clear that God is the origin, sustainer, and redeemer of all human knowledge. God reaches out with His Word and reveals Himself to us. He does so through His created physical world (Psalm 19:1–4), through His written Word (2 Timothy 3:15–17), through His Son (John 1), through special revelation (Acts 9), and through the mediation of other people (2 Timothy 3:14). Full understanding comes about not just through reason and empirical evidence (although these have important roles). We also need God's revealed truth in the Bible in order to have knowledge of God and the greatness of His power (Ephesians 1:17–19) and to interpret our world and our place in it. "The fear of the Lord is the beginning of wisdom," says Psalm 111:10. The book of Proverbs tells us that knowledge, discernment, and wisdom are closely intertwined (Proverbs 1:7, 14:6, 24:3–4). God's revelation in the Bible makes clear to us who He is and His calling to us to use our thoughts, words, deeds, and affections to serve Him and our neighbor obediently and responsively.

> **Word alert**
>
> A curriculum that incorporates a *biblical view of knowledge* will help students understand that
>
> - Knowledge is rooted in God's revelation.
>
> - Knowledge points to God's providence and marvelous deeds, and instructs us in His ways.
>
> - Knowledge involves a person's whole being, not just the intellect.
>
> - Knowledge leads to response, commitment, and service.

Knowledge in the biblical sense reveals the praiseworthy deeds of the Lord as well as God's ways of righteousness. That is why, as Samuel was teaching the Israelites "the way that is good and right," he directed them to consider the great things God had done for them (1 Samuel 12:23–24). Our science, art, and history lessons must proclaim God's marvelous handiwork. At the same time, they must help and encourage children "to act justly and to love mercy and to walk humbly with your God" (Micah 6:8).

Scripture also makes clear that knowledge involves our whole being, not just our intellect. Knowledge is more than absorbing facts and concepts. In Hosea 4:6, for instance, God accuses His people of being destroyed from a lack of knowledge. That does not mean that they didn't know their Bible lessons or were school dropouts. Rather, they had rejected what they had learned. They ignored God's law of life. They were unfaithful to God and to one another. They failed to integrate their "mind knowledge" into their everyday life. Lack of knowledge in Scripture means a lack of commitment, a failure to put learning into practice.

Knowledge that does not include committed service is no more true knowledge than faith without works is true faith. God searches hearts and minds. He evaluates how we act on what we know (Jeremiah 17:10, Revelation 2:23). In the last five chapters of Job, God teaches Job that his knowledge was too cognitive, too intellectual. Job needed to transcend his conceptual learning, see the greatness of God, and respond with his heart. In school, the content we choose, how we think about situations and issues, and the attitudes and dispositions we engender through what and how we teach—all these must reflect our dedication to hearing and doing the Word of the Lord.

Reflect and respond 3-2

Discuss how the example below takes into account a biblical view of knowledge. If you taught the unit, what changes or improvements would you make?

Jason Szabo, in his fourth-grade unit on weather and climate, shows that weather is not just part of a closed, autonomous world of cause and effect. Rather, it functions in all aspects of created reality. His students learn how weather acts upon our environment and therefore affects plants, animals, and human life. They discuss how weather affects people's feelings and moods. They explore how weather and climate influence transportation, human survival, and agriculture as well as plans for daily and seasonal life. Jason teaches the basics of the physical aspects of weather and climate. He does so, however, in a context that makes the topic personally meaningful for the students. At the end of the unit, his students make a large mural in the hall of the school that they call "Living with Our Weather."

The biblical metanarrative and its implications

We can think of the biblical "grand story" as a drama in four "acts":
1. God's creation of the world (Genesis 1 and 2)
2. Humanity's fall into sin (Genesis 3)
3. God's redemption of the world through Jesus Christ, enabling humans to be God's ambassadors (2 Corinthians 5:16–21)
4. Jesus' return to earth to establish God's kingdom in all its fullness (2 Peter 3:10–13, Revelation 21:1–5)

Since Jesus' death and resurrection, we live in the third act. Each act, however, leads to a curriculum question as well as to a God-given mandate that has implications for our curriculum.

METANARRATIVE "ACT"	CURRICULUM QUESTION	GOD-GIVEN MANDATE
Creation	What is God's intention for the particular area of reality or culture that we will investigate?	The Creation or Cultural Mandate: to care for and be stewards of the earth.
Fall into sin	How has God's purpose been distorted by human disobedience and sin?	The Great Commandment: to love God above all and our neighbor as ourselves.
Redemption through Christ	How does God want us to respond? Can we restore, at least in part, the love, righteousness, and justice that God intended for the world?	The Great Commission: to make disciples of all nations and teach them everything that Christ commanded us.
Fulfillment when Jesus returns	How can we instill in our students a sense of hope, strength, and courage despite the many problems and struggles we all face?	To be revealed when Christ returns!

What do these questions and injunctions mean for our school's curriculum? First, in the Creation Mandate, God calls humans to develop the possibilities of His creation, to fulfill its intended function. God has entrusted humans with the complexity of His creation for the benefit of all creatures. The fall into sin did not negate that call, even though sin will continue to undermine our efforts until Christ's return. As we saw in chapter 1, four types of learning enable students to be involved and contribute to society in worthy and upright ways:

- *Learning-that:* intellectual, cognitive content (e.g., understand the components and processes that make up a chemical reaction)
- *Learning-how:* skills and abilities (e.g., balance chemical reactions)
- *Learning-why:* beliefs, values, and dispositions (e.g., appreciate how chemical reactions sustain life)
- *Learning-with:* interpersonal relationships, collaboration, empathy (e.g., working helpfully and productively with a laboratory partner)

All four categories include problem-solving and creative activities. All are geared toward enabling students to engage in authentic life experiences: applying technology, cultivating family life, acting in dramatic productions, working to overcome a community's poverty, and so on.

After the fall into sin, humans could no longer fulfill the Creation Mandate. Still, it remains God's mandate. But now God needs to remind us that love for Him and for our neighbor are the keys to being transformed and no longer conforming to sinful patterns. So our curriculum content must take into account how personal and societal sin affects all aspects of life from personal relationships to government decisions to the running of business. However, we also include content related to the Great Commandment: situations where *agape* love can make a difference. The curriculum helps students explore what it means to love God and our neighbor in all places and situations: for instance, in strategic areas of society such as law or the media.

The Great Commandment suggests that students should not just learn *about* a Christian vision of life, but they should also *experience* it in the way teachers plan and implement learning activities. That is why biblical love must also characterize the classroom itself. Teachers are attentive to the needs of their students. They are charitable persons who give students meaningful responsibilities in a setting where they nurture respect and support. The curriculum helps students unfold their gifts to serve one another, to share their joys, and to bear one another's burdens. Teachers foster Christlike learning communities.

Jesus came to earth to restore the kingdom of God. While sin still wields great power, God now allows us to be His ambassadors and coworkers. So after His resurrection, Jesus added the Great Commission to the Creation Mandate and the Great Commandment. The Great Commission demands that we hold before students the importance and consequences of committing their lives to Jesus Christ. Together with our students, we explore what Jesus commanded us. That means we investigate a Christian vision of life as it relates to both personal and societal issues and phenomena.

So we do not choose learning experiences just for the sake of attaining cognitive and ability outcomes. Our aim is to develop tendencies and dispositions that encourage students to believe, value, and act on the basis of the biblical principles that Christ taught us. In the Gospel of Matthew, for instance, Jesus promoted humility, mercy, peace, forgiveness, generosity to the needy, justice for the oppressed in society, and faithfulness to one's marriage partner. Such dispositions, in turn, foster a commitment which, if the Holy Spirit grants conversion and regeneration, enables students to take on their God-given calling as responsive disciples.

The implication of all three mandates is that Christian school curricula facilitate and call students to be faithful in doing the truth, in reconciling and healing what sin has distorted and ruined, and in promoting integrity and justice in their communities. Programs help students acquire the discernment and abilities necessary for standing in the world as dissenters and reformers. Graduates should be able to offer fundamental critiques of secular society, its institutions, and its values.

Moreover, a Christian curriculum orientation fosters knowledge that, by God's grace, leads students to active service. Students relate to others. They develop a

Christian lifestyle. They serve society without compromising their commitment. They develop their abilities and insights in order to become vibrant Christians as family members, friends, consumers, workers, citizens, and church members. They learn and experience the rightful place of science and technology, leisure and labor, communications and aesthetics, and justice and love. Throughout, they learn from teachers who model that submission to the Lord is the beginning of wisdom.

Reflect and respond 3-3

Does the example below do justice to the biblical metanarrative? Why or why not? Some teachers and parents might not consider this minicourse to be sufficiently academic. What do you think?

A weeklong minicourse makes eleventh- and twelfth-grade students aware of stewardship and lifestyle responsibilities. They learn about transportation, land use and shelter, food and nutrition, clothing and appearance, and time and leisure. For each topic, students ask questions like these: What positive and negative features of the topic do we experience in life? Why? How are biblical values upheld and undercut in our society? What does it mean to respond positively to God's Word about stewardly living? How can we personally contribute to hope for the future? The students begin to realize that Christians do not have all the answers to the many problems faced by our technological culture. But they begin to ask penetrating questions. They make everyday decisions using God's Word to guide them in the stewardly use of their time, talents, and resources. The students critique their own lifestyle and explore some positive alternatives. Through a hunger-awareness dinner, they learn to understand that our personal and communal decisions affect people throughout the world. They also plan and experience a Christian celebration. The unit clarifies some important components of a Christian vision of life.

Embedding biblical values in the curriculum

God implanted values in His creation, values by which life can flourish. A good place to begin is to take the biblical principle that Paul calls the fruit of the Spirit: love, joy, peace, patience, kindness, goodness, faithfulness, gentleness, and self-control (Galatians 5:22–23). However, throughout the Bible we find other values that God wants us to espouse and practice: holiness, integrity, responsibility, marital faithfulness, authentic communication, beauty, respect for life, compassion for the poor and exploited, and so on. We also nurture values such as accuracy in mathematics, creativity in art, and trustworthiness in interpersonal relationships. In literature we choose selections that promote respect and compassion. In social

studies we discuss questions of social justice, as well as values dilemmas faced by
historical figures. In science we promote precise and truthful reporting of data. In
mathematics we have students research and plot morally significant social trends.

Throughout the curriculum, we can explicitly plan to develop students' sense
of responsibility, combining high expectations with love, encouragement, and
support. For every topic, we ask which value outcomes can be a natural part of
the learning. We give reasons for endorsing certain values. We introduce cases
that lead students to consider how such values apply in specific circumstances. In
these ways as well as through our modeling, we help students replace selfishness
and faith in the autonomy of the individual with self-sacrifice, humility, and
servanthood.

Reflect and respond 3-4

Discuss how the unit described below promotes biblical values. What changes or
improvements would you make if you taught the unit?

*Elaine Brouwer teaches a sixth-grade unit called The Book Company. The students explore
what the Bible says about God's norms for economic life. They use biblical teaching to operate a
book company that produces and markets a book. The students buy shares for ten cents each.
They raise additional capital for materials by visiting a local bank and taking out a loan. They decide
the content of the book. Elaine helps students see that their business should serve people by making and selling things that help them, such as durable toys, healthy foods, and worthwhile books.
Once the students have decided their book's content, they collect, write, edit, organize, typeset, and
illustrate the material. They design a cover and make plans to print and bind the books themselves.
They decide how many books they need to produce and plan a marketing strategy. Elaine makes
suggestions about using resources responsibly. She guides them in setting the price: businesses may
make a profit but may not charge exorbitant prices. At the end of the unit, the students decide how
to divide and use their profits. Throughout, Elaine stresses that if we really try to serve God in business, we must love our customer as ourselves. The students learn not only how a business operates,
but also how their attitudes and ways of going about business can obey or disobey God's norms.*

Designing and adapting unit plans

As a teacher, you likely plan your curriculum at four different levels:
1. *You develop yearly overviews or course outlines* for each subject or time block.
   Such outlines generally contain topics and overall goals; main content, concepts, understandings, and values; key skills and abilities; student assessment
   strategies; and a time schedule. You may also show how the outline links to

government-prescribed standards or learning outcomes. Often a school has an overall scope and sequence chart to ensure that there is a balanced consideration of topics, without excessive repetition.

2. *You then plan "units"* that may take anywhere from one week to one or even two months. These usually focus on a particular theme.

3. *You do your daily preparation and lesson planning* within the framework of your yearly and unit plans.

4. *You make on-the-spot decisions as you teach,* basing those decisions on student reactions, informal observation and assessment, or flashes of insight.

It is usually at the unit level that your planning best comes to grips with implementing a Christian vision of life. Jumping directly from a yearly outline to making daily lesson plans usually results in a hit-and-miss or superficial approach to implementing a biblical perspective. It may also lead to the implicit inclusion of textbook perspectives at odds with the school's basis and aims. So the remainder of this chapter deals with unit planning. It shows one way (not the only way!) to design a classroom unit rooted in a Christian worldview. The next chapters will then look more specifically at day-to-day planning and student assessment strategies.

In the chart and in the descriptions that follow, I describe eleven steps for planning a unit. Often you will adapt existing units to fit your school's requirements and aims and your class's needs. Even when you rework a unit

Word alert

A classroom *unit* is part of a course that focuses on a specific topic or theme. It often but not always focuses on a topic within a particular subject area (e.g., weather and climate in science, World War II in social studies, a specific novel in literature). The term *unit* has the same root as the word *unity*, implying that

- Units should be integral in that they possess internal unity. That is, everything in the unit is geared toward a clear theme and focus. Without internal unity, a unit becomes a sequence of possibly interesting but disjointed or even purposeless activities (see the section on thematic statements).

- Units should be integrated in that they help students see the "whole picture" and experience the wholeness of life. They avoid dealing with concepts in isolated, fragmented fashion. Since situations in life are usually multifaceted, they seek out significant, natural interrelationships between the unit's subject-centered concepts and other areas of reality (e.g. weather is a science topic that has a great deal of relevance for geography, work and leisure, and our whole way of life).

from other sources, however, it is still important to go through these steps, for you yourself need to decide your theme, learning outcomes, suitable learning activities, resources, and assessment strategies. Note that you will seldom do the steps in the exact order shown. Likely you already have many good ideas for steps 4 through 8 even before you develop your thematic statement. But don't neglect the first three steps! Completing those steps makes it far more likely that your specific learning activities will contribute to your overall aims.

PLANNING A CLASSROOM UNIT
1. Consider the significance and relevance of your topic.   Whether the government, your school, or you yourself choose the topic or theme, consider how it can lead to significant, meaningful learning for your students.   Ask, How can the topic advance understandings of a biblical worldview and values as they apply to students' personal lives and to society? How is the topic suitable and relevant for your students? How can the topic meet diverse learning needs?   Consider whether the topic needs modification because it is too narrow (e.g., apples), too broad (e.g., progress), not significant enough (e.g., kites), or not suitable for your grade level (e.g., World War II in second grade).
2. Brainstorm ideas (if possible with some partners).   Ask, where applicable, questions such as these: What is God's intent or purpose and function for this area of reality or society that we will investigate? What has gone wrong as a result of human sin? How does God want us to respond? How can human activity be restorative? How can we give students hope for the future? How can the unit contribute to a deeper understanding of and commitment to a Christian way of life?   Generate ideas about the unit focus, the key values you want to emphasize, the skills to be incorporated, some sample activities, possible assessment strategies, and so on.
3. Formulate your unit theme and focus.   On the basis of your brainstorming in step 2, determine the unit's "big ideas," or enduring understandings. Use them to write a thematic statement that includes enduring understandings, key concepts and skills, and the main values, dispositions, and commitments you want to foster. Ask, Does my focus reflect my school's vision and aims and uphold a biblical worldview? Will it help my students become responsive and responsible disciples? (See section below for details.)
4. Formulate your intended learning outcomes (ILOs).   On the basis of the ideas you wrote for step 3, specify your intended learning outcomes. Balance them reasonably among learning-that ("to know"), learning-how ("to do"), learning-why ("to value"), and learning-with ("to be"). Include some expressive/creative outcomes. Use the general statement "It is intended that students will . . ." with each outcome beginning with a verb. (See section below for details.)
Steps 1 through 4 in this section are sequential, although you may later come back and revise your thematic statement and ILOs as you develop your unit. The steps below can be done in various orders.
5. Design, choose, balance, and sequence learning activities.   Ensure that each activity links with one or more ILOs and with one or more student assessment strategies.   Ask whether the set of activities as a whole meets all your intended goals for the unit, is balanced, and provides for the needs of students with different learning styles and aptitudes. (See chapter 4 for details.)
6. Plan student assessment. For each intended learning outcome, ask how students will demonstrate the outcome's attainment.   Develop suitable and varied assessment strategies for each learning outcome. Ask how your assessment encourages student learning. (See chapter 5 for details.)

7. Consider your learners.
    Find out what your learners know, need to know, and want to know in relation to your topic and unit focus.
    Determine your classroom setting, the characteristics of your students, and your own personal characteristics; adjust your unit accordingly.

8. Incorporate government standards.   Adjust your unit to ensure that you include government requirements.
9. Plan a time schedule.   Develop weekly schedules and/or lesson planning sheets. (For the latter, see chapter 4.)
10. Select curriculum resources.   The resources you use must contribute to your outcomes. Therefore ask these questions: What topics does the resource consider important? Does it deal with significant issues and do so fairly? Do the values, priorities, and goals of the resource match yours? If not, can you still use it? How? Are the learning activities thoughtful, varied, and suitable for your students? (See section below for details.)
11. Review the effectiveness of the unit.   During and after your teaching of the unit, review its effectiveness. Ask the following: What can I celebrate? What content and which strategies were most relevant and effective? What improvements can I make next time? Make and keep some notes for future use.

Formulating a unit theme and focus

Usually it is not necessary to start from scratch in planning a unit. Often you will have various resource units and other materials available, either in your school or from Internet sources. However, the quality of such resources varies widely, and they may not match your school's or your own intended outcomes. It is useful, therefore, before looking too closely at available resources, to complete steps 1 through 4 described in the unit planning chart. After some initial brainstorming, you'll want to compose a thematic statement for your unit. Your thematic statement describes the unit's overall aim and approach. It includes what you intend your students to learn and acquire: basic understandings and concepts, abilities and skills, values and beliefs, and dispositions and commitments. In this way you will put your own stamp on the unit. You are then more likely to meet your intended learning outcomes.

Consider, for example, a fifth-grade or sixth-grade unit on government. In your brainstorming you determine that the unit is a significant one. In order for students to become responsible and active citizens, they should know how governments function and how the students can become involved. You may choose as your main theme "God intends governments to render justice and to allow citizens to live responsibly in peaceful and free settings." But you also recognize that, regrettably, governments have often abused their power. Corruption may exist.

Leaders may have seized undue powers. They may let people carry out unjust economic policies or unethical acts. They may limit basic freedoms. Therefore, Christians, both as citizens and as politicians, witness to government leaders about what it means to rule with justice and righteousness. They also uphold the need to obey lawful authorities. You want your unit to help students begin to take on their role as citizens who contribute to their nation and community according to the biblical guidelines and values that relate to life in society. Your brainstorming no doubt has given you ideas about meaningful activities: a simulated session of a town council debating a current issue, a visit by a local mayor or city council member to answer students' questions, and so on. But first you develop your thematic statement to give focus to your ideas:

God instituted governments to preserve order and harmony in our society. The task of governments is therefore to provide and coordinate services that (1) promote and develop justice, (2) uphold good, and (3) restrain and punish evil caused by brokenness and sin in society. God calls Christians to be responsible citizens who strive for just laws and who obey governing authorities. In this unit, students will learn about the three levels of democratically elected governments (federal, state or provincial, and local) and their respective tasks. They will explore how democratic elections are held, the role of politicians and government employees, and government services and taxes. The students will compile a portfolio of assignments and hold a simulated session of their city council. Finally, they will investigate some current political issues and present their views on one of those issues to a political leader. Throughout, they will consider what it means to govern justly, honestly, and compassionately. At the same time, they will learn what it means to be proactive citizens who exercise their rights and responsibilities in positive and respectful ways.

Word alert

A *thematic statement* describes the basic approach and scope for a unit's teaching and learning. It includes the enduring understandings, major concepts, and key abilities to be acquired, as well as the basic values, dispositions, and commitments to be fostered. The first part of a thematic statement may be a rationale describing why the unit is a significant one.

Intended learning outcomes specify and extend a thematic statement. They identify the desired result of classroom learning. They may be categorized, for instance, as content, ability, and value-related outcomes. They will be at different levels of complexity and will include some that lead to expressive and creative activities.

Let's look at one more example of a thematic statement. Businesses and governments use statistics regularly to make decisions. Statisticians use powerful tools to collect and analyze data. However, statistics are often applied and used in questionable ways. For example, government leaders may decide an issue on the basis of fickle public opinion rather than taking a principled stand and guiding opinion toward what is right and just. Statistics can also be used to distort reality, for instance, by asking leading questions in surveys. God wants us to gather and apply statistics in ethically responsible ways, and to base our decisions on social, moral, and aesthetic factors that go beyond statistics:

In an eleventh-grade unit on statistics, students experience how statistics can be used to gather and interpret large quantities of numerical data. They read and draw statistical graphs. They calculate averages and standard deviations. They use sampling techniques and explore normal distributions and their uses. They discern underlying patterns and trends and how to draw conclusions from them. The students examine how statistical analyses and conclusions are applied in various everyday situations. They investigate how statistics can be used as a foundation for making economic, social, and political decisions. They consider how statistics can be used in both ethically responsible and irresponsible ways. The students design a project in which they use and apply statistics responsibly in a relevant setting.

Reflect and respond 3-5

For a unit at a grade level you teach or intend to teach, carry out steps 1, 2, and 3 of the unit planning chart. If possible, do this in a small group. First discuss what is important about the topic. Then, after some brainstorming, develop a thematic statement.

Learning outcomes

Once you have written a thematic statement, you prepare your intended learning outcomes. Some of these you write yourself. Others you select or modify from curriculum guides and available units. Learning outcomes elaborate your thematic statement and further articulate what you intend your students to learn. They provide direction for choosing learning activities and resources, and for the nature and means of your student assessment and evaluation.

Learning outcomes have different emphases. Some focus on *learning-that* (cognitive knowledge); some on *learning-how* (intellectual, aesthetic, and physical abilities); some on *learning-why* (values and commitments), and some on *learning-with* (relating positively to others). They include some outcomes relating to *posing and solving problems* (which is part of *learning-how*) and some leading to expressive and creative experiences, where the specific outcome may be uncertain. Note that all of these may take place at varying levels of complexity. There should be *learning-that* outcomes, for instance, at the recall, comprehension, interpretation, application, and evaluation levels. Learning, in other words, should be well balanced. It should not overemphasize, for instance, *learning-that* nor only recall and comprehension within *learning-that*.

Learning outcomes should not be so general that they do little but restate your thematic statement. Nor should they be so specific that you get swamped in details. The latter problem can occur with performance outcomes that reflect a reductionist view of learning and a deterministic view of the person (e.g., "The student will identify three deciduous and five coniferous trees in the coastal forest"). Learning outcomes should be written in terms of what the students will learn and do (not what you as a teacher will do!).

These learning outcomes for a first-grade unit on the seasons are categorized into three general outcomes, each with several related, more specific outcomes.

It is intended that students will ...

1. *Distinguish how and why God has provided different seasons, each with special features.*
    a. *Identify the four seasons in their order.*
    b. *Observe God's faithfulness in the reliable order of the seasons.*
    c. *Understand and explain why we have seasons.*
    d. *Contrast weather conditions in different seasons, both locally and elsewhere in the world.*
2. *Investigate the effects of seasons on the local area.*
    a. *Determine which special days and events occur in each season.*
    b. *Find out and explain how and why the length of days and nights changes with the seasons.*
    c. *Observe and describe how the colors of nature change with the seasons.*
    d. *Describe how seasons affect water, plants, animals, and humans in the local area.*
    e. *Describe how plants are grown and used throughout the seasons.*
3. *Recognize that each season gives unique opportunities to enjoy and work in God's world.*
    a. *Share and record why people like (or do not like) winter, spring, summer, and fall.*
    b. *Enjoy poetry, art, songs, drama, and music related to the seasons.*
    c. *Identify how the seasons affect the bodies, clothes, and activities of children and their parents.*
    d. *Share seasonal activities, and delight in doing some of them together as a class.*
    e. *Communicate their observations and experiences in writing and art, including making a scrapbook about what they have learned about the seasons.*
    f. *Experience and praise God for opportunities to demonstrate love for others in all seasons.*

To obtain a balanced set of learning outcomes, you could develop a chart with three or four ILO categories. The chart below is based on a unit prepared by Leigh-Ann Teichrieb (2006). You will note that some ILOs are put in one category but include several, and that *learning-with* ILOs are included in both the *learning-how* and *learning-why* columns.

UNIT ON JAPAN: 6TH GRADE		
It is intended that students will ...		
Learning-that	**Learning-how**	**Learning-why**
Demonstrate an understanding of the unique aspects of Japanese culture including religion and cultural values, celebrations and aesthetic expression, homes and family structure, and food and clothing.	Research, evaluate, organize, and present information about Japan in a variety of forms, including charts, posters, descriptions, essays, and maps.	Value the richness of ethnic and cultural diversity throughout the world, and the contributions the Japanese have made to Canadian society.
Link Japanese cultural values to their traditions, beliefs, aesthetic expression, and daily living routines.	Create Japanese-type haiku poems, origami, family crests, and kamishibai folktales.	Realize how the Japanese express themselves spiritually, and be thankful for Christian witness within that culture.
Recognize the main features of Japan's geography and climate, and relate Japan's geography, climate, and population settlement patterns to resource consumption and depletion.	Research a chosen aspect of Japanese culture and make an oral presentation that uses posters.	Learn to appreciate the value of interdependence and community bonds.
Identify some key historical events in Japan and the chief features of its government.	Participate in and contribute to small-group work, a tea ceremony, and a martial arts session.	Evaluate mass media stereotypes of Japanese society and recognize the dangers of stereotyping and its related preconceptions and prejudice.
Examine Japan's economy and its exports to and imports from Canada.	Learn and enjoy using selected commonly used Japanese words and songs.	Appreciate the value of clarity, accuracy, correctness and meaningfulness in all assignments.
Compare Japan's geography, environmental issues, family structure, education systems, and art and literature with those of Canada.		Become committed to showing respect for all humans as image-bearers of God.

Reflect and respond 3-6

Discuss the effectiveness and balance of the intended learning outcomes in this section. Then write a set of intended learning outcomes for the topic you worked on in the previous *Reflect and respond* assignment. If possible, compare yours with those given for your topic in a curriculum guide or other teacher resource unit.

Choosing and using resources

Your resources, including your textbooks, should help you attain your learning outcomes. However, they should not determine your teaching content or methods. Resources are tools, not masters. True, your learning activities sometimes depend on the resources you have available. But as a teacher *you* decide when and where to use the available curriculum materials and which ones will contribute to your intended learning outcomes.

Carefully consider the appropriateness of materials for your classroom. Some books, for instance, promote ethical relativism. These suggest that students should choose their own values. Science books usually present an evolutionary explanation of human origins and development. They also often assume that through science and technology we can control our destiny. Textbooks published by Christian publishers also need careful examination. Some are excellent. However, others are poorly designed, deficient in their analysis of issues, or too difficult for students' reading levels. Here are some questions to ask as you examine curriculum resources (including ones from the Internet):

- *What values, commitments, and goals do the authors state or assume? What do they think is important in society, in the way we live, and in the way we view the world? Do my faith and worldview correspond or conflict with that of the resource? Look especially at introductions and endings and analyze the choice of content. Note also what is missing. History books may minimize the importance of religion, for instance. Books whose worldview differs from yours may still be useful. But think about how to use them to support your thematic statement and achieve your learning outcomes.*
- *Does the type of learning suggested encourage responsive discipleship? Do the books actively engage the students? Can you use the material to plan a variety of activities that suit different needs and that help children take responsibility for their learning?*
- *How is the material put together? Is it motivational? Are the important themes and concepts highlighted and reviewed? Do the layout and illustrations promote learning, or do they just "decorate" the print materials?*

- *Do mathematics materials teach new concepts in a meaningful setting, showing the relationship between mathematics and society? Do science materials develop a sense of excitement about science as an exploration of our wonderful creation? Do they also show the limitations and dangers of uncritical application of science and technology? Do reading and literature materials present significant content with role models that reflect biblical lifestyles or content that leads to discussions about basic values and beliefs? Do social studies materials show that cultures are rooted in beliefs and values that shape a way of life? Do the materials state their biases openly, or do any biases remain hidden?*

Often teachers do not have the luxury of choosing their main resources. For instance, the school may have purchased materials several years ago and cannot afford to buy new ones. Examining the books carefully is still useful, however. You will see their strengths and weaknesses more clearly and can then plan teaching and learning accordingly.

Reflect and respond 3-7

With a small group, examine one or two commonly used textbooks or another significant resource in a subject and at a level of your interest. Use the questions above to draw conclusions about the suitability of the materials and the ways in which you would make use of them (if at all).

To what extent should schools and individual teachers be able to choose their own curriculum resources? Is there a need for common textbooks so that children in different communities receive similar content instruction? Or should teachers use a variety of resources rather than one textbook even within their classrooms?

Subject-area considerations

The Bible does not contain "recipes" telling us what content we should or should not teach. It helps us understand the basic themes for life: creation, fall, redemption, the coming kingdom of God, and how God calls us to live. We therefore infer that the school curriculum should help students develop their God-given calling and that our content and pedagogy should encourage students to respond in obedience to God's mandates.

More specifically, curriculum content should point to the *vertical unity of knowledge* proclaimed in Colossians 1:16–17, "All things were created by [Christ] and for him. He is before all things, and in him all things hold together." It is in Christ, Paul continues in Colossians 2:3, that all the treasures of wisdom and knowledge are hidden. True wisdom and knowledge have their source in Christ. Through Christ all things were made. Through Christ we were given life. Through Christ we received the light that has brought us grace and truth (John 1:4–5, 14). Secular approaches to education overlook this centrality of Christ in the world. To make this unity clear to students and to show that Christ is preeminent and gives us direction for all aspects of life is not an easy task. Yet many Christian teachers do plan units that make clear how Christ as the creating and redeeming Word for life puts our schoolwork into a perspective that allows us to be God's fellow workers (1 Corinthians 3:9). They hold God's Word to be "a lamp to [their] feet and a light for [their] path" (Psalm 119:105). Examples of such teachers are those whose lesson approaches, based on actual classroom situations, are used in this book.

Often we teach curriculum content most easily within the framework of established school subjects. We must also make clear to our students, however, the *horizontal unity* of knowledge. Many significant topics and issues in life cut across disciplines. We should include those in our curriculum, either within a subject or as an interdisciplinary or "integrated" unit. For instance, we may not neglect issues such as our environmental crises, the mounting violence in the world, and the increasing gap between the rich and the poor in society. Our content must also expose the many natural interrelationships between different disciplines. In science, for example, mathematics is not only an essential tool but also a vehicle for interpreting scientific phenomena. Moreover, economics and ethics proclaim limits to the applications of science.

Here I give some very brief guidelines for teaching various subjects (for more detail, see, for instance, Van Brummelen 2002). In the next section I then give an example of a humanities unit that cuts across several subject areas.

In biblical studies students read and interpret the Bible as God's revelation of His plan of redemption. They practice biblical interpretation, studying the literary forms and cultural background of individual Bible books as well as tracing significant biblical themes. In addition, they apply the biblical message to their personal lives, to their relationships with others, to contemporary issues, and to life in the community. Throughout, teachers confront their students with the biblical call to personal repentance, faith, and discipleship.

Language arts/literature helps students grow as they enhance their ability to relate to and communicate with others in positive, meaningful ways. Language is a beautiful and exciting means to serve God and our neighbors and to build community. Students learn to listen thoughtfully, speak effectively, read critically, enjoy imaginatively, and write competently and creatively. In literature, students develop spiritual, moral, and social maturity as they learn to discern the worldview visions that are presented and promoted.

In *science* students learn that their inquiry about physical reality assumes that God's laws and precepts are trustworthy (Psalms 111 and 146). They observe, experiment, and draw conclusions about our creation structure. They also begin to recognize, however, that human investigation and formulation reflect the unchanging laws of God only in limited ways and that science can never be our ultimate authority in life. Moreover, they see how God created each living being to fit the environment in which He placed it, with each having a special purpose in God's plan for life. Through science, students become aware of their personal and our collective roles as caretakers of our planet: to maintain healthy bodies, make stewardly lifestyle decisions, maintain harmony among living things and their environment, and deal responsibly with social issues that have a scientific component.

The basis for *mathematics* lies with God's wise and orderly decrees (Psalm 33:6–11, Jeremiah 33:25). Children initially discover God's created order about number and space from concrete, hands-on experiences. Only slowly do teachers introduce and reinforce more abstract conceptualization, formal reasoning, and algorithms. Even then, they continue to show how society uses the methods and conclusions of mathematics as essential tools in various areas of life.

In the *fine arts* (visual art, music, drama, creative movement, film) teachers provide children with rich experiences in which they look, listen, and feel. They introduce students to the artistic statements of other people, both past and present. Students experience the power of aesthetics to shape people and their values. They respond artistically, with originality, within a framework of purposeful development of concepts and skills. In music, for instance, the students listen, perform, compose, and improvise. They learn to appreciate how music is an important part of life and culture. They learn how to use music in praise to their Creator as they express joy and sadness, faith and doubt, obedience and disobedience in imaginative ways.

The starting point for *physical education* is the belief that God calls us to honor Him with our bodies as well as our minds (1 Corinthians 6:20). Human beings are a unity, and their physical health affects their emotional, mental, and spiritual state. As such, physical involvement is part of a Christian lifestyle. Therefore, the aim of physical education is that students develop and maintain acceptable motor proficiencies, health fitness, and physical skills in a variety of activities. Physical education encourages and enables all students to incorporate wholesome physical activities in their everyday routines.

Reflect and respond 3-8

For one or two subjects in which you are interested, discuss how the above guidelines would influence the teaching and learning in your classroom. Are there additional or alternate guidelines you would suggest?

An example of a classroom unit

Units usually fit into a specific subject discipline. Often teachers ensure that they bring in authentic connections to other subjects for the topics studied. For instance, a history unit on the Renaissance would likely include an analysis of Renaissance art and perhaps would have students paint a Renaissance-style painting. A science unit on electricity might include discussions of the environmental, economic, and social considerations of generating electricity in different ways.

However, since most knowledge arises from and is applied to multidimensional phenomena, not all learning should take place within well-defined "subjects." At times we need to transcend subject-centered knowledge and have students interact with reality in a holistic way. The minicourse on stewardship and lifestyle responsibilities described earlier in this chapter is one example. Another is a unit about the local city; it can look at transportation, the economy, government, people's lifestyles, environmental concerns, and the city's cultural expressions.

Below I describe a unit called *Taking a Stand*, developed by teachers from three Christian schools in British Columbia (Koole 1996). The principal of each school gave pairs of teachers some joint planning time. Once the teachers had tried various approaches, they saw the benefit of getting together during a summer and pooling insights and experiences. The result is a unit that reflects biblical views of knowledge and of the person while avoiding the secularism and relativism of our age. The unit helps students see the connections between themselves and the world around them by exploring and examining their relationships with God, one another, the past, their own and other cultures, and creation. The content comprises themes and issues from biblical studies, English, and social studies.

Taking a Stand

The teachers who developed this unit wanted their students to consider how people's beliefs influence their lives. What are the characteristics of individuals who make a difference? And what kind of stand does Christ call us to take? They worked out their thematic statement and intended learning outcomes as follows:

In each generation and culture the Spirit of God moves people to take a stand in pursuit of truth. Taking a stand involves personal commitment and a willingness to question those traditions that distort the discovery of truth. A personal relationship with Jesus Christ is the foundation of all truth: His Word illumines all human understanding.

It is intended that students will ...

- *understand the gospel's message of salvation by faith alone as expressed in Paul's letters*

- *understand that the pursuit of truth, which drives many individuals to observe, question, challenge, experiment, and defend their convictions, often involves personal suffering*

- *see the sovereignty and love of God as He continually calls His Church to repent and to proclaim His message through a walk of faith*

   The unit consists of four main parts:

- *Paul's life, how he took a stand, and, specifically, his letter to the Galatians. The study of Galatians not only provides the link between Paul's writings and Martin Luther's ninety-five theses but also confronts students with questions about their own life: How did Paul take a stand? What is the depth of Paul's message for you and us today? What beliefs and practices do you think are necessary to being a Christian (e.g., praying to God, baptizing believers, marrying a Christian)? One student assignment is to create a brochure promoting the Christian faith using the theological themes of the letter to the Galatians.*

- *The Renaissance and Reformation, focusing on why individuals such as Wycliffe and Luther took certain stands. Students write a research paper and a biography. They also write reports on how a historical or current religious leader has made a difference in people's lives and how a religiously based group such as World Vision has improved the lives of others in our world.*

- *The novel* Cue for Treason.

- *The television play* Twelve Angry Men, *with students learning about television as a medium and focusing on the statement of one juror: "It takes a great deal of courage to stand alone."*

A concluding activity entitled "How Should We Then Live?" is described as follows: We seek to discover patterns, themes and trends. We would like to learn from the victories and the mistakes of others. Begin by thinking about the things that interested you most about the areas we studied. Then search for an underlying theme: for example, loyalty, cowardliness, courage, perseverance, compassion, integrity, creativity, godliness. You will use the theme you choose for both your position paper and your speech. The examples you use should come from the cultures we have studied. The application should be specific to what you feel is important for us to remember in the way we live our lives today. Choose a topic that is important to you. Your speech and position paper will be more powerful if you believe in your topic.

Topic ideas include the following:
- *It is more fun to live today than at any other time in history.*
- *I believe our society has lost the faith that Christ, Paul, and the Reformers died for.*
- *We need to follow the example of our Christian forefathers and make a difference in our world.*

Note how the unit takes a very different view of knowledge and values than does constructivism and yet allows for a great deal of student response. God's Word is held central as the authoritative truth for our lives. History is looked at in terms of human response to God's Creation Mandate and His Great Commandment. The study of a historical novel enriches the discussion of the historical time period. While human interpretation and bias are not denied, the unit recognizes the importance of actual historical happenings and cultural development. It holds that history is more than arbitrary human constructions. Students grapple with their personal beliefs and values. They do so within the context of the existence of certain absolutes that they can follow or rebuff in their lives. Yet the learning goes far beyond passive memorization or simple interpretation. The unit includes a wide variety of learning activities and continually calls for personal response and action. In that sense it is soundly rooted in a biblical understanding of knowledge.

Reflect and respond 3-9

The Taking a Stand unit integrates aspects of biblical studies, English, and history (sometimes collectively referred to as humanities). Do you like this approach, or would you prefer to teach the subjects separately?

A spectrum of subject integration is possible in schools. Schools can teach school subjects in completely separate time blocks. On the other hand, they can have an "integrated day" in which all learning is thematic, without any subject distinctions. At the grade level you teach or intend to teach, how much subject integration is desirable? How much is realistic?

Chapter 3 enduring understandings

- Traditional education does justice neither to the unique giftedness of learners nor to the response and commitment demanded by a biblical view of knowledge. On the other hand, radical constructivism is rooted in relativism of truth, knowledge, and values ("there are no right answers"), and, if solely used, its learning strategies are unduly time-consuming.

- A biblical view of knowledge affirms God's revelation and providence, and it embraces human response, commitment, and service as integral elements.
- A Christian curriculum orientation takes into account the Creation Mandate, the Great Commandment, and the Great Commission. It includes, where applicable, God's intent for the theme studies, how humans have distorted that intent, and what our response ought to be. It also holds that all learning activities, including cognitive- and ability-focused ones, ought to foster dispositions and commitments consistent with biblical guidelines and values.
- To ensure that teachers plan their classroom units to reflect a distinctively Christian approach, they ought to develop a thematic statement and a set of related intended learning outcomes (ILOs). They also carefully consider what learning activities are appropriate, how they will choose and use learning resources, and how they will assess their students in terms of the ILOs.

References

Baker, D., and M. Piburn. 1997. *Constructing science in middle and secondary school classrooms.* Boston, MA: Allyn and Bacon.

Fosnot, C. 2005. *Constructivism: Theory, perspectives and practice.* 2nd ed. New York: Columbia Univ., Teachers College Press.

Koole, R., ed. 1996. *Humanities 8: A resource guide.* Langley, BC: Society of Christian Schools in British Columbia.

Phillips, D., ed. 2000. *Constructivism in education: Opinions and second opinions on controversial issues.* Chicago, IL: National Society for the Study of Education.

Steffe, L., and J. Gale, eds. 1995. *Constructivism in education.* Hillsdale, NJ: Lawrence Erlbaum.

Teichrieb, L. 2006. Learning from Japan (unpublished sixth-grade curriculum unit). Langley, BC: Trinity Western University.

Todd, D. 2007. Seeking solid ground in a pluralistic world. *The Vancouver Sun.* November 17: D4.

Van Brummelen, H. 1997. Curriculum development is dead—or is it? *Pro Rege* 26, no. 1:14–23.

_____. 2002. *Steppingstones to curriculum: A biblical path.* Colorado Springs: Purposeful Design.

How Do We Prepare for Meaningful Learning?

4

Chapter 4 guiding questions

- Which metaphors for human beings inform teaching and learning?
- How do we take into account students' developmental growth, learning styles, and aptitudes as we plan for learning?
- Can we develop a model for learning that takes into account that every student uniquely bears the image of God?
- How can we plan our daily lessons to support meaningful learning?

Melissa Hildebrandt has to teach elementary equations to her ninth-grade class. This is her second year of teaching, and last year she heard some of her students— particularly the ones who often did not do well in math—mutter under their breath, "What's the use of this stuff?" Reflecting on last year's experience, she decided that this year she will use more variety in her teaching strategies. In this way, she hopes to meet the needs of students with different learning styles. Also, she will try to motivate her students by regularly including relevant applications. In addition, she will plan for more differentiated learning, in which students with different aptitudes work on different levels and types of problems.

Ms. Hildebrandt begins her unit by dividing the class into small groups to solve several problems. She explains to the students that they likely can solve the problems by trial and error. They can take that approach if they wish. However, in order to solve more complex problems in the future, they must also develop a system for solving them using algebraic language.

After giving the students an example of what she expects, they work on problems like the following:

- *If a 450 gm bag of cookies says that it contains 28 percent more than the former size, how many grams did the former size contain?*

- *If a driver drives to a city 200 km away at a speed of 50 km/hr and returns at 80 km/hr, what is her average speed for the round trip?*
- *A car's cooling system holds 8 liters of a mixture of water and antifreeze, of which 20% is antifreeze. How much of this mixture must be drained and replaced with pure antifreeze so that the resulting 8 liters will be 50% antifreeze?*

At a table Ms. Hildebrandt also has a science balance and two sealed bags of marbles as well as fourteen loose marbles. On a card she has explained that she divided her original marbles into equal groups. In one bag she put two of the groups, in the second she put four groups. Then she took three of the second bag and added them to the first bag. How many marbles were there in each original group? [The students add eight marbles to the first bag to balance the second bag. They then write this as $(2x + 3) + 8 = 4x - 3$.]

After debriefing the solutions, she teaches solving simple equations in a more structured way. But she begins each lesson with an authentic problem that students translate into an equation and then solve. For students who need concrete visualizations, she again uses the example of the scale in which x represents an unknown number of marbles in a bag. She asks other students who are having difficulty to write out how they are thinking about a problem, or to draw a representational picture.

Each period, the students practice solving equations, including ones that involve practical situations. They solve a number of specified problems, but Ms. Hildebrandt provides additional problems and suggests strategies that focus on the needs of certain groups in her class. She supplies a number of applications at different levels of difficulty for students with various levels and types of aptitude. She also has weaker students explain their strategies to a partner who may help them overcome hurdles. Some application problems involve situations in which a solution may not be the best one to put into practice because of value considerations (e.g., manufacturers reducing sizes of food containers but not lowering prices). The students also construct some problems for others to solve, and pose problems to be solved in consultation with others.

Overall, the unit allows for exploration and discussion in small groups. It includes structured instruction and conceptualization. Ms. Hildebrandt complements problems that require practice and simple applications with those that require creative thinking. While not all students like algebra at the end of the unit, the variety of activities has enabled all students at times to use their preferred learning style. Moreover, they understand the usefulness of algebra, and have solved problems and applied their new knowledge in a variety of ways.

No two persons learn in exactly the same way. Also with respect to learning, each person has unique gifts from God. "One has this gift, another has that" (1 Corinthians 7:7). Humans are not limited to one gift but have unique degrees and combinations of many gifts. Some persons learn better deductively; others, inductively. Some learn better through visual stimuli; others, through aural-oral ones; still others, through kinesthetic ones. Some persons need to try things out in concrete settings; others reflect abstractly. Some persons learn well through individual study; others prefer the give-and-take of discussions with others. Some like to sketch about what they're learning; others benefit from explaining their strategies orally or in writing.

A Christian approach to classroom learning needs to take into account these complex variations. It serves no purpose to decry the fact that some students do not learn well with a particular approach. Instead, we need to plan learning so that it celebrates the diversity with which God has created us.

This chapter considers various views about the nature of human beings and the classroom implications of each view. It discusses how the experiential backgrounds and developmental phases of students affect their classroom learning. Then it describes a model for planning learning that takes into account the rhythm of learning as well as the needs of students who prefer different ways of approaching learning. Finally, it presents how to plan for meaningful learning on a daily basis.

Views of the person: Implications for learning

The Bible views humans as created in the image of God. To do justice to a discussion of classroom learning, we need to expand upon this idea and its implications for learning. First, however, it is useful to sketch the four main ways in which educators have looked at human beings during the last three hundred years. This process will help us see more clearly the distinctiveness and importance of looking at students as bearers of God's image.

Traditionalists in education often look at children as *blank slates* on which adults write knowledge, or as *piggy banks* into which we deposit facts and concepts. Learning becomes, to a large extent, a teacher-centered "pouring in." Teachers present, and students memorize. Traditionalists correctly see that learning needs a conceptual base. However, they overlook students' personal responsibility for learning. They also neglect the fact that students learn from experience and investigation, posing and solving problems, interacting with peers, and creating products. Moreover, students respond to teaching in unique ways, both in how they interpret knowledge and in how they apply it.

Students are more than blank slates that teachers fill with whatever they desire. They are personalities with their own beliefs, traits, abilities, and capacity to make decisions. All these influence learning. Christian teachers who tacitly regard their students as half-full piggy banks to be "topped up" may transmit information, including specifics about God's creation and His love. But they will fall short in helping them discover, interpret, extend, and apply knowledge in loving, responsive, and creative service.

Behaviorists look at human beings as *trainable objects*. They emphasize rigid learning structures. They present knowledge step by step and bit by bit. They use frequent stimuli and reinforcements (rewards and punishments) to condition students. Students may learn some basic concepts and skills efficiently. However, this approach reduces education to training and even manipulation.

There are some special circumstances in which behaviorist methods can be useful. I have known students, particularly in the lower grades, who could not function normally in a classroom. They disrupted learning for everyone. In such cases I have seen teachers use stickers to reward such children whenever they behaved and learned in positive ways. I have also seen kindergarten and first-grade teachers use small rewards to encourage fearful or clinging students to go out and play at recess and lunch hour. Gradually, however, teachers should wean such children away from extrinsic rewards. For example, they could begin to ask them to decide for themselves when they deserve a reward. Gradually they give the rewards at longer intervals, and then stop giving them altogether.

Behaviorist methods are limited in effectiveness. Their mechanistic strategies keep students from becoming choosing, responsive persons. They leave little room for personal responsibility and creativity. They fail to recognize sin and its consequences. They believe the right stimuli can resolve all problems. They also neglect the community context of learning. They assume that learning takes place individually using stimulus-response techniques. Wise teachers use behaviorist strategies only to solve immediate problems, not to motivate long-term learning.

Educators from Pestalozzi to Piaget have viewed young persons as *unfolding plants*. Teachers assist their natural and preordained development as they move through the universal stages. They see human life as a unity, a wholeness. Humans, they believe, have some inherent thought structures. As these develop, persons move from one psychosocial, rational, lingual, or moral stage to the next.

The stages most commonly applied in education are Piaget's cognitive ones. Piaget held that cognitive intelligence organizes the world around us. Learning, however, involves more than cognition. It also has emotional, social, and creative dimensions. Thus Piaget's stages overemphasize the rational dimension of life at the expense of other, equally important ones. Moreover, his stages are not as inevitable or as fixed as his followers would have us believe. Unlike plants, humans can make personal choices and decisions about learning and about life. They may revert back to earlier stages from time to time, depending on the situation.

Finally, progressive educators like John Dewey and critical theorists like Paulo Freire consider students to be *primary agents of social change*. They emphasize problem solving and critical thinking. They use inquiry and other strategies that help students transform society. They see schooling as a journey in which the process is as important as the destination. They use learning as a means to improve society. However, they put the child rather than God at the center of the universe. They assume that the innate goodness of students will motivate them to study and learn what is good for them. They hold that inquiry leads to truth. But such truth and values may work only for particular persons in particular circumstances. Their efforts to improve society may shipwreck on a lack of agreement on moral, economic, and social values.

All these metaphors for the learner contain kernels of validity. Each says something of value about learning. That this is so is understandable, since all educators deal with the data of God's reality. Sometimes learners benefit from receiving information and concepts in a structured way. Sometimes students benefit from a carrot-and-stick behaviorist approach. Sometimes it helps to know that students are not yet ready to learn abstract algebra. Further, the processes of inquiry and problem solving and critical thinking are important if students are to contribute to society.

In short, we can learn something from each metaphor. As we will see, however, each falls short of the rich biblical conception of humans as image-bearers of God. None admits that in the end learning is meaningful only when it leads to an understanding of God's call that impels us to responsive discipleship and responsible action.

Reflect and respond 4-1

On a large sheet of paper, complete the following chart:

METAPHOR OF CHILD	CLASSROOM STRUCTURE	TEACHING STRATEGIES	CURRICULUM CONTENT
Blank slate			
Trainable object			
Unfolding plant			
Agent of social change			

Then discuss which one of these four metaphors, or what combination of metaphors, you would favor for your own classroom. Justify your position

Students as image-bearers of God

God created all persons, including teachers and students, in His image and likeness (Genesis 1:26–27, James 3:9). Being image-bearers of God and reflecting God in our lives is not an option for us. God created us that way. We display His image as we use our unique freedom and abilities. We honor and reflect God's majesty by ruling over the works of His hands in responsive ways (Psalm 8).

Yet the extent to which we exercise our calling to be image-bearers of God depends on several factors. Are we wholeheartedly devoted to the one true God? To what degree are we committed to God's Creation Mandate (Genesis 1:28, 2:15)? the Great Commandment (Matthew 22:37–39)? the Great Commission (Matthew 28:18–20)? To what degree do we even understand them? Living as *obedient* image-bearers means first of all looking up to God as we serve Him and our neighbor. We must depend on God, in whom we live and move and have our being (Acts 17:28).

We may not divide our lives into separate secular and spiritual sectors. God calls us to serve Him in *all* that we do, with undivided hearts. Students are holistic, integrated beings whose religious "heart" governs all dimensions of life. Some educational leaders absolutize one or another of these dimensions and equate it with our religious heart. John Dewey, for instance, made the social dimension the focus of all of life. Some educators emphasize preparing students mainly for economic life. Others focus on rationality as that which will save humanity. All of these espouse a reduced view of what persons really are. More seriously, all posit a secular faith in human abilities that replaces faith in God.

Scripture makes clear that humans have a *religious* and not a social or economic or rational heart. Our religious core governs all dimensions of life: the spiritual, moral, political, economic, social, linguistic, logical, aesthetic, emotional, biological, physical, and mathematical aspects. The heart is the wellspring or source of life (Proverbs 4:23). Faith in God leads to singleness of heart in all our actions. Obedient faith and action lead, for example, to God's blessing in business and agriculture (Jeremiah 32:38–44). A false religious heart, on the other hand, is a deluded heart without understanding or true knowledge (Isaiah 44:19–20).

Word alert

Many books have been written about what it means that humans were created in the *imago Dei* or *image of God*. What is clear is that this phrase was radical in the human-servitude context of the Middle East. God, the Bible proclaims, is a generous Creator who shares power with humans. He trusts humans to be His representatives on earth and gives them a responsible task (the Creation Mandate). Humans are not God or gods, but they are called to imitate and continue God's creative work by unfolding the potential of creation in ways that promote God's purposes for justice and shalom (Middleton 2005). Graham (2003) adds that we can do so because God has endowed us with small measures of His own character—purposefulness, creativity, rationality, faithfulness, morality, mercy, and so on—even if in us they are flawed because of the effects of sin. .

Schools highlight explicit growth in a number of identifiable (though inseparable) dimensions of human life. These include the social, economic, and rational aspects of life. However, our religious heart rules all these facets of life. If students do not share our biblically based commitment, they may well also reject a biblical approach to social or economic issues. Therefore, teachers need to take into account the faith and worldview groundings of their students. Christian schools need to teach and demonstrate how basic commitments affect how we live all of life.

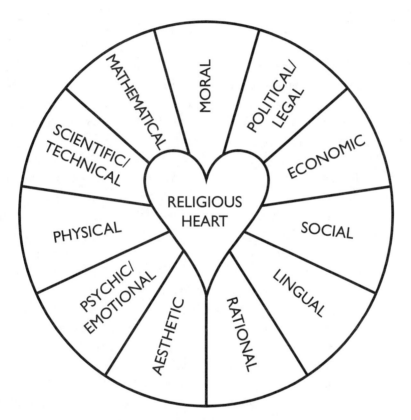

Figure 4.1. Dimensions of Human Beings

Further, even when a school subject focuses only on certain aspects of life, students learn as total, integrated beings. We teach logical thinking, for instance, to students who have brought their whole being to class. Not only their rational ability but also their physical, emotional, social, and moral characteristics will affect how well they learn—and how well they reason. Similarly, if students' physical or emotional or social needs are not met at home or in their peer group, they will find classroom learning difficult. That is why schools in challenging socioeconomic areas provide breakfasts and start the day with sharing sessions that try to offset a lack of healthy relationships, security, and support.

All dimensions of students' lives are interrelated. Each dimension affects all the others. An incident on the playground, the loss of a prized possession, the scoring of a goal in a soccer game, a forthcoming visit by a divorced parent—all affect learning. While such events are often beyond our control, we can be sensitively alert to them and to their effects on classroom learning.

Being image-bearers of God also means that students are responsible and accountable for their actions. God has established norms and guidelines for our lives. There are rights and wrongs. Absolutes do exist. The Word of God stands forever (Isaiah 40:8). This truth is a source of comfort and security for both students and teachers. At the same time, as bearers of His image, God holds us accountable for living according to His norms. Starting with Adam and Eve, God allowed persons freedom to choose. Students can make decisions. They can choose to obey or disobey. They can decide how to respond to God's calling. Students need to experience being responsible and accountable for their actions. This means that we give them appropriate responsibility and hold them accountable for their learning efforts as well. We use our God-given authority to enable students to become ever more responsible for themselves. Kindergartners already can learn to keep checklists of center work they have done and to solve conflicts with other students.

Students, like teachers, will fall short, even when they have turned their lives over to Jesus in trust and service. They are sinners in need of redemption and daily renewal (Romans 3:23–24). This does not mean, however, that they are corrupt and can do no good. Rather, it means that they will fail from time to time even when they try to make good decisions or take correct action. Their conduct, effort, and relationships with others will not always reflect a biblical lifestyle. Therefore, students need guidance, supervision, and discipline. A key role of teachers is to direct their students "in the way [they] should go" (Proverbs 22:6). Teachers do so within an atmosphere of security, lack of fear, and mutual respect for others' dignity and property.

We must not forget that students through conversion and regeneration become *fellow workers* with God and *co-heirs* with Christ (Romans 8:17, 1 Corinthians 3:9). When they turn their hearts to God, they can work with true purpose and meaning, although, like us, they still fall short in their service. Our teaching helps them become transformed through the renewing of their minds (Romans 12:2). They learn to pitch in to help make God's creation a better place.

Despite their sin and weakness, God extends to students the gift and the mandate of His kingdom. This makes their task in school and life a far richer one than that proposed by the traditionalist or the behaviorist. Seize opportunities to help students see how important and enriching it is to be touched by the Holy Spirit. Plan your pedagogy and choose content so that you encourage students to take up their intended calling as bearers of God's image.

The Bible also makes clear that each person is unique. All are able to contribute to life in community in a special way, using their distinctive gifts (Romans 12:4–8). In the classroom, expect all students to be actively engaged. Not all students, however, can achieve equally. Therefore, use diverse approaches. Modify assignments for students with different abilities. Otherwise, you may not be bringing up children and adolescents "in the training and instruction of the Lord." Rather, you will exasperate at least some of them (Ephesians 6:4).

Build on students' strengths! Enable them to understand and develop their particular gifts. Encourage them to do things they can do well. Thus students may acquire and maintain a sense of worth. All of us need success before we can confidently explore unfamiliar or difficult areas. When students, with suitable effort, successfully complete tasks, they develop self-confidence and look forward to future growth. Give all students meaningful roles as participants in classroom and school activities and events. They need to know that you appreciate them for being contributing members of a learning community in which they image God in all aspects of their lives.

Reflect and respond 4-2

This section outlines (but does not exhaust) what it means that students are created in the image of God. What is central is that God calls each student—and teacher!—to commitment and service. Discuss the implications and give some classroom examples for each of the following student characteristics:

- Multidimensional and yet holistic
- Uniquely gifted
- Responsible and accountable
- Sinful but living under God's common grace, with the possibility of redemption

Are there other characteristics of being image-bearers of God that have implications for the classroom?

Experiential background and developmental layers

One of the marvels of childhood is the powerful ways in which young human beings learn through their everyday experiences. Before children attend school, they have already learned an amazing amount about quantity and space, movement and speed, warmth and light, rocks and water, plants and animals, human emotions and interrelationships, right and wrong, and beliefs and faith.

It is also humbling for teachers to realize how much school-age children learn without being taught, both inside and outside school. Once they attend school, students continue to develop their insights through the countless experiences they have at home, on the street, in parks, in church, and in shopping malls. They also learn through exposure to printed, visual, oral, and computer-based materials.

That does not mean that schools are unimportant for learning. Schools are more than just institutions that socialize students. The more formal, focused learning that schools provide plays an important role in students' development. But we need to take into account what our students have learned and are learning through their everyday experiences. We use students' experiential knowledge as a starting point for more focused learning. Through guided questioning, we deepen and formalize what students already know. We ask them to stand back and study God's world as a place with structure, patterns, and relationships. We help them apply the resulting insights to various life experiences.

Teachers cannot assume, of course, that all students have similar experiential knowledge backgrounds. Homes vary a great deal in how much and what types of stimulation they provide. These differences affect both the readiness and the ability of students to learn. For instance, some children enter school without any experience with books. Such children know nothing of the rewards of reading. They are not ready to learn decoding skills. If their experiences have not given them any reason for needing or wanting to read, decoding for them may be a rote activity with little point except to please the teacher. A defeatist attitude can easily result.

Therefore, we plan many experiential activities, especially for children with limited literacy backgrounds. We base more formal, focused school learning on students' own background knowledge, whether gained outside school or through activities we provide. Neglecting experiential learning for children who lack it will result in rote learning that is not personally meaningful.

We nurture a learning context for students by giving rich experiences with the primary "stuff" of reality. We provide activities with concrete, manipulative, and imaginative materials. Before we formally teach new content and skills, we give our students activities in which they themselves explore, generalize, and make informal inferences. Meanwhile, we observe, interact with, and guide them. We note how they think and whether they are ready for more focused learning. We try to find out whether they are gaining meaning. We allow inexact thinking and products early on. Kindergarten teachers, for instance, give many opportunities for emergent reading and writing as well as informal exploration with numbers and shapes. Tenth-grade science teachers encourage students to experiment with lenses and prisms. It is useful for students to draw interim conclusions before concepts are formally taught.

It is easy to fragment learning to the point where students see little relevance in school learning. They experience life as a whole. The mathematical, physical, emotional, social, aesthetic, and moral dimensions of life all impinge on real-life situations. We separate them for the sake of analysis, but students do not experience them separately. Therefore we teach even specialized topics in a meaningful context. How does the topic relate to other aspects of knowledge? to life in culture? How does the topic relate to biblical themes and norms that set the direction for our lives? Can the topic help students see the unity of creation and of life? How can students respond to and use the new knowledge in a personal way?

We are sensitive not only to the traits and backgrounds of our students, but also to their developmental levels. Effective learning activities take into account students' current conceptual and thinking abilities. We need to avoid labeling students too soon, however. Some develop early; others, late. Some learn to read slowly and find the early years of school difficult. Yet they may be very intelligent in other ways and become perceptive and creative persons.

Developmental stage theories like that of Piaget are not as helpful as is sometimes assumed. Teachers do not know precisely their students' levels of cognitive development. Even if they did, they would still face a wide spectrum of stages in their classrooms. Moreover, Piaget's stage theory concerns itself mainly with logical thinking, which "represents only a small part of the intellectual equipment children bring to making sense of the world and their experience" (Egan 1983, 96).

Kieran Egan (1997) suggests instead three developmental "layers of understanding" that may help you in planning: *primary* or *mythic, romantic,* and *philosophic* understanding. Successive layers do not replace previous ones but fuse with them, giving deepened understanding and insight. According to Egan, at the mythic or primary level of understanding (ages 5–9), students can already deal with deep and abstract concepts and themes. To help students do so, teachers design units as "stories" that communicate meaning and values in terms of "binary opposites" such as love and hate, honor and selfishness, or dominance and submission. He adds that children at this age are intrigued by what is remote and imagined, by what expands their horizons. Stories or myths provide children with causal explanations, prediction, and control. Egan emphasizes not only the importance of telling stories to children of this age group but also of structuring units in story form.

Once students move into the romantic layer (ages 8–15), they do not lose their interest in story or narrative formats, but they now look for adventure, imagination, and idealism. They enthusiastically explore the world and their experience in it. They are fervent in their quest for knowledge about the extreme and the exotic. Facts and explanations of how and why things happen fascinate them. Teachers make the familiar strange. They stimulate romance, wonder, and awe. At the same time, they develop units around basic "transcendent" human values.

In the philosophic layer (ages 14–19), students understand and develop causal chains of reasoning and interrelationships within networks of concepts and knowledge. Here students move beyond detail and set out to draw general conclusions. They want to explore and understand what causes phenomena so that they can prepare to live independently in the real world. Teachers focus their planning on underlying questions and issues.

Consider teaching about honeybees, for instance. In kindergarten, you may emphasize the cycle of life and death. Children may experience how each bee has a special function in the life of a hive. While the activities are concrete, the unifying "story" may be how, over one year, a hive cares for and renews itself. In fifth grade, you may have students explore the unexpected order and intricacies of the life of bees in a hive (e.g., how complex dances indicate the location of flower nectar). God's gracious provision for pollination of plants becomes the underlying value that students learn to

---

Word alert

For planning classroom pedagogy, Kieran Egan's three layers of understanding for school-age children are helpful (Egan 1997):

Primary or *mythic understanding*: Children aged 5–9 learn abstract concepts, causality, and values from stories and units taught in story settings with dramatic opposites.

Romantic understanding: Students aged 8–15 benefit from learning transcendent values, often in narrative settings. They love the unexpected (including details), idealism, and imaginative activities.

Philosophic understanding: Students aged 14–19 can deal with the meaning and purpose of life in terms of general explanatory schemes (beliefs, worldviews, theories). They like to consider and draw causal connections.

These three layers build on top of each other, but the higher does not replace the one below it. This model helps us teach a biblical worldview and biblical values in ways that are appropriate for different age groups.

---

appreciate. In eleventh grade, teachers would put the study of bees in the context of genetic developments and our ecosystem. What will be the effects of African bees slowly moving north in North America? What impact will beehive devastation caused by mites have on crops and our ecosystem? Can genetic engineering develop mite-resistant bees? Is this desirable? What are the causes, the far-reaching consequences, and the possible solutions to bee colony collapse?

Students have different experiential backgrounds and operate at varying levels of cognitive, social, and moral development. Observe your students and listen to them carefully to check whether their learning is meaningful for them. At the same time, do not trivialize educational content because of dubious claims made about children's cognitive development. Young children can enjoy, deal with, and learn about profound themes and values as long as they are presented in concrete settings and as long as we do not expect them to reason about those themes and values in the formal ways that we can expect from young adults.

Reflect and respond 4-3

Choose a topic that can be taught at different grade levels (e.g., the family, China, or magnetism and electricity). Discuss how you would teach the topic in first grade, sixth grade, and eleventh grade. How do your suggestions relate to Egan's layers of understanding?

The complexity of learning

God has created us as complex beings, and thus we learn in complicated ways. Despite a great deal of research on learning over the last half century (including research on brain-compatible learning), we still know surprisingly little about effective pedagogy. Educators who have evaluated a large spectrum of research studies agree on a few general principles. Often good teachers have used these already for many years on the basis of their own experience and reflection (e.g., Cotton 1999; Marzano et al. 2001; Van Brummelen 2002; Willis 2006).

- *Interact with students in respectful and caring ways.* Create an atmosphere of openness, trust, and security, with efficient routines and clear discipline policies.
- *Engage your class* in planned, purposeful, relevant, challenging, and imaginative learning. Use clear but flexible goals. Set high but realistic expectations.
- *Balance clear and focused whole-group instruction with small or cooperative learning groups* for reinforcement and higher-level thinking skills.
- *Have students summarize what they have learned, generate and test hypotheses, and explain their reasons.*
- *Provide adequate practice* to reinforce concepts and skills.
- *Reinforce student effort* and provide recognition in terms of specified intended outcomes.
- To *consolidate learned material into long-term memory*, use surprise to motivate students, introduce information when you have students' focused attention, use

multiple and multisensory exposures, and have students use the information in real-world settings.

There are two aspects of learning that have received much attention over the years. One is that we often go through a pattern of steps, or phases, as we learn. We first build on our experiential knowledge, explore a new topic informally, or carry out an investigation. We then learn in a more focused way by hearing a presentation, reading about a topic, or discussing our findings in a structured way. Next we check and reinforce what we have learned by summarizing, answering questions, or practicing. And finally we generalize and apply our learning in what for us are new and possibly creative ways.

A second facet about which much has been written is the fact that students learn differently. They prefer learning in different ways (learning styles), and they have different types of aptitudes (multiple intelligences). For instance, some students enjoy working on structured worksheets. Others thrive on more open-ended, creative activities. Some learn math strategies through writing out how they solve problems. Others like to sketch out the problem and the steps they use.

I believe that both of these factors relate to the fact that students have been uniquely created in the image of God. Therefore, both need to be taken into account when planning classroom learning. But here I need to sound three cautions. First, I base the next two sections on the implications of a biblical view of human beings and of knowledge and not on research that demonstrates that my suggested model leads to higher student achievement. In fact, despite many studies over a thirty-year period, it is not possible to conclude that implementing a pedagogy based on learning styles or "multiple intelligences" increases the attainment of standards or outcomes (e.g., see Coffield et al. 2004). A second caution is that learning styles and a preference for certain "intelligences" depend on many past and current influences: personal predilections, age, family and cultural background, and contextual influences. So they may change over time, and even from one situation to another. Finally, learning is far too complex to suggest that one model can or should be used at all times.

Nevertheless, the planning model I describe in the next two sections is a defensible one that many teachers have used constructively. It can benefit students as long as it is used flexibly and as long as it is remembered that certain learning situations call for different approaches. The model encourages students to affirm and use what they have already learned and experienced. It also gives them the background to use and apply their learning in meaningful ways. In addition, it takes into account that students are uniquely gifted and should be able to use and develop their special gifts in optimal ways.

Learning styles

Students differ greatly in their preferred learning styles. It is neither feasible nor desirable to provide all students with experiences during each class that match their particular learning style. Yet knowing the features of diverse learning styles makes us sensitive to students who prefer to approach learning in different ways. So in each unit we should try to provide some learning activities in which learners can use their favored learning style. At the same time, to enable our students to function in society as balanced persons, we stretch them by helping them become comfortable with diverse approaches to learning. Surveying your students' favored learning styles and planning your teaching on that basis is unrealistic. It has, in any case, far less payoff than judiciously using informal assessment to enhance learning (Coffield et al. 2004). However, being aware of different learning styles and analyzing your own preferred learning style(s) helps you plan a balance of learning experiences. Otherwise you may leave out activities that do not match your own preferred style(s).

No one classification of learning styles captures all the nuances of differing preferred approaches to learning. Some emphasize that learners favor visual, oral, or kinesthetic means. Others base their classification on the fact that pupils may prefer kinesthetic, logical, linguistic, interpersonal, or aesthetic learning. Still others include as many as twenty factors.

Let me give an example. Our two sons both have strong mathematical intelligence (the oldest has a PhD in math; the younger, an undergraduate minor). But they learn very differently. The older is an analytic learner who reasons things out very carefully, step by step, until he solves a problem or reaches a conclusion. Our younger son is an inventive or imaginative learner. One of his professors once said to me, "I love marking your son's exams and assignments. He jumps to conclusions in creative and often surprising ways, only later filling in the gaps. He falls flat on his face 20 percent of the time, but the other times he comes up with remarkably imaginative and original solutions." Both our sons have mathematical intelligence. But when our older son tried to help our younger one with some high school math problems, frustration

Word alert

The terms *learning styles* and *multiple intelligences* are sometimes used interchangeably. However, as this chapter points out, they are not the same. Learning styles refer to the favored ways in which students like to learn. Multiple intelligences refer to students' aptitudes and types of intelligence. Sometimes a type of intelligence may naturally lead to a preferred way of learning, but that is not always the case.

resulted. Neither one had the patience to put up with the other's way of trying to solve problems. Their learning styles were at opposite ends of the spectrum.

Bernice McCarthy (1997, 2005) has applied learning styles to classroom learning in helpful ways. Her work has its roots in the Myers-Briggs classification of personality types as well as the work of David Kolb (1984). McCarthy begins by considering how humans *perceive* and how they *process* experiences as they learn. Some persons perceive new situations more intuitively, by sensing and feeling them concretely. Others analyze experiences more abstractly, thinking and reasoning about them. Persons also process experiences and information differently. Some actively jump in and try things out. Others stand back and reflect on their experiences (or those of others). In general, schools have favored abstract perception and reflective processing. Yet students need to feel as well as think, do as well as reflect. Society needs persons with all these abilities.

If we superimpose these two dimensions of learning, four learning-style categories result, as shown in figure 4.2.

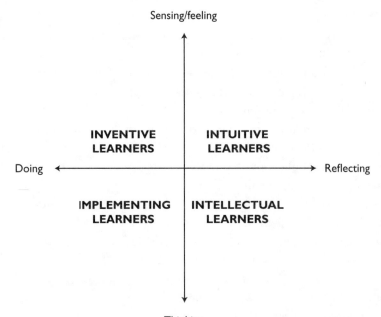

Figure 4.2. Learning Style Categories

The upper right quadrant contains learners who prefer to perceive information concretely and process it reflectively. I call these *intuitive* learners (these are my own, not McCarthy's terms). Intuitive learners are personally involved in their learning. They view concrete situations from different perspectives. They reflect on their own experiences to seek meaning and reach conclusions. They enjoy social interaction and involvement. They learn by listening and sharing ideas. They ask questions and learn through responding to and discussing their perceptions. A key question for intuitive learners is *Why?* Intuitive learners benefit from looking at phenomena and problems in the light of their previous experiences and exploring causes and effects in social settings. Intuitive learners often include counselors, sociologists, and elementary school teachers.

The lower right quadrant contains *intellectual* or *analytic* learners. They perceive information abstractly and process it reflectively. They are interested in concepts and ideas. They collect, analyze, and conceptualize knowledge. They find satisfaction in thinking through problems and issues and in determining the validity of a thesis. They learn well in traditional classrooms from presentations, explanations, and readings. A key question for intellectual learners is *What?* Teachers help them gather, digest, and process facts, concepts, and theories. Unlike intuitive learners, they may not enjoy group work or open-ended tasks. Planners, philosophers, and mathematicians often favor this learning style.

The lower left quadrant contains *implementing* learners. They perceive information abstractly and process it actively. They revel in hands-on experiences and in solving real-world problems. They want to know how things work and how to apply concepts in everyday situations. They enjoy learning by testing theories and applying ideas to practical situations rather than by being given answers. The key question for implementers is *How?* Teachers must let them move around and do things as they construct, manipulate, and demonstrate. They tend to act before they reflect. Implementers include many nurses, technicians, and engineers.

The fourth category, in the upper left quadrant, is that of *inventive* learners. These learners perceive information concretely and process it actively. They are also people of action. Rather than implementing the ideas of others, they prefer to let their own ideas take flight. They can work with people, though others sometimes see them as too pushy in their enthusiasm and drive. They are entrepreneurs who like to make things happen. They test experience and excel in situations that call for flexibility, improvisation, and creativity. They seek out possibilities through trial and error and experimentation, often reaching accurate conclusions without linear, rational argumentation. Inventive learners ask *What if?* Teachers must let them discover and seek out hidden possibilities. Many marketing and sales people as well as artists are inventive or imaginative learners (McCarthy 1996, 2005).

Students and their teachers may lean heavily toward one orientation, may have two or even three strong ones, or they may be balanced in all four. Moreover, learning-style preferences may well change with age and with different types of experiences. Analytic high school learners, for instance, may have preferred a hands-on approach in kindergarten. Schools traditionally have emphasized learning activities that particularly fit intellectual or analytic learners. Yet to celebrate that students are unique image-bearers of God, students should, on a regular basis, be able to use their own preferred learning styles.

Reflect and respond 4-4

Where are your strengths as a learner in the four described categories? What are the implications for your classroom? (If you do not know, you may want to complete a learning style inventory.)

Choose a unit topic for a particular grade level. Construct or find some activities that would suit learners who prefer each of the four learning style categories.

Phases of learning

Pentecost morning, as described in Acts 2, provides an example of four more-or-less distinct phases of learning: setting the stage, disclosure, reformulation, and transcendence. The apostle Peter first provided the setting. *He waited until the people had experienced the morning's strange events and had asked one another, "What does this mean?" He then related his remarks to what people were thinking: "These men are not drunk, as you suppose ..." (Acts 2:15). Next, he put forward* disclosure, *analyzing and building a conceptual structure. He recounted that the events were taking place in historical context, showed that they fulfilled prophecies of old, and proclaimed the good news of Christ. The listening learners then* reformulated *the concepts themselves. Their thinking and reflection led them to be "cut to the heart." They asked, "What shall we do?" (Acts 2:37). Finally, they had an opportunity for* transcendence, *for acting on what they had learned in a personal way. Many accepted the message. They were baptized, they devoted themselves to the apostles' teaching and to the fellowship, and they gave as people had need (Acts 2:41–47). Their acceptance of knowledge led to commitment and obedient response.*

Many years ago Alfred North Whitehead (1929) wrote that there is a natural rhythm in learning. It moves from what he called romance, to precision and, finally, to generalization. In thinking about this I came to the conclusion that a better categorization for the phases of learning would be a fourfold one: setting the stage (*preparing*), disclosure (*presenting*), reformulation (*practicing*), and transcendence *(responding by going beyond)*.

A few years later, I saw McCarthy's categorization of learning styles. I realized that I could superimpose her template on my four phases of learning. Each phase lent itself to activities particularly suited for one of McCarthy's learning-style categories. I also saw, however, that learning is too complex to categorize completely. I do not intend my phases to represent a rigid, foolproof formula for lesson planning. But the schema is helpful for checking whether in teaching a topic you are providing for all phases of learning and for all learning-style categories. The four-phase model stands independent of a consideration of learning styles, but is enriched by it. It encourages students to use their diverse gifts to exercise responsive obedience to God's call in life, no matter what their learning styles may be.

Let me give a classroom example of these four phases. You may want to ask how these relate to McCarthy's learning styles.

A seventh-grade teacher first engages her students by reading aloud a number of pages of the novel A Wrinkle in Time. *The students read the rest of the novel themselves. They respond to their reading by drawing a picture of a favorite scene, creating a collage showing their feelings about the novel, or writing another ending to it. Later, as an introduction to more formal work on characterization in the novel, some students dramatize certain scenes to show the uniqueness of the characters. Others do an interpretive reading. The activities are open-ended and allow for much exploration and imagination before the novel is discussed formally in class. The activities emphasize the students' own enjoyment and personal reaction. The teacher encourages informal reflection by asking questions.*

The teacher then introduces a handout, "A Way of Responding to Literature." Using this handout, the class develops a plot graph, discusses the conflicts in the novel, and learns what is meant by the plot climax. The students write a paragraph organizing their reasons for believing that the climax occurs at a particular point in the novel. Later, the teacher analyzes with the class how the author portrays love and evil, writing the main points on an overhead transparency. In a small-group discussion, the students compare these main points with what the Bible says about evil and love. They then make a summary statement comparing and contrasting the two views.

At the end of the unit, the students write an essay on the characteristics of the evil that exists on the planet Camazotz. The teacher asks the students not only to compare the author's view of love and evil with a biblical view but also to state how they would respond to the Camazotz-type evil we find on earth. The class holds a discussion about how people in society and the students themselves can be more accepting of one another as unique image-bearers of God. The teacher invites them to write one or two specific ways in which they will try, during the next week, to show Christian love in an area where they have a difficult time so doing. Finally, the unit provides personal choice and open-ended response about other novels and poems by the same author.

Phase 1: Setting the stage (preparing)

The first phase of learning attempts to make the learning that is to take place personally meaningful. It makes use of the students' experiential knowledge. It encourages them to enjoy, to discover, to imagine, to search for relationships, and to draw conclusions without approaching a topic deductively and formally. This phase of learning is a time for exploring, for asking questions, for delighting in immediate response.

In this phase, provide a meaningful setting by encouraging your students to react, to express their feelings, to make suggestions, and to draw their own conclusions—even if those are unpolished at this stage. Help them reflect on the knowledge they already have and explore the limits of such knowledge in nonthreatening ways. Dialogue with students to find out what they are thinking so that you can plan the other phases of learning to meet their needs.

In this first phase all students should experience, as Whitehead called it, some "romancing" with academic content. Especially here, make use of imaginative materials, real-life objects and situations, field trips, and film and drama. Blomberg (2007) refers to this phase as *play*. He emphasizes the importance of students' playful initial encounter, engagement, and exploration of what, for them, are new facets of God's creation. This phase, he adds, enables students to draw new connections, see things from different angles, and connect school learning with everyday experience. Such play can nurture students' imagination and creativity. Seerveld (1980) calls this phase one of *surprise*. He suggests that you amaze the students by having them creatively pioneer, detect, and imagine unfamiliar things. While play and surprise are not always necessary, we use this phase to motivate students to become involved in and excited about the learning that is to take place. The students' informal work during this phase prepares them for more complex formal work.

Intuitive learners especially shine in the setting-the-stage phase. Here students check out their feelings and ideas, often interacting with other students. Students try to answer *Why?* questions in personal ways. They step into and reflect on concrete situations, integrating personal meaning with the experience. You encourage them to use their imagination and innovation. You are the facilitator and motivator who helps them analyze concrete experiences in meaningful ways.

A unit on the natural history of the British Columbia coastal forest begins with a class activity in which students answer the questions What do we know? *and* What do we want to know? *The students categorize their answers and then plan a field trip in which they begin to seek answers to some of their initial questions. During this trip, on the basis of their previous knowledge and current information, they also record the relationships they discover among plants, animals, and their physical environment. They discuss their experiences and findings as they draw an informal web showing forest relationships, a web that they will expand and correct as the unit progresses. Other unit sections start with an open-ended investigation of the properties and importance of water and a film on (and subsequent discussion of) communities of living things.*

The setting-the-stage phase may last one or several days at the beginning of a topic, or it may consist of short activities at the start of individual lessons. How long this phase lasts and when activities take place will vary considerably. What is important is that the students themselves become engaged in their learning. They need to reflect on their own experiential knowledge, their present action, their own feelings, and their own beliefs.

Phase 2: Disclosure (presenting)

It is insufficient for schools to have students do no more than explore and reflect informally using their experiential background, even when you structure and guide such activities. To understand God's complex creation and the role of humans in serving God in it, schools must systematically disclose, analyze, and evaluate significant aspects of that creation and how humans respond to their calling. If learning does not go beyond the setting-the-stage phase, students will have hazy insights, fuzzy thinking, and an inability to distinguish peripheral from central concepts. Precise, well-organized instruction must follow the first phase of learning.

The second phase of learning, *disclosure*, builds on the students' experiential knowledge, including that gained in the first phase. In disclosure the topic is unfolded and disclosed to the student in a carefully structured manner. You supersede the explorative nature of phase 1 with systematic and focused teaching modes: oral and visual presentations, demonstrations, class discussions, readings, computer-based instruction, collaborative small-group work, tutoring, and so on. This phase emphasizes careful conceptual development. It acquaints students with the common symbolic representation structures (e.g., language, mathematics, music, graphics). You encourage and assist students in using reasoning strategies to systematically process information and develop cognitive structures.

Avoid two pitfalls here. First, do not *close* the topic instead of *disclosing* it. Continue to involve and challenge your students. Ask penetrating questions. Encourage them to ask questions in turn. Phase 2 is not just a one-way presentation. Students are not passive receptors of information. They must actively process concepts and ideas. Meaningful learning demands active involvement.

Second, most teachers know how to organize, present, and explain concepts and information very well; therefore, they may be tempted to overemphasize phase 2. Yet disclosure must not become the sole or principal focus of learning. Gradually, as students get older, teachers may give more time to this phase. Yet even college students regularly and legitimately complain that instructors shortchange them when a course consists mainly of lecture °presentations (including or sometimes especially PowerPoint ones!). At higher grade levels, students can do more phase 3 and phase 4 activities outside of class. However, always strive for an appropriate balance of the four phases of learning. Regularly ask whether you are putting too much stress on phase 2 learning. Remember that only a minority of students prefer this type of learning, and that even they need to process, interpret, extend, and apply the ideas and their meaning themselves.

An important and integral part of disclosure is *conceptualization*. Students abstract concepts from experiential knowledge. They develop and refine them during disclosure, building their conceptual structures. As a teacher you present and explain information selectively so that you highlight core concepts. You consciously relate main and subordinate concepts so that students see interconnections. You help students assimilate concepts in meaningful, non-verbatim ways (Steensma and Van Brummelen 1977).

Precise conceptualization involves hard work. Often you must take concepts out of context to develop them further, resulting in an additional level of abstraction for students. You and your students need self-discipline and patience. However, if you regularly include all four phases of learning, your students will understand the purpose and place of conceptualization. They will recognize that it is a necessary prelude to further generalization and application.

It is the intellectual/analytic learners who delight and excel in the disclosure phase of learning. They enjoy learning and thinking about new concepts and hypotheses and their implications. They have the inclination and facility in analysis, classification, drawing conclusions, and theory construction. They examine and critique ideas. Often they are collectors of information. In the past, because schools have emphasized phase 2 of learning, and to an extent phase 3, it is these students who have been especially successful in school.

The disclosure phase of learning may take five minutes or several weeks, depending on the topic and the students' developmental level. It leads directly into phase 3, reformulation. Usually, in fact, reformulation activities are closely integrated with or closely follow each disclosure activity. Therefore the example of the forest unit continues in the next section.

Sensing/Feeling

4. TRANSCENDENCE

TEACHERS:

- ✓ provide opportunities and choices
- ✓ stimulate and encourage
- ✓ encourage open-ended exploration
- ✓ assess and evaluate
- ✓ look for originality, new insights, willingness to push limits

STUDENTS:

- ✓ make and exhibit personal products
- ✓ choose and commit
- ✓ improvise and invent
- ✓ imagine and create
- ✓ pose and solve difficult problems
- ✓ evaluate their own products
- ✓ set future goals

Doing

1. SETTING THE STAGE

TEACHERS:

- ✓ provide concrete setting for learning
- ✓ draw out experiential knowledge
- ✓ pose questions and problems
- ✓ motivate, facilitate, and guide reflection
- ✓ encourage questions, explorations

STUDENTS:

- ✓ reflect on experiential knowledge
- ✓ observe and gather information
- ✓ search for relationships and theorize
- ✓ infer and draw conclusions
- ✓ listen, question, discuss
- ✓ imagine, conjecture

Reflecting

3. REFORMULATION

TEACHERS:

- ✓ question and discuss
- ✓ provide reinforcement and practice activities
- ✓ coach
- ✓ check for understanding and accuracy

STUDENTS:

- ✓ rephrase, explain, summarize
- ✓ apply concepts and theories to real-life situations
- ✓ solve simple problems
- ✓ experiment, manipulate
- ✓ put into practice or show use
- ✓ worksheets, end-of-chapter questions

2. DISCLOSURE

TEACHERS:

- ✓ present, explain, and disclose
- ✓ show interconnectedness of ideas
- ✓ demonstrate, analyze, synthesize
- ✓ develop enduring understandings, key concepts, and theories

STUDENTS:

- ✓ collect and acquire knowledge
- ✓ conceptualize and theorize
- ✓ see relationships and patterns
- ✓ draw inferences and conclusions
- ✓ gain theoretical understanding
- ✓ construct models and nonverbal representations

Thinking

Figure 4.3. Four Phases of Learning

Phase 3: Reformulation (practicing)

The presentation and analysis of the disclosure phase does not become personally meaningful until students can *reformulate* the main concepts. That is, they must demonstrate that the concepts are integrated into their conceptual schema. This does not mean that they just parrot what has been disclosed. Rather, it means that they have fitted the pieces into their conceptual framework and that they can use and respond in their own way to what they have learned. During this phase, you follow up (and often intersperse) your disclosure with interpretation and inference questions. You ask for general and specific reactions. You ask students to explain their new knowing and use it in simple applications. During this phase, students "reinvent" and begin to use the disclosure phase.

During disclosure and reformulation you may use resource materials and reinforcement activities to good advantage. These materials can clarify concepts, give further information, pose questions, and, especially, provide activities to strengthen and sharpen what has been learned. Exercise material gives students opportunities to reformulate key concepts in a variety of ways and provides necessary reinforcement and drill. You should be careful not to use such exercises as the basis of a course or a program. They have a legitimate place in furnishing reformulation experiences, but they are only one part of meaningful learning. If such work becomes the main focus of learning, you impoverish education. Students then tend to become passive rote learners, not responsive image-bearers of God. At the same time, during this phase you encourage students to memorize with understanding. Whenever possible, they do need to develop an information base for future use in active and pleasurable ways.

Students who learn best as implementers appreciate the reformulation phase. They are the ones who like to do things themselves. They try out and apply concepts and theories. During this phase, therefore, provide activities in which students apply concepts and theories and solve related problems. Allow them to manipulate and experiment, to do things on their own in a step-by-step fashion. Facilitate students' progress by giving directions and constant encouragement. Involve them actively, usually individually but sometimes in small groups. In this phase students manipulate prescribed materials related to the disclosed concepts. Their knowledge grows in small steps. They make the material their own, and they begin to add something themselves and to use it in personal ways.

A unit on the natural history of the British Columbia coastal forest contains many disclosure and reformulation activities. In a discussion, for instance, the class lists the characteristics of all ecosystems and classifies the characteristics into major concepts (disclosure). When finished, the students use the creatures found in the forest during phase 1 of the unit to draw a large model ecosystem to show these characteristics (reformulation). The disclosure phase in the section on the food pyramid involves doing a number of experiments and readings. The reformulation phase includes a class question-and-answer section, making some notes that summarize presentations and discussions, and summary diagrams of the food chain made by individual students.

Phase 4: Transcendence (purposeful responding)

The final phase in the rhythm of learning is *transcendence*. I use the word in its original meaning of "going beyond." In this phase students move beyond and rise above disclosure and reformulation. During transcendence theoretical reflection becomes purposeful response and reflective action. It is an integral and crucial part of meaningful learning. One of my acquaintances once characterized the four phases as *hello, know, show*, and *grow*. It is in this fourth phase that students grow in using their insight and skills in what for them are new contexts.

Without transcendence, schooling may fail to touch students personally. Students are less likely to develop the dispositions and commitments we cherish. Learning may then be little more than controlled regurgitation. Without this fourth phase, your students are unlikely to exercise their talents in school in the full, rich way God intends those talents to be used. Yet, as teachers we easily leave out transcendence. Many of us like the neat packaging that is possible for disclosure and reformulation. We may find it difficult to find time to do justice to this phase. That is partly the case because of the traditionalist overemphasis on phases 2 and 3.

Nevertheless, transcendence is as important as the other phases of learning. During this phase, students may respond to what they have learned in deeper and more creative ways. They apply concepts and principles in their own unique ways, often in what for them are original situations. They develop personally meaningful products and choose responses that affect their own lives. They commit themselves to certain dispositions, values, and courses of action. Students now offer to others the results of their learning and thinking in various forms. They have frequent opportunities to share and display the results of their learning. Especially in this phase, students may experience how humans can live in obedient response to God and accept the mandate of God's kingdom for themselves. Their work may reflect their understanding of their religious calling and set out their own positions.

The products that students create during this phase should be their own, reflecting reality and their place in it as they perceive it. Such response may involve answering open-ended questions in class: What does this mean for you? How can you use it? It may be applying mathematical concepts in new contexts. It may be a science investigation that goes beyond class discussions and demonstrations. It may involve writing an essay, doing a project, or making an object. As teachers we ask initial questions. We provide guidance and incentive for thinking and exploration to continue when needed. We recommend resource materials.

At the same time, especially in the transcendence phase, students need to share in choosing and planning their responses. Enable them to capitalize on using and developing their unique gifts. Encourage them to use not only conventional but also new, expressive representations. Support them in creating new perspectives on seeing and responding to God's Word and world. Writing and painting, for instance, are means through which students refine and transcend the reformulation phase. Students may also share their knowledge or teach it to others.

Inventive learners do well in this phase of learning. They are able to compose and fashion products with imagination, using learned concepts in singular and original ways. They enrich reality and animatedly try out new possibilities. As teachers we stir interests, make suggestions, guide thinking, and evaluate products. On the whole, however, inventive learners want to learn by themselves. They take their own initiative and develop ideas on their own. You help them by providing opportunities and choices, and by having them set goals.

The coastal forest unit has far more transcendence activities than students in a particular class can do. Of the fifteen learning activities on the role of government management of the forest, the whole class does three or four activities that involve the first three phases of learning. Individuals or small groups of students then choose several others. (Having a choice helps make the chosen activities personally meaningful.) Most of these activities include several phases of learning besides transcendence. For example, the instructions for "Debate the statement: The only good wolf is a dead wolf" ask students to read a book and watch some videotapes (setting the stage and disclosure), identify and analyze the issues (reformulation), and respond personally to them (transcendence). Other parts of the unit suggest meaningful transcendence products that will appeal to students with different interests and abilities. Students may write or give reports. They may write psalms similar to Psalm 104 using forest creatures. They may draw a scale diagram of a model garden landscaped with plants native to the forest, or they may experiment with different kinds and cuts of wood from the forest and investigate their uses.

A model for meaningful learning

The four-phase model of learning described in the previous section is summarized in figure 4.3. The model assumes several biblically based premises:

- *Students are responsive and unique image-bearers of God.*
- *Knowledge entails far more than learning concepts. Knowledge involves values, dispositions, and commitments. It intends to lead to service.*
- *The dimensions of teaching embody teacher guidance through unfolding, structuring, and enabling.*

Note that the *type* of structuring tends to differ in the four phases of learning. As learning moves from the first to the second phase, the learning activities become more teacher directed. As learning moves toward transcendence, the classroom structure allows for more student initiative and choice. Also, while the four components of teaching occur in all four phases, there is more emphasis on unfolding in the first two, and more on enabling in the last two.

The four-phase model of learning does not put teachers and students into a straitjacket. Rather, it allows them to use the flexibility and freedom in teaching and learning that God provides in their particular situation. You can use a great variety of strategies and techniques in each phase. Your choice depends on the subject matter, your personality, the nature of the class, and the time available. While some types of learners seem to "fit" into one quadrant better than the others, there is no precise one-to-one correspondence. Students never exhibit learning characteristics solely in one category. Moreover, each phase of learning can include some activities that are suitable for each type of learner.

Further, despite a natural rhythm, the phases described do not necessarily always follow one another sequentially, nor are they always given equal weight. The phases also operate at different levels. In the whole school curriculum, we gradually move through the year from a greater emphasis on setting the stage and reformulation to more on disclosure and transcendence. In particular courses, early units may set the stage, with later ones stressing transcendence. Each unit, if well designed, has a cycle that moves from setting the stage to disclosure and from reformulation to transcendence. And, in a more limited way, many (but certainly not all!) lessons quickly set the stage, involve some disclosure and reformulation, and at least hint at some transcendence. Thus the phases may overlap, may occur in a variety of forms, and may not always follow one another in exact sequence.

What is important, however, is that as a teacher you deliberately plan learning to include all four phases of learning in your units. Provide an adequate, experience-based setting. Accompany disclosure with a variety of reformulation activities that help students assimilate and reinforce new concepts. Give students opportunities to transcend the precision learning by applying their learning to new situations and responding in their own distinctive ways.

Traditional schools have emphasized phases 2 and 3, downplaying phases 1 and 4. As a result, learning often failed to become personally meaningful. Constructivist approaches, on the other hand, easily overemphasize phases 1 and 4, with students not sufficiently developing an understanding and appreciation of our cultural heritage, or the clear conceptual and value frameworks that they need in order to function well in society. Regular inclusion of all four phases is most likely to lead students to knowledgeable, insightful, reflective, and committed involvement and action.

Reflect and respond 4-5

Choose a unit topic and suggest learning activities for each of the four phases of learning. Discuss whether each activity also suits the type of learner that, according to the previous sections, "fits" that particular phase.

Now consider two or three specific class periods in the unit. Which phases of learning would be included in each period? Is it possible to include all four phases of learning? Is it desirable? Why or why not?

Multiple intelligences

When I Googled the phrase *multiple intelligences*, I got almost 8,000,000 hits! Clearly, since Howard Gardner first proposed his theory of multiple intelligences in 1983, it has received enormous response and debate. One reason that educators have generally reacted favorably is that they have always recognized that persons have different types of abilities. They know that it is simplistic to describe their students in terms of a "general" intelligence quotient.

Howard Gardner (1999) argues that persons possess nine different types of intelligence:

- *Existential*: the ability to pose and ponder questions about life, death, and ultimate issues; to use spiritual resources to solve problems; to be virtuous
- *Interpersonal*: the ability to understand and interact with other people
- *Intrapersonal*: the ability to understand yourself, know who you are, and what you can do (self-reflection)
- *Verbal/linguistic*: the ability to use spoken and written language to express what is on your mind and to understand other people
- *Musical/rhythmic*: the ability to think in music; to be able to hear, recognize, and manipulate tonal and rhythmic patterns
- *Naturalist*: the ability to discriminate among living things and be sensitive to creatures and features of the natural world
- *Bodily/kinesthetic*: the ability to use your whole body or parts of it (physical movement, athletics, making something)

- *Visual/spatial*: the ability to visualize objects and spatial relationships, and create and manipulate mental images related to the spatial world
- *Logical/mathematical*: the ability to reason inductively and deductively and to recognize underlying principles and abstract patterns.

These intelligences, according to Gardner, are only slightly interdependent. Most persons, he adds, develop some intelligences highly, other modestly, and the rest hardly at all. But we must remember that students' intelligences and their ways of using them shift, grow, and vary over time (Hatch 1997). Controversies also exist about Gardner's categorization. His nine intelligences may not be the only ones. Indeed, Gardner added the naturalist and existential intelligences later (rejecting moral and spiritual intelligences, even though those are clearly closely connected with an existential intelligence). Further, a numerical intelligence may well differ from a logical one. As well, some question whether the bodily/kinesthetic and intrapersonal categories are actual intelligences. More seriously, there is a lack of empirical research support for the theory and its application (Denig 2004; Waterhouse 2006).

Despite these limitations, what has become clear from Gardner's theory is that learning is complex and needs to take into account not only students' learning-style preferences but also the intelligences or ways of knowing they favor. Gardner's followers reject the question *How smart are you?* They replace it with *How are you smart?* That is, they rightly point out that all students have specific gifts of intelligence. They then design learning to take into account the diversity of intelligences and to enable students to capitalize on their strengths. Gardner's work reminds us that teachers need to celebrate diverse patterns of intelligence gifts. They need to try to arrange learning contexts in which students feel free to develop their personal ones.

Multiple intelligences are not the same as learning styles. Multiple intelligences include students' abilities; learning styles are the ways in which students prefer to learn. No doubt there are some interconnections, but they are complex. For instance, persons with high verbal/linguistic intelligence may well learn best through reading, hearing, speaking, writing, and debating. And there is some evidence that students with high mathematical/logical intelligence benefit from learning through working with patterns and relationships. But it has been shown that bodily/kinesthetic students do not necessarily have a preference for learning through movement. And in one study, students high in musical intelligence preferred kinesthetic learning (Denig 2004).

Where the linkage of multiple intelligences to classroom pedagogy has had positive effects, the results can be ascribed to teachers' taking into account students' diverse abilities, and to the excitement generated by teachers trying something new (Waterhouse 2006). And because it is so difficult to link learning styles and multiple intelligences, most curriculum planners take into account either learning styles or Gardner's intelligences, but not both. (But for one interesting, complex attempt to do so, see Silver, Strong, and Perini 2000.)

It isn't that Gardner's theory is not useful for teachers. It helps them see the need for a curriculum that goes beyond developing verbal/linguistic and logical/ mathematical abilities. It gives them a basis to broaden their focus so that they provide learning activities that develop all intelligences. It encourages them to prepare their students to develop well-rounded lives. It makes them emphasize that students should not look at certain gifts as better or worse, but that their various abilities complement one another and can all contribute to a healthy community. As such, it is worthwhile to keep in mind and provide for the spectrum of intelligences among your students as you plan activities in each of the four phases of learning.

Reflect and respond 4-6

For the same topic you chose in 4-5, complete the lines in the following chart that are applicable:

INTELLIGENCE	CORRESPONDING LEARNING ACTIVITY
Existential	
Interpersonal	
Intrapersonal	
Verbal/linguistic	
Musical/rhythmic	
Naturalist	
Bodily/kinesthetic	
Visual/spatial	
Logical/mathematical	

For which intelligences was it easy to find an activity? For which was it difficult? Would you have the same difficulty for other topics? Why or why not? Is it possible to find activities for each intelligence for all topics? Is it desirable? In that connection, consider the value of teaching knowledge through rap songs, as educators promoting the inclusion of all multiple intelligences often recommend.

Motivating learning

Learners bear the image of God; they were created to respond to His call. This truth implies two guidelines for motivating them to learn. First, help students to appreciate the value of their learning activities. Second, enable students to achieve success if they put forth reasonable effort. In other words, the best motivation for students is to master tasks in a supportive setting. Learning tasks should also have inherent interest or value and should lead to worthwhile learning outcomes.

Within such a context, use the following specific strategies to motivate students (see also chapter 5 in Good and Brophy 2007):

- *Model interest in learning. Project enthusiasm. Convey that what is learned is important. Ask students to list what they already know about a topic and what they would like to learn.*
- *Treat students as eager learners as you induce curiosity and interest. Keep them actively involved. Help them set and commit to appropriate learning goals. Allow them to respond actively and to make choices.*
- *Encourage students to succeed and to learn from mistakes. Affirm good performance and build confidence.*
- *Make content personal, concrete, or familiar, and bring out the unusual and unexpected.*

Note that intrinsic motivation is more effective in the long run than extrinsic motivation. Extrinsic motivation (e.g., stickers, grades, threat of punishment) may improve performance in routine tasks. However, it affects learning negatively when a learning task is interesting in itself, when it involves problem solving or open-ended learning, or when students perceive that a teacher is using the reward to control behavior (Graham 2003).

Therefore, as teachers we strive for intrinsic motivation. Intrinsic motivation comes about largely when teachers deal with what children believe to be important and relate it to their sense of purpose and values. Students want to learn about things that matter to them, so we demonstrate how learning tasks have inherent meaning and value. We foster, for instance, curiosity and a sense of achievement in successfully completing a task. As image-bearers of God, students intuitively know that God's reality has meaning and purpose. They want their learning to relate to the meaning they have experienced and to deepen and broaden their perspective.

Reflect and respond 4-7

Think of occasions in school when you were motivated to learn. List the factors that led to a high level of motivation. Compare your list with those of others, and try to find common patterns. How does your list compare with the items mentioned in this section?

Day-to-day planning

Appropriate unit planning makes your daily preparation easier and more focused. However, you still need to prepare every day. Even if you include many of the items below in your unit plan, you still need to make daily adjustments. Your lesson plans might include the following:

Intended learning outcome(s): These are taken from your unit plans, or are closely related to them. You do not need a long list of very specific learning outcomes. Those will be self-evident from your learning activities. They also take much time to write. You do need to state your main intents, however, so that you can keep them in mind as you teach. Make clear what you expect your students to learn. Can you achieve the outcomes? Take into account the dynamics of your classroom. Be flexible if things don't work just the way you had hoped.

Introduction. You need an introductory activity (a) to motivate students, (b) to help them see the value of what they are to learn, and (c) to relate the learning to previous experiences. Phase 1 (setting the stage) activities are often useful here.

Learning activities. Ask yourself what type of activities will attain your learning outcomes. Include activities suitable for diverse learners. Do you want activities in all four phases of learning? Or does this lesson call for only one or two phases? Will you actively involve your students throughout the lesson? Plan a variety of activities for longer time blocks. Even in high school, a "disclosure" presentation should normally not exceed ten minutes. Note any independent work and follow-up that needs to take place after the class period. Write down the key questions you will ask. Include some questions that go beyond recall and simple comprehension. Ask students to give reasons, to draw conclusions, and to support or refute arguments. Also ask them to extrapolate ("What would happen if ...?"), to assess, to justify viewpoints and opinions, and to suggest solutions. Give students enough time to think about their answers, and ask follow-up questions to help them develop their insights.

Conclusion. Don't leave your lesson "hanging" at the end. Pull together the main points that you want students to learn. Ask the students, for instance, to write down the two most important things they learned. Or conclude with some review questions that will indicate whether the class has attained your intended outcomes.

Resources and materials needed. List the resources you need: books, pamphlets, computer files, physical materials, chart paper, audiovisual equipment, and so on. Use a variety of resources, but choose judiciously.

Assessment. How do you plan to assess students' learning both during and at the conclusion of the lesson? Sometimes this may involve little more than informal observation. Plan to monitor student interest and response. Also plan to check the quality of assignments done prior to, during, and after the lesson. Leave some space on your planning sheet to jot down what went well—or poorly—in the lesson.

Notes and reminders. You may want to design your own photocopied (or computer file) lesson-planning outlines with the above headings. This last heading is useful for reminding yourself about special notes and instructions that you must give to the students, contacts you must make with specific students, special supervisory duties, and so on.

On the next pages I will show a possible template for a daily lesson plan as well as a completed one for a sixth-grade lesson on Japan. (The template is based on one used in my university's teacher education program.) You may want to develop one that you feel comfortable with. If you are a pre-service teacher, find an opportunity to speak with several teachers to see what type of daily planning works well for them, and in what ways they ensure that their planning focuses on the attainment of their intended learning outcomes.

Reflect and respond 4-8

Pick a topic for which you have some resources available, perhaps within the same unit you have been working on in previous activities. Develop one or two daily lesson plans for the topic, using the outline given above or the template on the next pages.

If you are a pre-service teacher, once you have written the plan and discussed it with several other persons, teach the lesson to a small group. Afterward, analyze with the group how successful you were in attaining your intended learning outcomes. Revise your plan accordingly.

LESSON PLAN TEMPLATE

Date	Time
Curriculum area	Unit topic

Key enduring understandings, concepts, abilities, and/or values

Intended learning outcomes (to know, to do, to create, to value, etc.)

Assessment strategies: How will you assess attainment of the intended learning outcomes?

❑ Observation	❑ Anecdotal notes	❑ Work samples/portfolio
❑ Checklist	❑ Focused questions	❑ Self-assessment
❑ Peer assessment	❑ Interview/Conference	❑ Learning log/journal
❑ Presentation or performance	❑ Rubric	❑ Other (explain)

Materials/preparation

Introduction	*Setting the stage*: engaging, motivating, experiencing, connecting with prior knowledge, reflecting, conjecturing, posing problems
Guided learning steps	*Disclosing*: acquiring knowledge/skills, conceptualizing, developing, understanding, integrating
	Practicing, reinforcing: modeling, giving instructions, checking for understanding, guided practice, independent practice, applying, posing and solving problems

Closure	*Transcending*: summing up, responding, creating, performing, committing, evaluating

Modifications: How will you change the lesson to meet the needs of individual students?

❑ Increase time, space, amount	❑ Scribe	❑ Include visuals
❑ Decrease	❑ Oral explanation	❑ Use manipulatives
❑ Change	❑ Peer/tutor/partner	❑ Extend

Who will require lesson modifications?

Personal notes/reminders/homework

Post-lesson reflections

LESSON PLAN EXAMPLE: VALUES OF JAPANESE CULTURE
(based on Teichrieb 2006)

Lessons 16 and 17	**Time:** Two 50-minute periods
Curriculum area: Social studies	**Unit topic:** Learning from Japan

Key enduring understandings, concepts, abilities, and/or values
• Japanese cultural values are reflected in beliefs, traditions, daily living routines, and aesthetic expressions.
• By comparing and contrasting Canadian and Japanese cultural values, we appreciate how some Japanese values are in harmony with a biblical lifestyle.

Intended learning outcomes (to know, to do, to create, to value, etc.)
• Investigate and understand how cultural values are embedded in Japanese beliefs, traditions, daily living routines, and aesthetic expressions.
• Analyze the similarities and differences between Japanese and Canadian values, and compare each with biblical values.
• Record and summarize group and class findings accurately and clearly.
• Appreciate that our understanding of other cultures enriches our own lives.
• Become committed to a set of values that "borrows" from several cultures but, at the same time, reflects those that the Bible upholds.

Assessment strategies: How will you assess attainment of the intended learning outcome(s)?		
❑ Observation	❑ Anecdotal notes	❑ Work samples/portfolio
❑ Checklist	❑ Focused questions	❑ Self-assessment
❑ Peer assessment	❑ Interview/conference	❑ Learning log/journal
❑ Presentation or performance	❑ Rubric	❑ Other (explain)

Materials/preparation
Photocopy and cut apart Japanese values sheet. Have chart paper and markers ready.

Introduction	*Setting the stage*

Tell the students that one of the best ways to understand a culture is to examine and know its main values. For this reason they will be recording Japanese values throughout the unit. We live by our values. They reflect and affect everything we do, say, and believe.
   Show two TV video clips of Japanese adults being introduced to each other, and then American ones. What are the differences? Why?
   Give students a few minutes to take out their "Japanese Values" sheet, review it silently, and write a summary sentence on what they have learned.
	engaging, motivating, experiencing, connecting with prior knowledge, reflecting, conjecturing, posing problems

Guided learning steps Break the class into groups of four. Give each group two paragraphs cut from the Japanese Values sheets and have them determine the main value the paragraphs reveal. Have one member from each group read the group's paragraphs and identify the value. Students add these values to their personal "Japanese Values" sheet. Use a jigsaw technique. Give the number *1*s from each group a sheet on the Japanese emphasis on harmony; *2*s, a sheet on time and decision making; *3*s, communications; and *4*s, respect and position. Each group discusses its sheet. Then students go back to their original groups, where they take turns explaining the related Japanese values to the others. On the basis of their personal Japanese Values sheets and the presentations and discussions on the four sheets, the group then makes a poster titled Japanese Cultural Values.	*Disclosing*: acquiring knowledge/skills, conceptualizing, developing, understanding, integrating *Practicing, reinforcing*: modeling, giving instructions, checking for understanding, guided practice, independent practice, applying, posing and solving problems
Closure The students walk past the displayed posters. The teacher then develops a chart on the board in two columns headed *Japanese cultural values* and *Canadian cultural values*. The teacher tries to elicit at least the following Japanese values from the students: appreciation of beauty and of nature; respect for position; emphasis on detail, accuracy, and punctuality; emphasis on community, living in harmony, and conformity. Lead a discussion of key questions: What would you find attractive about living in Japanese society? What would be difficult? Which Japanese values could benefit Canadian society? Why? Which Japanese values are also affirmed in the Bible? Students write a short essay about the values they would espouse if a group of Canadian sixth-graders and a group of Japanese sixth-graders camped together for a week.	*Transcending*: summing up, responding, creating, performing, committing, evaluating

Modifications: How will you change the lesson to meet the needs of individual students?

❏ Increase time, space, amount	❏ Scribe	❏ Include visuals
❏ Decrease	❏ Oral explanation	❏ Use manipulatives
❏ Change	❏ Peer/tutor/partner	❏ Extend

Who will require lesson modifications?

Personal notes/reminders/homework

Ask that students discuss Japanese values with their parents to see whether the parents have any experiences and/or insights.

Post-lesson reflections

Meaningful learning

Meaningful learning in the classroom does not just come about by chance. It presupposes careful planning. Educators do not achieve meaningful learning by simply following a textbook or by providing interesting learning activities. As a teacher you must consider all aspects of the learning environment. Carefully plan your intended learning outcomes, ways to assess their attainment, and relevant teaching and learning strategies. And take into account the characteristics and needs of individual students and of the whole class within the context of the vision of the school and government expectations.

For meaningful learning to take place, you need to be sensitive to students' experiential backgrounds, developmental levels, aptitudes, and preferred learning styles. Plan to balance different phases of learning. Think about how you can motivate your students to learn. Create a classroom atmosphere in which students feel secure enough to take risks as they learn. Recognize students for the contributions they can make to the learning community. Encourage reciprocal trust, respect, and responsibility. Reflect on the positive and negative effects your own personality may have on the learning atmosphere. It may take a lot of work, but there is nothing as rewarding as seeing that your teaching has made a real difference in the lives of your students, especially when that difference helps them to follow our Lord.

Remember also that there is no single best teaching strategy. Effective teachers use a wide range of strategies. Sometimes you use direct teaching in which you systematically explain new concepts or skills and follow up with practice. At other times you use indirect strategies such as question/discussion sessions, simulations, the analysis of case studies or problems, guided student inquiries, or learning centers. Or you may use group explorations or lab partner investigations, literature circles, cooperative learning, or structured dialogue in which students articulate and question one another's insights and experiences (Van Dyk 2000). You need to choose different instructional strategies for different subjects and topics as well as for different phases of learning. The key is to choose those strategies that enhance learning for responsible and responsive discipleship.

Even with all your planning, necessary as it is, learning will be successful in helping students be responsive disciples only to the extent that the Holy Spirit takes hold of you and your students and enlivens both. When that happens, learning will truly enable your students and you to walk in God's truth with undivided hearts (Psalm 86:11).

Reflect and respond 4-9

This chapter has not said anything about the place of technology in learning. Yet the use of computers and other technologies is common in the schools. Make a list of the types of technology that are frequently used in the classroom. In what phase or phases of learning can each be used most effectively? Why? Consider the advantages and disadvantages of the use of each type of technology. Ask questions such as the following:

- In what ways can the technology contribute to meaningful learning?
- Is the technology being used effectively in classrooms that you are familiar with? Why or why not?
- In what ways is the technology changing learning and the curriculum? What are the positive and negative aspects of such changes?
- Could the funds spent on the technology be spent in more effective ways? Are there times when less or no technology would be better?
- Is the technology available equally to schools in diverse socioeconomic neighborhoods? What are the implications?
- How does the technology enhance communication? In what ways does it curtail meaningful communication?

Our students are part of a world that cannot function without technology. Therefore, we must familiarize our students with common technologies and enable them to use those technologies in appropriate ways.

On the other hand, remember that there is no research evidence that greater access to computers in schools has a positive correlation with academic achievement. This apparent lack of positive benefits may result at least in part from the fact that in school, students use computers mainly for word processing, getting information, sending messages, and playing games. What is clear is that frequent use of computers in schools leads to declines in academic performance, downplays the importance of conversation and careful listening, and limits the development of children's imaginations (Angrist and Lavy 2002; Oppenheimer 2003; Fuchs and Woessmann 2004; Ferguson 2005).

Zwaagstra concludes from his analysis of research studies, "While it may make sense for students in higher grades to become computer literate, the same does not hold true for those in earlier grades. Introducing computers at too early an age can have a negative consequence on academic achievement" (2008, 4). The promoters of the latest technology often are large corporations that stand to profit from its implementation. When using technology, always ask, "How does this help my students attain the aims of my school?"

Chapter 4 enduring understandings

- Educators have seen learners as blank slates, trainable objects, unfolding plants, and primary agents of social change. All these metaphors contain some kernels of truth, but they all limit human potential in significant ways.
- Humans are created in the image of God. That is, God has endowed them with a sense of purposefulness, creativity, rationality, faithfulness, morality, and mercy that they can use to further fulfill God's intent to unfold the earth so that it is a place of justice and shalom. Despite human sinfulness, God wants learners to fulfill His calling by developing and using their unique gifts optimally in service to Him and to their fellow humans.
- A model for learning that takes into account learners as unique and responsible image-bearers of God includes four phases: setting the stage (preparing), disclosure (presenting), reformulation (practicing), and transcendence (responding).

References

Angrist, J., and V. Lavy. 2002. New evidence on classroom computers and pupil learning. *The Economic Journal* 112, no. 482:735–65.

Blomberg, D. 2007. *Wisdom and curriculum: Christian schooling after postmodernity.* Sioux Center, IA: Dordt College Press.

Coffield, F., D. Moseley, E. Hall, and K. Ecclestone. 2004. *Should we trust styles? What research has to say to practice.* London: Learning and Skills Research Centre.

Cotton, K. 1999. *Research you can use to improve results.* Alexandria, VA: Association for Supervision and Curriculum Development.

Denig, S. 2004. Multiple intelligences and learning styles: Two complementary dimensions. *Teachers College Record* 106, no. 1:87–95.

Egan, K. 1983. *Education and psychology: Plato, Piaget, and scientific psychology.* New York: Teachers College Press.

_____. 1997. *The educated mind: How cognitive tools shape our understanding.* Chicago: University of Chicago Press.

Ferguson, S. 2005. How computers make our kids stupid. *Maclean's,* (June 5): 24–30.

Fuchs, T., and L. Woessmann. 2004. *Computers and student learning: Bivariate and multivariate evidence on the availability and use of computers at home and at school.* CESifo Working Paper No. 1321. Munich: CESifo.

Gardner, H. 1999. *Intelligence reframed: Multiple intelligences for the 21st century.* New York: Basic Books.

Good, T., and J. Brophy. 2008. *Looking in classrooms.* 10th ed. Boston, MA: Allyn and Bacon.

Graham, D. 2003. *Teaching redemptively: Bringing grace and truth into your classroom.* Colorado Springs: Purposeful Design.

Hatch, T. 1997. Getting specific about multiple intelligences. *Educational Leadership* 54, no. 6:26–29.

Kolb, D. 1984. *Experiential learning: Experience as the source of learning and development.* Englewood Cliffs, NJ: Prentice-Hall.

Marzano, R., D. Pickering, and J. Pollock. 2001. *Classroom instruction that works: Research-based strategies for increasing student achievement.* Alexandria, VA: Association for Supervision and Curriculum Development.

McCarthy, B. 1996. *About Learning.* Barrington, IL: Excel.

_____. 1997. A tale of four learners: 4MAT's learning styles. *Educational Leadership* 54, no. 6:46–51.

McCarthy, B., and D. McCarthy. 2005. *Teaching around the 4MAT cycle: Designing instruction for diverse learners with diverse learning styles.* Thousand Oaks, CA: Corwin Press.

Middleton, J. R. 2005. *The liberating image: The* imago Dei *in Genesis 1.* Grand Rapids, MI: Brazos Press.

Oppenheimer, T. 2003. *The flickering mind: The false promise of technology in the classroom and how learning can be saved.* New York: Random House.

Seerveld, C. 1980. *Rainbows for a fallen world.* Toronto, ON: Tuppence.

Silver, H., R. Strong, and M. Perini. 2000. *So each may learn: Integrating learning styles and multiple intelligences.* Alexandria, VA: Association for Supervision and Curriculum Development.

Steensma, G., and H. Van Brummelen, eds. 1977. *Shaping school curriculum: A biblical view.* Terre Haute, IN: Signal.

Teichrieb, L. 2006. Learning from Japan (unpublished sixth-grade curriculum unit). Langley, BC: Trinity Western University.

Van Brummelen, H. 2002. *Steppingstones to curriculum: A biblical path.* Colorado Springs: Purposeful Design.

Van Dyk, J. 2000. *The craft of Christian teaching.* Sioux Center, IA: Dordt College Press.

Waterhouse, L. 2006. Multiple intelligences, the Mozart effect, and emotional intelligence: A critical review. *Educational Psychologist* 41, no. 4:207–225.

Whitehead, A. 1929. *The aims of education and other essays.* New York: Macmillan.

Willis, J. 2006. *Research-based strategies to ignite student learning: Insights from a neurologist and classroom teacher.* Alexandria, VA: Association for Supervision and Curriculum Development.

Zwaagstra, M. 2008. Computers in the classroom: Technology overboard? *Frontier Backgrounder: Brief Analysis.* Winnipeg, MB: Frontier Centre for Public Policy.

How Do We Assess to Enhance Student Learning?

5

Chapter 5 guiding questions

- How can we assess to improve learning?
- How can assessment be a blessing and encouragement while promoting excellence and justice?
- Which assessment and grading strategies supportively and fairly communicate what students have learned?

Middle school teachers Connie Clements and Jim Vance discuss their students' report cards in the teachers' workroom.

"My students did poorly this term," Connie laments, "I'm afraid quite a few parents and maybe our principal will be upset with the many Cs, Ds, and even Fs I've given. But it's better to give these marks now than at the end of the year. Maybe they'll shock my students into better effort."

Jim asks, "But isn't positive reinforcement more effective if you want to stimulate learning?"

Connie ponders the question. Then she answers, "Well, that may generally be true. If my students have done poorly, though, their parents must know the truth. And then they can put on some pressure to see that their children do their work."

Jim persists, "All right, so parents need to know. But what about parents who say—or think—that if so many of your kids have poor marks, you as the teacher are the problem?"

"I'll give them a piece of my mind," Connie shoots back. "My students generally did well on daily seatwork. There I could supervise them closely. But their test results were poor. They sure didn't focus on their work consistently."

Jim replies, a bit hesitantly since he risks collegial friction, "But couldn't a parent then ask, 'Did you teach the concepts thoroughly? Did you review enough?' Or even, 'If students are achieving your outcomes and standards on everyday work, is there something wrong with the tests? Are you failing to match testing to teaching?' I don't know your class that well, Connie, but it seems to me that parents may have some valid questions if the marks of the whole class have dropped sharply."

Connie, stung, quickly recovers, "Well, some of their questions may be valid. But shouldn't report card grades show how much my students actually know? And I believe mine do!"

Jim doesn't want to prolong the discussion. Like Connie, he has to finish his report cards before the deadline. He still has to think through what comments he will put on them. So he says, appeasingly, "Well, you know, for quite some time our staff hasn't discussed how we should assign grades or what they reflect. Our principal only asks us about an unusual number of high or low marks, or about comments that don't seem to match our grades or are too harsh. We all do our own thing. I myself, for instance, emphasize informal observation and assessment of daily work more than you do. And your B doesn't mean quite the same thing as mine, I suspect. I'm not saying that either of us is right or wrong. But should we suggest a staff discussion about how we assess and grade students? After all, students and parents have a right to expect some consistency, especially if we expect them to interpret our evaluations properly."

Teachers constantly assess students' behavior, aptitudes, interests, achievements, and dispositions. They base assessments on their own and society's beliefs about the aims of schooling. Both what and how they choose to assess and evaluate reflect what they hold to be important. Teachers who use mainly short-answer factual test questions, for instance, value different things than those who often give questions that require critical thinking. Also, teachers may evaluate a score of 85 percent on a science test quite differently. One may conclude that the student has mastered the material very well. Another may decide that the student has memorized the content but has not grasped how to apply the concepts in new situations. These teachers implicitly value different dimensions of learning. They therefore interpret the results differently. Assessment and evaluation are valuing activities.

The importance teachers attach to assessment and evaluation and how they go about those activities create meaning for their students. Some teachers make recall the focus of assessment. Students may then decide that memorization is of prime importance in learning and in life. When teachers often ask students to evaluate and apply what they have learned, however, their students are likely to conclude that knowing concepts and skills is a basis for solving further problems or analyzing complex issues. The kinds of assessment strategies we use have a substantive effect on students. Therefore, they ought to reflect a biblical understanding of the nature of persons and of knowledge. In this chapter we will consider how the Bible can inform our assessment practices.

The strategies teachers use and how they report their evaluations to students and parents also affect learning and classroom relationships. If a student feels that a teacher's assessments are unfair, he may defy that teacher's authority. A student who tries her best but still gets Cs and Ds may well give up. On the other hand, when a teacher makes clear her expectations for assignments and tests, and uses both informal and formal assessment to help students improve, students will usually accept the results and use them to further their learning.

Word alert

Assessment means gathering data that gauge student achievement of learning outcomes. *Evaluation* interprets such data and makes resulting judgments and decisions. For instance, a kindergarten teacher may determine that a student recognizes twenty of the twenty-six capital letters in the alphabet (assessment). Near the start of kindergarten she may interpret that as very good progress, but at the end of the year she may consider the same thing to be a cause for concern (evaluation).

The Latin roots of *assess* and *evaluate* are "to be seated beside" and "to determine worth," respectively, implying that we work together with our students to add worth or value to their learning as we assess and evaluate. Which students are ready for more advanced learning? Which ones need additional help and support? How can we stimulate students' grasp of concepts, their problem-solving ability, or their creativity?

Even when students feel that teachers have treated them fairly, however, assessment may take place without a good understanding of what its aims are or which assessment strategies encourage learning. We still need to ask questions like the following:

- How can we relate assessment procedures to standards and intended learning outcomes?
- How can assessment lead to excellence, and how do we define excellence?
- Should we sample student work for grading? If so, how?
- Is it possible to evaluate compositions and reports fairly?
- What weight should we give to final exams?
- Is it meaningful to assess effort and learning skills as well as achievement?
- Is marking "on the curve" fair? Or should we mark only on the basis of whether students have met certain standards?
- Are there assessment approaches informed by biblical principles that lead to better relations among teachers, students, and parents?

The list of questions is inexhaustible. This chapter does not give all the answers or lay all the arguments to rest. Rather, its intent is to stimulate thinking and suggest some biblical metaphors and principles that are helpful to keep in mind as we assess learning.

5.1 Reflect and respond

Read the following statements about student assessment. With which ones do you agree? disagree? How would you rephrase the latter to reflect your beliefs?

- Assessment must help all students succeed.
- All student work must be assessed.
- Not everything that counts can be counted, and not everything that can be counted counts.
- Assessment is an integral part of teaching and learning.
- Students should be involved in setting assessment criteria.
- The main goal of assessment is to inform parents how well their children are doing.
- Grades are so imprecise that they are almost meaningless.
- Percentage grades are more accurate and therefore better than letter grades.
- Anything complex in life has many answers and often no "right" one. An emphasis on objective assessments sends the wrong message to students about life.
- Grades should reflect effort and participation as well as achievement.
- Grades on assignments and tests motivate students to do their best.

How assessment is often used

In North America today, student assessment is often used mainly for two purposes. First, schools use the results of assessment to inform both students and parents how well children are doing in school. Teachers well know that students ask each other, "What did you get?" And most parents and guardians, understandably, are interested in their children's progress. Second, in many places the most talked-about assessment tools are "standardized" tests that all students must take. Such tests assess whether students and schools meet specified standards, particularly in language arts and mathematics.

Standards vary widely in how broad or narrow they are. They usually include benchmarks or performance indicators. They are guideposts for student achievement and can lead to more uniformity in expectations. Schools and teachers can make them part of their intended learning outcomes. Students can achieve standards through creative and engaging teaching approaches. The standards can be assessed using a variety of strategies (e.g., open-ended questions, rubrics, student explanations, tests). Used within such a context, these strategies enable schools and teachers to determine to what extent students are learning key concepts, understandings, skills, and values.

However, the "high stakes" tests based on standards and developed centrally often restrict the scope of the curriculum. The test questions, based on the standards, reflect only the simple concepts and skills that can be tested and graded for a large population. Because the tests rank schools, teachers begin to teach to the tests. Even when unintended, assessment is seen as a cudgel rather than as a support to improve learning.

Assessment rightly communicates learning achievement to students and parents in terms of specified outcomes or standards. However, assessment has a more basic purpose. And if the focus of assessment becomes teaching to external tests, then the cart is before the horse, and the school's vision and aims may no longer drive its program.

5.2 Reflect and respond

Views on the aims of student assessment have changed over the years. As high school teacher Don Aker (1995, 11–12) put it: "[When I began teaching,] I thought that . . . teachers assessed for three reasons: to bring about closure to a unit of work ("We'll finish this off with a test on Friday"), to maintain control of the classroom ("You'd better pay attention because this could be on the test"), and to reward or punish students for learning or not learning ("Maybe next time you'll study harder"). For me, assessment was something that ended with a mark in my record book and on a report card. Fortunately for my students, I know better now."

In what ways was Aker's view of assessment a limiting one? How do you think his views of assessment changed over the years? Before you read the next section, make a list of what you consider to be the aims of student assessment and evaluation. Then after you've read the section, review and refine what you wrote.

The aims of assessment

Our starting point for thinking about student assessment is that it is an integral part of learning. Therefore, like all learning, assessment aims to help students become knowledgeable, discerning, competent, and responsive disciples of Jesus Christ. That means that we assess in ways that nurture meaningful learning and foster students' gifts. That includes helping them become knowledgeable, discerning, competent, and creative. It also involves becoming disposed to apply biblical commitments and values. All this implies that assessment goes beyond asking students to repeat information or demonstrate specific abilities. It does much more than merely enable us to assign grades. Through assessment, we celebrate student accomplishments and support those who face learning challenges.

There are three different types of student assessment, each with its own purposes:

Assessment *of* learning (or summative assessment) sums up student achievement at the end of a unit or year. This type of assessment monitors how well students have learned what we have taught. To what degree have students met preset standards or learning outcomes? Assessment of learning is often reported as a score or a mark. Final exams at the end of a school year, for instance, assign students a mark but give no feedback or help for future improvement.

Assessment *for* learning (or formative assessment) provides descriptive feedback to improve learning and the learning process. It helps students clarify meanings and overcome obstacles to learning. It recognizes and builds on achievements. It diagnoses learning difficulties in order to give students another chance to demonstrate success. Teachers ask questions that lead to further student reflection. They comment on drafts of compositions so that students can improve their final product. They praise students for particular achievements to build on and develop student strengths. Teachers and students interact to adjust or plan further suitable learning activities, or to overcome weaknesses. If done well, assessment for learning creates confidence in students about their ability to learn and challenges them to continue and improve their learning.

Assessment *as* learning takes place when students learn from assessing their own progress. Here they practice self-appraisal of their learning—their knowledge, abilities, creativity, and dispositions. They develop insight into the attributes of high-quality work. On the basis of their self-assessment, they learn to set meaningful and realistic goals. They make decisions about and assume responsibility for improving their work. Here teachers need to provide a framework for self-assessment. They may discuss the qualities of anonymous work samples. They may help students develop self-assessment guidelines. They may give students opportunities to construct test items related to specified learning outcomes. And they may consult with individuals about their self-assessment and the resulting goals.

These three types of assessment are not always distinct. Assessment for and of learning overlap, for instance, when a teacher provides useful feedback on a project but also assigns a mark. Similarly, when a teacher holds an individual conference with a student about a checklist of language arts skills displayed in an assignment, she may suggest how the student can improve (assessment for learning). She may ask the student to write an answer to "If I were to do the assignment again, I would . . ." and to self-assess another similar language arts assignment (assessment as learning). She may also use the checklist to report to parents at a "meet the teacher" evening (assessment of learning).

Appropriate assessment tries to find out how well students have attained the intended learning outcomes. Not all learning outcomes can be fully measured.

Take, for instance, an outcome in a unit on multiculturalism such as "to exercise respect and compassion toward others." Its realization will not become clear unless a teacher happens to observe an unsuspecting student in a real-life, relevant setting. And no teacher can adequately measure creativity in an essay or a work of art. Also, assessment should take into account that learning activities may have outcomes that were not intended. Suppose students develop and put on a skit to show differing attitudes toward forestry practices. In some circumstances the activity may run aground unless the teacher helps students develop conflict resolution skills. The latter may even become the focus of the learning activity.

A summary of the purposes of student assessment follows below. The first main aim stresses assessment for and as learning, while the second highlights assessment of learning.

Aims of student assessment

1. To encourage and improve student learning
a. To assess the extent to which students have met the intended learning outcomes, and to look for and evaluate unintended outcomes
b. To recognize achievements and diagnose learning difficulties so that students learn to build on their strengths and overcome or cope with their weaknesses
c. To refine instruction and other learning experiences in order to improve both individual and class learning
d. To help students develop and practice self-appraisal and self-understanding about their learning
e. To help students set meaningful and realistic learning goals and assume responsibility for their own learning
2. To communicate meaningful information to students, parents, and school authorities about student learning
a. To give realistic and helpful feedback about achievement, capabilities, behavior, attitudes, and dispositions
b. To put teachers, students, and parents/guardians in touch with one another about progress over time
c. To provide guidance for educational and vocational choices
d. To report learning achievement to school authorities such as school boards and governments

5.3 Reflect and respond

Consider the balance between assessment *of* learning, *for* learning, and *as* learning in your elementary and your high school experiences. Was the balance appropriate? Would you strive for a similar balance in your own classroom? Why or why not?

In the list of aims of student assessment, are there any that you would revise? add? delete? Why? Now jot down some of the implications of these goals for classroom learning and assessment. Keep this list and add to it as you continue reading this chapter.

Biblically informed metaphors for assessment

In what ways can the Bible inform our approach to assessment and evaluation? First, I'll consider several biblically informed metaphors for assessment: assessment as a gift, as a blessing, as grace, and as justice. Second, I'll describe what the biblical principles of encouragement and excellence mean for assessment. Finally, I'll reflect on the implications of treating students as image-bearers of God.

Metaphors are windows to knowledge and meaning. They shed light—often in unexpected and enriching ways—on the essence of a concept or idea. And as we saw for the metaphors about teaching, different metaphors can enlighten different aspects of a notion. By looking at several metaphors, we can enrich our understanding of the intent and the implementation of student assessment in the classroom. Note that the metaphors and principles overlap. In that way, they are like different facets that enrich one another.

Assessment as a gift. Elaine Brouwer writes that the best gift in life is "the opportunity to live life fully, joyfully, and purposefully in God's presence," made possible through God's gifts in creation and in redemption. Assessment, she continues, should therefore be a gift we extend to learners to help them grasp that goal. It means that "we think carefully not only about the content or form of the gift but of the receiver of the gift" (2006, 2.1–2.2).

For many of us, thinking of assessment as a gift rather than as judgment involves a paradigm shift. Just think of the consequences of this metaphor. Assessment will serve mainly as a way to support rather than test student learning. Students will sense that teachers use assessment to work with them to develop and apply concepts, abilities, and creative gifts that enable them to contribute positively to God's kingdom and to society. Assessment enables. It offers growth. It's a gift that leads to new and deeper learning.

In 2 Corinthians 9 the apostle Paul discusses the principles of Christian giving. Gifts must supply the needs of others, particularly the deprived, in cheerful and generous ways that reflect the indescribable gift God gave us in Jesus Christ. While Paul was not thinking of assessment, our viewing of assessment as a gift will enrich our students. Then God's grace will abound to us for our "good work" of assessment (2 Corinthians 9:8).

If we see assessment as a gift, we will foster and support student growth in caring and collaborative ways. Assessment becomes a process that enables students to unwrap their God-given gifts with joy, even though no doubt both learning and assessment will continue to produce challenges at times.

Assessment as a blessing. Gary Smalley and John Trent describe how bestowing the blessing in the Old Testament included five elements: a meaningful touch; a spoken message; attaching a high value to the one being blessed; an image of a special future for the one being blessed; and an active commitment to fulfill the blessing (Smalley and Trent 1986).

If we view assessment as a blessing, we first provide our students with a meaningful "touch"—which, in today's society, has to be a figurative one. Our starting point for assessment is that we communicate warmth, personal acceptance, and affirmation to our students. Research on assessment shows that students not only learn more but also do better on tests when they feel that the teacher encourages their efforts in a sincere and friendly way during all assessment processes.

Second, a blessing involves a spoken message—words that indicate that each student is worthy of some attention. Plan your schedule so that you hold a brief conference with every one of your students once every two weeks about how you and they have observed their progress. The spoken message may be "tough love"—truth that is not pleasant but is spoken in love and with encouragement. Ensure that students realize that because you value their learning, you try your best to assess their work carefully and fairly in ways that will help them improve.

Third and closely connected is that a blessing celebrates that the person receiving the blessing is valuable and has redeeming qualities. Our assessment strategies include helping students see that they have many gifts they can develop to contribute to society for God's glory. I remember a weak math student wanting to participate in a national mathematics contest. I encouraged her and gave her some extra help to prepare even though we both knew that her final score would not be high. But afterward, while she came in below the national average, I could praise her for her diligence and perseverance, two qualities that, I added, would stand her in good stead later in life (besides the fact that the extra work she did helped her in her regular math course!). I also remember the time when as a high school staff we chose a student to be valedictorian who academically had barely received her diploma. We chose her because her gifts of compassion for others, her involvement in community service, and her personal positive influence on the class and school atmosphere had made her the outstanding student of the year. We needed to bless her in a special way for the way she had used her God-given gifts to impact the school—and to show other students what we considered most important in assessing potential valedictorians.

A fourth element of a blessing is how it pictures a special future for the person being blessed. Our evaluation of assessment results must hold before our students the possibilities of what they can do with their special gifts. Those prospects may not be what the student has dreamed of (if so, we'd have one veterinarian for every three or four dogs and cats!). Nor can we predict a student's future accurately. However, our assessment can lead us to help students set meaningful goals based on their strengths. A former student of mine, now a senior pastor of a large church, shared with me an experience in high school. I had long forgotten the incident, but it had affected him a great deal. I had made a written comment on a math test on which he got an A minus. My comment was that he needed to start using his God-given abilities more effectively. I said he was just marking time and should turn his life around—and he did as a result of our discussion. My assessment held before him a picture of what was possible in his life, and in that way the assessment (in a subject he seldom used after high school!) became a blessing for him.

Finally, a blessing entails an active commitment. Words alone cannot communicate the blessing. As teachers, we need to back assessment with a commitment to do everything possible to help the student being blessed to be successful. We must provide the tools. We must provide the time. We must provide the second and third chances. We must remain actively committed to our students with insight and staying power. We become students of our students in order to grasp how our assessment can genuinely bless them.

Assessment as grace. Donovan Graham points out that "perhaps in no other dimension of school life is it more difficult to put grace into practice than [student] evaluation" (2003, 256). God evaluates our actions, he continues, but God has infinite patience with us and in His grace always gives us another chance. Similarly teachers should use assessments to produce eventual success and use evaluation as a means of grace. Assessment as grace implies that students who do not do well at a task be given other opportunities, with appropriate help from the teacher or others.

That does not mean that we do not maintain standards for learning: "God has standards, and He demands that we live up to them.... Jesus Himself did not hesitate in evaluating the work and attitudes of both His disciples and His enemies.... So we need not avoid the evaluation of our students' outward work or of their inner attitudes" (Graham 2003, 256).

Graham's point is that we can maintain standards and at the same time use assessment as a means of grace. We do so if, like God, we affirm our students as human beings—unconditionally, no matter what their grades. At the same time, we help them turn bad into good and mistakes into successes. Then they can steadily come closer to meeting the intended learning outcomes.

What does that mean for our assessment strategies? We give students, where possible, multiple opportunities to attain the intended learning outcomes. We clarify the criteria for assessment at the start of an assignment so that students are not "ambushed." We make self-assessment and peer assessment integral parts of the learning process. Our observations lead to constructive help. Our tests assess attainment of key concepts and understandings, skills, and values. But students do not just regurgitate. They also respond to and apply what they have learned. We give students ample opportunity to demonstrate their learning achievements. We assign grades only at the end of the assessment process. Moreover, we recognize grades as imperfect and not always valid or reliable summaries of complex learning achievements.

Assessment as justice. By now you may ask, "All right, so we look at assessment as a gift, as a blessing, and as grace. But doesn't there come a point when we just have to say to a student, 'You didn't meet the standards, and therefore you fail'?" When Jesus said, "Do not judge, or you too will be judged" (Matthew 7:1), He was speaking about judging others on lifestyle standards that we are not willing to apply to ourselves. But it is clear that elsewhere Jesus Himself, as well as the apostle Paul, did judge the actions of others (e.g., Matthew 23 and 1 Corinthians 5). Therefore, it is not wrong to conclude that there does come a point where, for whatever reason, we have to tell a student that he did not make the grade.

After a considerable formative process, we do need to make a judgment about students' progress and their ability to move forward. Now, telling students this can still be a blessing or a sign of grace. Students may see, for instance, that they did not put forth the effort of which they were capable, and they may change their ways. Or they may begin to realize in what areas they can better use their gifts.

The key question here is whether we have made such a judgment fairly. Has the decision been reached impartially and justly on the basis of clear criteria? Have we applied our assessment as justice?

In the Bible, the same word denotes justice and righteousness. Particularly, the Old Testament prophets insisted on right action and fair dealing within a framework of grace:

But let justice roll on like a river,

righteousness like a never-failing stream!

(Amos 5:24)

And what does the Lord require of you?

To act justly and to love mercy

And to walk humbly with your God.

(Micah 6:8)

After God condemned spiritual leaders for stressing trivialities, He made clear that for Him justice and righteousness are the measuring lines (Isaiah 28:10, 13, 17).

So, if we look at assessment as justice, what are the implications for our classrooms? We treat all students justly and fairly:

- We assess all students on the basis of clearly defined criteria.
- We avoid prejudgments made on the basis of previous performance.
- We do not penalize students for taking risks.
- Our formative comments are fair and constructive.
- Whenever possible, we do not "count" first efforts for final grades.
- Our test content represents a fair sampling of the important learning outcomes and provides different questions for students with different strengths.
- We are willing to explain why we reached certain conclusions, and we admit when we have made mistakes.
- Our grading procedures are linked to stated learning goals, and grades are a fair reflection of students' most recent performance.

5.4 Reflect and respond

The metaphors we have considered are assessment as a gift, as a blessing, as grace, and as justice.

- Can you give examples of specific assessment strategies that illustrate each metaphor?
- What are the strengths of each metaphor? the shortcomings?
- Are there other metaphors that you would add? or ones that you would drop? Why or why not?
- If you had to choose one metaphor that you felt gave the best image for your beliefs about student assessment and evaluation, what would it be? Why?

Biblical principles that inform student assessment

Biblical principles do not tell us exactly what to do in a classroom. Yet there are principles commended for living as a Christian community that also apply to how we go about assessment. Some have already become clear in our discussion of assessment metaphors. We have seen, for instance, how the biblical norms of both justice and grace affect assessment. Here I consider the principles of encouragement and excellence, and the implications of treating students as image-bearers of God during assessment.

The principle of encouragement. With respect to student behavior and achievements, God calls teachers, like pastors, to "correct, rebuke and encourage—with great patience and careful instruction" (2 Timothy 4:2). We evaluate, give feedback, and correct in a loving, helpful, and patient way, in a context of supportive but persistent and well-planned instruction. In both 2 Timothy and Titus, Paul says that as we correct, we must always encourage. As we assess, we recognize accomplishments and challenge students to further learning and growth.

We do not assess in order to judge personal worth. Rather, we are to prepare our students for works of service. Speak the truth in love, but say only what is helpful for building them up according to their needs (Ephesians 4:12, 15, 29). Regularly make notes about your students' progress, difficulties, and behavior. Probe students' understanding. Use your observations to revise your teaching. Have discussions with students about their progress. Provide extra help for students who need it. At the same time, hold them responsible for their efforts at improvement. Help them reflect on their learning, and encourage them to learn from their mistakes. Ask them to complete checklists indicating the completion of specific tasks, with their comments about how well they feel they have completed the tasks. When you need to confront students about work not done well, continue to encourage them even as you criticize. Give them multiple opportunities to achieve.

Encouraging students as we assess helps them discover, develop, and use their talents. This method requires far more than "pigeonholing" students. The latter, research shows, can easily become a self-fulfilling prophecy, especially for weaker students. It is possible for our assessment methods to lead "little ones to sin," especially by discouraging them from using their abilities in enriching ways. Jesus points out that teachers bear a heavy responsibility in this respect (Luke 17:2).

The principle of excellence. The concordance in the back of my Bible lists only seven texts that use the word *excel* or *excellent*. Yet I believe that God wants us to strive for excellence as we live in and unfold His creation. The Bible makes clear that we must work with all our heart to use our God-given abilities to contribute to society in God-glorifying ways (e.g., see Genesis 2:15, Romans 12:1–8, 1 Corinthians 14:12, and Colossians 3:23). But then we must ask, What is excellence? How can our assessment methods lead to such excellence?

True excellence, according to the apostle Paul, is rooted in love: "If I have ... all knowledge ... but have not love, I am nothing" (1 Corinthians 13:2). Excellence in a biblical sense cannot exist without a deep love of God, wonder and love for His creation, and respect and love for all people. It is within this context that Paul in Philippians 4:8 writes that "whatever is true, whatever is noble, whatever is right, whatever is lovely, whatever is admirable—if anything is excellent or praiseworthy—think about such things." Excellence therefore includes truth, justice, beauty, and worthiness.

What is clear is that excellence in the Bible is much deeper and much broader than doing well on tests and academic assignments. In a biblical sense, excellence is not just being in the top 10 percent of students academically or winning the highest award. The Bible does not exclude a thorough grasp of knowledge, skills, and values. However, it goes far beyond that. Also, Jesus makes clear in the parable of the talents (Matthew 25:14–30) that He expects us to assess excellence against potential. Richard Edlin (1999) argues that this parable shows that the class plodder would have received Jesus' approval long before the "smart kid" who with little effort still achieved an A.

The apostle Peter similarly says that within the context of loving one another deeply, each of us should use whatever gifts we have received to serve others "with the strength God provides" (1 Peter 4:8–11). Paul adds that the person who plants and the person who waters "have one purpose, and each will be rewarded according to his own labor" (1 Corinthians 3:8). So our assessment should help students reach their optimal potential to develop and exercise their diverse abilities. However, we should praise the person who doubles his "one talent" as much as the one who doubles her "five talents." Moreover, if a student has only one talent, say in mathematics, we should do whatever we can to ensure that he can function in life with basic mathematics skills. But we should also find other areas where he can develop and apply his abilities in notable and joyful ways. At the same time, we must avoid reaching premature conclusions about particular weaknesses.

We value excellence. We want everyone in a school community to strive for excellence. But too often we base our evaluation of excellence just on our numerical assessment data. We also need to take into account the God-endowed abilities of a student. Excellence for one student may well be receiving, say, 16/25 on a rubric-marked essay, while for another it may be nothing less than 23/25. Our feedback to students must make clear not only how students can improve future work, but also, as far as we are able to determine, the extent to which we believe they have been faithful in using their abilities in achieving what for them is excellence.

The Bible makes clear that academic achievement in a narrow sense takes a backseat to the pursuit of purity, integrity, compassion, justice, loveliness, and nobleness. Biblical wisdom based on exercising such aspects is more difficult to assess than whether students can add or subtract. However, how students exercise (or fail to exercise) all facets of biblical wisdom reveals whether they practice what Paul calls excellence and commends as praiseworthy. Praiseworthiness in education includes (but is not limited to) a love for learning and cultural unfolding; curiosity, creativity, and aesthetic appreciation; social and emotional know-how; and a disposition to live in gratitude while promoting justice. Assessing students mainly on cognitive achievement fails to do justice to a biblical view of excellence.

Treating students as image-bearers of God in our assessment practices. We saw in an earlier chapter that all humans are created in God's image (Genesis 1:26–27). God, of course, is incomparably greater than any human being. Yet being His image-bearers includes the fact that God has endowed us with innate abilities that we can cultivate and apply in service to Him and to our fellow creatures. Doing justice to the biblical notion that each student is created in the image of God means that we use assessment and evaluation to strengthen students' sense of worth and calling even when God has not given them superior talents in certain academic subjects. And if we believe that students bear God's image, we will also involve them in responding to our assessments and in assessing their own learning.

We assess in order to encourage further learning, not to judge personal worth. In God's sight, what students are counts much more than what they know. Jesus makes clear that it is not our role to judge a person's heart (Matthew 7:1). Therefore, we need to be careful to evaluate students' behavior and products, not their personhood. Don't leave students with the impression that they are of little worth and not valued because they are "below average." A real and verified danger is that low assessments and resulting low expectations lead to low motivation and low achievement. Unless we evaluate the results in terms of students' abilities, we discourage them from functioning in their call as stewardly image-bearers of God.

You will not be able to overcome completely students' perception that letter grades indicate their worth as persons. However, try to minimize that notion. Discuss with your students how all of them are made in the image of God. Help them experience and use their personal talents and resulting responsibilities. For projects, give students your comments and discuss them before giving them their final grade. Display the work of all students when it represents their best effort. Do so without indicating grades publicly. In such ways, we help them realize as fully as possible their capacities as His image-bearers, using those capacities to the full and with joy out of humble devotion to God.

There is one other aspect to being bearers of God's image. Paul emphasizes that as image-bearers each of us is nonetheless unique and has unique gifts. Thus we assess different gifts and use varied assessment strategies. Students have different abilities. Therefore we need to give them different opportunities to demonstrate what they have learned.

Education calls forth three kinds of student responses. Teachers assess each kind differently. They assess *definite responses* with relative ease. They can use straightforward questions and answers because only one or two responses are right. In *nonprescriptive responses*, students display their unique abilities and creativity. Although teachers still use defined criteria, their assessment is more subjective. Here teachers give students thoughtful feedback that helps them grow.

Our ultimate aim in schooling includes positive *internal response*. We can evaluate this only partially, and usually not immediately. Yet we continue to encourage positive internal dispositions and commitments, even though these are not measurable. For some of the most important internal responses, we may not see immediate results, and yet God may use us as the Holy Spirit's instruments. For instance, I was disappointed with my lack of meaningful interaction with a troubled twelfth-grade student. I met him ten years later on a city street. He said it was only during the last year, after he had committed his life to Christ, that what other teachers and I had taught him about life became personally meaningful. After he had drifted for many years, what he had learned a decade earlier led him to a career in social services. He now helped others facing problems similar to those he had had.

Assessment and evaluation become more subjective as we move from definite to nonprescriptive to internal student responses. Yet assessing nonprescriptive responses, while time-consuming, is usually more valuable for student growth than assessing definite responses. Further, teachers and staffs ought to review from time to time the effect of their program on students' values, dispositions, and commitment to a Christian way of life.

A balanced student assessment program goes beyond definite responses. It also allows for a range of methods. Observe, reflect, and give feedback informally as students learn. Assess oral, written, and hands-on physical assignments. Assess daily learning tasks as well as longer projects and exhibits of student products. Include short and explicit responses as well as open-ended and searching ones. The latter may involve exploratory and creative inquiries, and worldview-based and values-based probing. Tests serve a purpose in encouraging students to review and understand course material in a broad context. However, they are only one part of assessment, and usually not the most important part. On tests, use both short responses and some open-ended questions, including some that require personal evaluative responses (e.g., "Based on your own beliefs, evaluate what happened during the storming of the Bastille at the beginning of the French Revolution").

In short, while treating students as God's image-bearers, strive to incorporate the interrelated biblical principles of encouragement and excellence. That way you are helping your students grow as disciples who will actively speak and extend their hands on behalf of Jesus Christ, in terms of their own potential. Our assessment encourages them to be stewards of their gifts and stewards of creation. We want them to do their best in acquiring knowledge and skills, exercising creativity, and developing dispositions that reflect biblical values. But we evaluate these, as much as we can, in terms of the students' God-given abilities.

5.5 Reflect and respond

Consider the following interaction of a kindergarten teacher with her children. How does the teacher apply biblical principles as she assesses?

> Kindergartners, I'm going to draw a picture of the fish in the sea that God created on the fifth day. I'm not very good at drawing, but I'll try my best. Will you promise not to laugh at my drawing?... Now, when you draw, what is important is that you try your best. Are you going to laugh at the drawings of others at your table?... Kevin, I really like how you've drawn all sizes and shapes of fish, just as God created them.... Stephanie, I like the different colors you used.... Megan, can you think of some more things to include in your picture? Why don't all of you at Megan's table give her some ideas about what else she can draw.... Jason, if you hold your crayon this way you'll do better.... Matthew, are you frustrated? OK, here's another piece of paper so you can start again.... Now when we are all done, we'll put all your drawings on the bulletin board. If you don't like your picture, you can try again if you wish.

5.6 Reflect and respond

For a curriculum topic (preferably one for which you have learning outcomes available), suggest some assessment procedures for activities involving both definite and nonprescriptive student responses. To what extent should a school try to evaluate students' internal responses?

Fenwick and Parsons (2000) mention four "traps" in student assessment:

- Measuring only what's easiest to measure
- Underestimating how the assessment itself affects learning and knowledge
- Failing to take into account that a teacher's role may be threatening for students, or that teachers fail to question the types of assessment they use
- Inadvertently reducing the curriculum to only what is being assessed

Do your suggested procedures avoid these traps? If so, how? If not, what can you do to change the assessment process?

5.7 Reflect and respond

This section contains a sample assessment policy that is based on the metaphors and principles presented in this chapter. It is a generic assessment policy for a K–12 school. If you teach or are planning to teach in an elementary, middle, or high school, what changes in the policy would you make to suit those grade levels?

Implementing an assessment policy

Assessment is an integral part of teaching and learning, and must be closely linked to them. Teaching and learning involve a spectrum of activities: discussing new ideas, holding debates, role-playing, solving problems, applying concepts to new situations, using creativity and imagination to make new products, and so on. Such a wide range of activities also calls for a variety of assessment strategies, from short and specific ones to long and reflective ones: informal teacher-student interaction, rubrics to give feedback on assignments and portfolios, concrete experiences, demonstrations and presentations, real-life tasks, self-assessment (including goal setting), and tests.

When you design an assessment process, ask questions such as these (Herman et al. 1992):

- Does the process match your intended learning outcomes? Does it adequately represent a cross-section of the important outcomes?
- Does the process enable students to demonstrate optimally what they have learned? Have you prepared them for the types of tasks required?
- Does the process use meaningful and authentic tasks? Do those tasks focus on enduring understandings? Does the process encourage teaching and learning excellence?
- Is the process fair and free of bias for students of different backgrounds, learning styles, and gender?
- Is the process worth the time spent on it, either by students or by you as a teacher?

In the remainder of this chapter, I will give some suggestions for implementing the ideas presented up to this point (as summarized in the sample assessment policy). The suggestions are only a sample, and far from comprehensive. School staffs and teachers will need to adapt and extend these suggestions to suit their individual contexts.

A sample assessment policy

The following is a sample school assessment policy based on the aims, metaphors, and principles discussed in this chapter. Schools may specify further details (e.g., the intent of student-led conferences, report card design, the use of standardized tests). Some of the grading suggestions are based on O'Connor (2002, Appendix 3).

Our school's student assessment practices ...

- Strive to be a blessing to students by encouraging them to be and become responsive and responsible disciples of Jesus Christ.
- Recognize achievements and diagnose learning difficulties so that students do their best in all aspects of life in terms of their God-given abilities.
- Help teachers and students set meaningful and realistic learning goals and assume responsibility, respectively, for teaching and learning.
- Help teachers refine instruction to increase opportunities for student success.
- Include making parents aware of our assessment practices, including grading, at "Meet the Teacher" night at the beginning of the school year.
- Regularly and clearly communicate meaningful information about student progress to students, parents, and school authorities.

Our student assessment ...

- Is always based on our aims, enduring understandings, and specified intended learning outcomes.
- Treats students with respect and fairness, avoiding bias and favoritism. Teachers explain and discuss assessment procedures with students at the start of the year, well before any major assessments are to take place. Students are given the rubrics for major assignments when they are introduced, and at times will have input into rubric criteria.
- Puts foremost emphasis on formative assessment for learning, while in the end providing summative assessment as well (e.g., final evaluations of projects, report cards).
- Supplements teacher assessment with student self-assessment.
- Leads to evaluations (but not grades) that take into account students' abilities, effort, and dispositions. Assessment encourages excellence that involves values and a lifestyle based on biblical ideals and service to others (Philippians 4:8–9), not just on academic achievement.

Our assessment strategies ...

- Are continuous, age-appropriate, and evenhanded.
- Are based on clear expectations and use a fair sampling of student work.

- Involve a range of appropriate methods to suit different learning activities and different learning styles, with frequent and timely feedback to students.
- Emphasize meaningful tasks, products, and performances at levels that challenge students to do their best at their level of ability, including opportunities to apply and respond to their learning.
- Include periodic completion of language arts, mathematics, fine arts, and social/emotional/attitude and disposition checklists, with results used to plan effective learning strategies for the class and for individual students.
- Take into account the results of standardized testing programs with a view to improving learning for all students within the context of the school's vision and mission.

Student learning products ...

- At times vary for different students to account for different learning styles and aptitudes.
- Are regularly self-assessed by students in order that students may set personal learning goals and take responsibility for enhancing their own learning.
- Are often shared with other students, classes, parents, or community members by means of displays, portfolios, exhibitions, and performances.
- Need to be completed, with students given opportunities to hand in work that is late because of absence or procrastination (without penalty under extenuating circumstances; otherwise with penalties not to exceed 10 percent).

Our classroom tests ...

- Assess what is important in a unit or topic: enduring understandings, intended learning outcomes, and key concepts, skills, and values.
- Balance recall/interpretation, simple application, and more difficult analysis, evaluation, and creative problem solving. (This will vary according to the age of the students.)
- Have different types of questions so that children with different learning styles or "intelligences" will have some questions favoring their preferred mode of knowing.

Our grades ...

- Are used only in fourth grade and above, with assessments indicated with anecdotal comments and checklists in grades K–3.
- Are related to stated learning outcomes, with weightings to arrive at a grade that reflects the importance of particular learning outcomes and the importance of the assessment.
- Are based solely on attainment of learning outcomes. Effort, participation, and attitude are reported separately.

- Use the most recent assessment for grade determination when students have had more than one assessment opportunity. Scores obtained in assessment for learning and assessment as learning will not be used to calculate grades.
- Can be interpreted as follows: The student has demonstrated ...

    A—achievement of all learning outcomes at a level that exceeds the expected standards.

    B—achievement of most learning outcomes at a level that meets the expected standards.

    C—achievement of a good number of the learning outcomes, but with a few below the expected standards.

    D—achievement of many learning outcomes at a level below the expected standards.

    F—a failure to achieve most of the learning outcomes at an acceptable level, with much remediation required.

Our communication with parents ...

- Includes individual contact whenever desirable, report cards, parent-teacher conferences, and a student-led conference.
- Includes four report cards every year that contain

Grades summarizing achievement of learning outcomes and standards, accompanied by comments on strengths and weaknesses.

Checklists and comments summarizing initiative, effort, and learning skills.

In grades 7–12, student response forms (in consultation with the teacher).

A section for comments by the parents or guardians.

Classroom observation

Formal and informal observation is often the most valuable method of assessing students for learning. Use various methods. Ask frequent questions to check whether students understand a concept. Check facial expressions for puzzlement, frustration, or boredom—reactions that may call for different strategies or activities. Walk past students to check whether they can apply the mathematical algorithm just taught. Observe students at learning centers to see what processes and skills they use. Look around the playground to understand pupils' interactions and to help those with special social or emotional needs. At times it is helpful to have support staff or other teachers observe for specific outcomes or behavior while you are teaching.

To make your observations systematic and helpful ...

- Interact frequently with your students. To check for understanding, ask students to think about a question or observation for a few minutes and then share their thinking, first with a partner and then with the class. As students work, check and extend ideas, strategies, and feelings. Use instructions and questions such as these: *Tell me what you mean. Tell me about your plans. How did you figure that out? Why did you do it that way? Look at that again: what do you notice? Help me understand: what was easy/difficult about this? How do you feel about ...? What other ways ...?* Use such conversations to give feedback and encouragement as well as extra help for students who need it. Assist students in making adjustments and overcoming roadblocks in a comfortable setting (Oakes and Lipton 2003).

- Regularly record anecdotes about students' academic progress, special achievement difficulties, learning skills, and behavior patterns. Record only what happens, not your inferences or interpretations. Keep a notebook handy. Alternatively, jot down notes about students on sticky notes, and transfer them to student files at the end of the day. At lower levels, choose two students daily whom you will observe with special care.

- Periodically complete checklists for reading, writing, and numeracy for each student, as well as ones for social skills, emotional development, learning skills, and work habits. In higher grades, use mastery charts for subjects that involve many skills.

- For learning-center work or major projects, prepare a sheet on which students indicate the completion of specific tasks. Hold students responsible for keeping track of their progress and for setting learning goals, but also monitor them yourself using their sheets.

- Regularly discuss observations with your students to help them improve their performance. Be positive even as you require students to do their best. Give your students the chance to think about and explain their work. Confront them about work not done well, but continue to encourage them. As Susan Brookhart puts it, "Being positive doesn't mean being especially happy or saying work is good when it isn't. It means describing how the strengths in a student's work match the criteria for good work and how they show what the student is learning. And it means choosing words that communicate respect for the student and for the work. Your tone should indicate that you are making helpful suggestions and giving the student a chance to take the initiative" (2008, 57).

5.8 Reflect and respond

If you are a pre-service teacher, discuss with one or two in-service teachers how they use observation as a daily assessment tool. Are there things they would like to assess but for which they don't have time in their regular routine? If you can visit a classroom, ask whether you can help observe and assess some aspect of learning of an individual student or of the class.

5.9 Reflect and respond

Look at some resources that contain assessment checklists that you can use to observe and conference with students. Two sources are the British Columbia Primary Teachers Association's *Evaluation: Techniques and Resources* (1992) and Burke's *How to Assess Authentic Learning* (2005). Discuss how, when, and to what extent teachers can make effective use of such checklists.

Assessing student products

Once you have decided on your intended learning outcomes for a unit or topic, ask yourself what evidence would show that a student had attained those outcomes. As you plan your learning activities, consider how students will demonstrate that they have reached appropriate standards. Both during and after learning tasks designed to display student achievement, you assess the learning product(s). You may want to consider the following questions (Aker 1995, 55):

- What do I consider a successful response to the task? What criteria will I use to assess student achievement? Are the criteria based on my intended learning outcomes? Do my students know and understand the criteria?
- Will I assess all students according to the same criteria, or will my expectations vary according to student giftedness?
- Which intermediate steps will I assess for feedback? After I assess the final product, will I give students opportunities to enhance their learning and improve their product?
- If students collaborate on this task, how will I assess each student's individual contribution fairly?
- Would I want to be assessed in this way? Would it allow me to demonstrate fully what I know and can do?

How teachers assess student products depends on their intended learning outcomes, the nature of the product, and the amount of available time. Assess student work on the basis of criteria that are based on your intended outcomes and have been discussed with your students. Your criteria for a book jacket drawing for a novel will differ from those for acting out a scene from the novel. And it is not appropriate to assess a map drawn by a student for effective use of color, for instance, when your intended learning outcomes and the work in class dealt only with accuracy of scale and the designation of physical features.

Use comments and simple scales to mark class work or overnight assignments. I often use a +, ✓, -, and 0 to indicate exceptional, satisfactory, unsatisfactory, and missing. I then supplement these symbols with comments. Here I try to be positive and encouraging, but also honest (e.g., "You did a good job in listing the main points, but you failed to give your personal views"). Focus comments on students' strengths and on how they can improve achievement. From time to time, review your comments to see whether they encourage students. For example, "You have written good sentences, but try to improve your neatness" will accomplish more than "Messy writing."

To assess major assignments, use a rubric. It gives a scale of values in several categories. The descriptions cover a range of achievements related to your standards and your intended outcomes. For a persuasive letter, for instance, one category could be "Develops a convincing argument." The rubric then lists and describes four standards: *expert* (clear logic; strong supporting evidence), *proficient* (absence of contradictions; acceptable supporting evidence), *developing* (no major inconsistencies; some gaps in supporting evidence), and *novice* (inconsistencies; little or no supporting evidence). The teacher assigns student work a 4, 3, 2, or 1, respectively, for this as well as each of the other categories. I give a sample rubric in figure 6.1. For other examples see chapter 11 of Stiggins (1997), Lewin and Shoemaker (1998), or Coil and Merritt (2001).

SAMPLE RUBRIC FOR HIGH SCHOOL SOCIAL STUDIES PROJECT

Criteria	1	2	3	4	5
Scope and choice of content ___/5	Choice of content inappropriate or far too little to do justice to the topic	Some of the content is relevant, but it is incomplete and/or some of it is inappropriate	Generally acceptable choice and range of content, but with some gaps or unsuitable selections	Proper choice and range of content	Skillful and judicious choice and range of relevant content
Grasp of content and issues ___/5	Incomplete understanding with many misconceptions	Basic understanding but some significant misconceptions and/or misinterpretations	Adequate understanding and analysis, but with some weak interpretations	Complete understanding with appropriate analysis of relevant issues	Insightful understanding, perceptive analysis of relevant issues
Use of resources ___/5	Used only one type of resource, or repeated or copied content indiscriminately	Several types of resources but not used effectively	A good range of suitable resources but with some gaps and/or ineffective use	A good range of resources, appropriately used.	Thoughtfully used a carefully chosen range of library, Internet, and in-class resources.
Structure and organization ___/5	Organization confusing and difficult to follow	Organization unclear in places, with abrupt or illogical transitions, and/or inappropriate headings; introduction and/or conclusion missing	Overall organization clear, but one or more of introduction, conclusion, headings, or logical flow awkward or missing	Generally well organized, but some improvement possible in one or two of introduction, conclusion, headings, or logical flow	Well organized with effective introduction and conclusion as well as clear headings; logical flow from one paragraph to the next
Writing effectiveness ___/5	Writing difficult to follow and understand, with a large number of errors in grammar, spelling, and/or diction	Writing lacking clarity in places, with many errors that lead to difficulties in understanding the meaning	Writing generally clear and fluent, but contains a significant number of spelling and grammatical errors	Writing generally clear and fluent, with only a few spelling or grammatical errors	Writing clear and eloquent, with no spelling and grammatical errors
Format and appearance ___/5	Title page missing; messy or incorrect format	Deficient title page; weak use of computer technology; inadequate format or neatness	Appropriate title page; adequate use of computer technology; some minor format flaws	Original title page; good use of computer technology; generally correct and neat format	Creative title page; resourceful use of computer technology; accurate and neat format throughout

TOTAL _____/30

Your project has the following strengths:

Your project can be strengthened and improved in the following ways:

Figure 6.1

Assessing assignments is time-consuming, especially for nonprescriptive responses. At higher levels, you may sometimes want to spot-check. For instance, collect all student journals but respond with comments for only five or six students. Then rotate this to different ones every ten days or so. The use of rating scales and rubrics reduces time spent writing comments and still gives meaningful feedback to students. In composition, use peer editing for specific skills that students have learned. This reduces your marking time, reinforces what you have taught, and develops student responsibility (even if at first you need patience!). Manage your time well. Schedule time for observation, for recording information, and for conferring with students when they do activities that require little intervention. Use peers and peer writing conferences to assess first drafts of compositions.

Self-assessment enables students to participate actively in their learning. It cuts down on time as well. More importantly, it makes students more responsible for their own learning. Paul enjoins all persons to test their own actions (Galatians 6:4). Students learn to set appropriate learning goals and develop realistic self-concepts. Students need your help to do this effectively. Primary children tend to think that the amount of work and neatness are more important than overall quality, so you have to help them set criteria for self-assessment. It is helpful to have students reflect on their progress in terms of weekly logs and daily goals. For projects, you might give them a sheet on which they describe the project and then complete open-ended statements such as these:

- What I enjoyed most about this project ...
- In this project I learned ...
- If I were to do this project again, I would ...
- I would like to find out more about ...
- What I did well in this project ...
- What I could have done better in this project ...
- What I found difficult about this project ...

Finally, note that when you assign tasks that require higher-level thinking or creativity, students achieve more when you give comments rather than grades. Comments lead to improved work; grades lead to reflections about self-worth. Good practice could include not disclosing a grade until students have responded to comments (Harlen 2007).

Portfolios of student work

Student portfolios are organized collections of sample student work, usually kept in folders, boxes, or computer storage devices. Students may include samples of their writing over a period of time, artifacts that showcase their work, annotated lists of books they have read, reflections and self-assessments, and goal-setting pages. These help students assess their daily work as well as their long-term progress.

Students who use portfolios frequently reflect on and revise their work, particularly when they are involved in selecting the key pieces for their final portfolios. As they add products, their portfolios show their growth over time. They can set goals that fit their individual abilities and achievements. Portfolios can also strengthen ties between home and school. For instance, they provide a meaningful basis for teacher-student, teacher-parent, and student-led parent conferences.

To use portfolios effectively, discuss with your students the purpose of the portfolio and which (dated) work samples they should include. If possible, show sample portfolios. Have students ask with you, Why is it important to include this product? What does it reveal about my learning? Evaluate the included work. Some teachers prepare cover sheets for portfolio entries (e.g., asking students to include items that demonstrate a strength, creativity, critical thinking, or improvement). On their cover sheets, students give reasons for choosing each item. The teacher, in response, indicates some positive features as well as one or two areas for the student to work on.

Review the items with the students from time to time, keeping only those that show significant growth. Limit the number of artifacts. The process of students' culling work to include what is most significant is metacognitive, and it leads to better-focused analyses of the remaining work (Burke 2005). When possible, affirm that student choices meet your expectations. Grade the portfolio in its entirety so that you assess overall learning progress (Fenwick and Parsons 2000). The final portfolio can be shared with parents and guests during an afternoon or evening.

5.10 Reflect and respond

Assessment and evaluation can affect the relationship between students and their teachers both positively and negatively. Have you had any assessment experiences that affected your relationship with a teacher negatively? If so, how could the teacher have used assessment in a more positive way?

For the grade levels you teach or intend to teach, discuss the assessment strategies that teachers can use with daily assignments as well as with larger projects in order to improve student learning and maintain good classroom rapport.

5.11 Reflect and respond

Before reading the next section, discuss in what ways tests and examinations can be negative experiences. Is it possible for them to be positive learning experiences? Write down four or five key points that you believe teachers should keep in mind when administering tests in order to make them effective experiences for students.

Constructing, administering, and scoring classroom tests

Ideally, tests help students reinforce, consolidate, and integrate what they have learned. They make connections between concepts, issues, and topics that previously may have appeared disjointed. Like other means of assessment, they serve both formative and summative functions. Formatively, tests help teachers diagnose learning so that they can improve follow-up instruction. Summatively, tests inform students, parents, and teachers about learning accomplishments.

Test results should lead to self-evaluation. Use them to help your students focus once again on the essentials of what they have studied and learned. Interpret the results in relation to the other assessment and evaluation methods you use, including your conclusions from observing and listening to students. How can you enable your students to improve their future results?

Testing is often a stressful occasion for students. I base the suggestions that follow on my belief that testing must be done in love and fairness, and must help students, not just rank them. To do so, you should keep the following in mind when preparing and giving tests:

- Use your intended learning outcomes and a description of the unit's content and skills to decide what types of questions to use and their balance. Relate test questions directly to your intended learning outcomes. Ensure that test questions reflect content and skills that have been part of classroom learning. For example, if your learning outcomes stress problem solving and critical thinking, don't emphasize low-level multiple choice questions, even if the former require more time to score. Test what counts!

- Test what was important in the unit. Avoid questions that trick or that deal with obscure points. Before finalizing a test, check whether the items represent a fair sampling of the unit content. Provide a proper balance of questions among recall, comprehension, and application of knowledge; reasoning proficiency and problem solving; abilities and skills; creative activities; and dispositions. Also check the growth of value judgments and dispositions to the extent it is possible.

- Use a clear, logical format. Provide space for the students' names. Indicate how much each item is worth. Group all items of the same format together. Give clear and complete instructions for each section. Within each section, sequence items from easy to more difficult ones, or in the same order as the learning took place. Arrange items on the page clearly for easy answering. Don't use separate answer sheets; they make tests more complex. Phrase questions and problems carefully. In short, help students show clearly what they have learned.

- For optimal response, put students at ease as much as possible during a test. Many students are anxious before a test, and their anxiety affects their ability to express their learning. There are a number of things you can do to help students give a good account of their learning. Before the test, give sample questions from previous tests so that students know what to expect. Acquaint young students with unfamiliar types of questions. For review, have small groups of students write sample test questions. Include one or two of those that are on the test. Suggest strategies that minimize stress such as doing the easiest questions first and briefly outlining an answer before writing it. Give tests reasonably often so that the result of any one test does not carry too much weight. Ensure that ventilation, lighting, and noise levels are acceptable. Tell students what they may do when they complete the test.

- Provide for students with different learning styles and for those with special needs. Include both lower-level and higher-level thinking questions. Where possible, include questions that do not emphasize just the linguistic/verbal (e.g., include visuals; provide manipulative tasks). Modify tests for students with special needs (e.g., provide alternative evaluations in another room; check whether students understand the directions; use oral assessment; use assistive technology; adapt in terms of an Individual Educational Plan).

- Monitor problems with tests and note what you can improve next time. Speed tests are designed to check how much work students can do in a given time. Otherwise, however, if more than one-tenth of the students do not finish in the allotted time, the test was too long. If many questions arise during test writing, you need to clarify some things for next time. Observe students who do well on everyday work but who do poorly on tests. Perhaps they have special difficulties that can be overcome. Some students may know the work but need to be tested orally, for instance.

- Mark tests fairly and quickly. Before students write the test, develop a detailed scoring key. This is important since it may show you that some unclear or ambiguous questions need revision. For longer questions, outline what you require for a full score. To maintain a consistent standard, score all students' answers for one question before going on to the next. Avoid bias by not looking at students' names. Shuffle papers between questions so that a particular test is not, for instance, always near the beginning or after the best student in the class. Score only positive points. Correcting for guessing is wasted effort. Feedback within one week is necessary if the test is to enhance learning. Give written feedback as well as final grades.

- Before you file away the test and forget about it, analyze how students answered questions. Write down what you can do to help your instruction and improve future tests. Also evaluate whether you assessed what you thought you did. For example, did your science test measure the students' comprehension and application of photosynthesis, or do the scores reflect deficits in other areas such as reading or writing ability?

- Standard books on measurement and evaluation contain many suggestions for writing effective test items (e.g., Stiggins 1997). Each type of question has strengths and weaknesses. The main advantage of true/false, matching, short-answer, and multiple-choice items is that they are quick to score. Such questions usually focus on low-level content, however. They also ignore the importance of writing to communicate insight. True/false questions are unreliable because of the guessing factor.

- Good multiple-choice items are difficult to write, especially ones that go beyond recall and simple comprehension. Also, creative and divergent thinkers see possibilities besides the ones listed and therefore may have difficulty with this type of question. If teachers give many multiple-choice questions, students conclude that teachers value predetermined answers more than students' own expression and thought. It follows that the number of multiple-choice questions should not exceed 20 to 25 percent of a test. If you use them to save marking time, create a bank of multiple-choice items and reject or revise those that prove to be unsatisfactory.

- Longer-answer questions take longer to score. They do allow students to analyze and evaluate as they formulate and organize ideas, however. They evaluate composition and critical evaluation skills, as well as the ability to assimilate, organize, and apply knowledge in new settings. Word your questions so that they present a clear, definite task (describe, explain, compare, interpret). For long answers, define the direction and scope of the response and the criteria used for scoring. Indicate how long an answer you expect and how much time students should spend on it.

- Use some creative questions that require students to apply and transcend knowledge learned in class. In a unit test on Mexico, for instance, you might ask the students to write a letter to the Mexican or the American president: "Describe the advantages and disadvantages of Mexican immigration to the United States. End your letter with a reasoned personal conclusion and advice for the president." Such a question assumes that you have discussed with the students the characteristics of a good persuasive letter and that you give them the criteria you will use to score their answers.

- Remember, finally, that tests alone do not give a valid basis for assigning report card grades. Tests have a valid but limited role in assessing learning. Don't make decisions about students too quickly on the basis of one or two tests. Testing cannot take the place of day-to-day assessment and evaluation.

5.12 Reflect and respond

Obtain some sample tests, preferably ones that have been scored. Analyze their effectiveness on the basis of the learning outcomes or standards for the topic tested (if available), and the suggestions given in this chapter.

Using standardized tests

Standardized tests are developed by test publishers or government agencies. They can provide a benchmark for schools in connection with their state's or province's curriculum. They can help to diagnose learning strengths and weaknesses for classrooms and schools as well as for individual students. They can help teachers design special strategies to suit the needs of their class or of individual students, and they can help teachers decide whether a particular student needs outside help.

Standardized achievement tests, especially if they "fit" a school's curriculum, may identify strengths and weaknesses of a program or a particular class. Some years ago, for instance, Christian schools in my area participated in fourth-grade mathematics tests. The results showed that students achieved well in all areas of the curriculum except geometry and probability. The schools took steps to improve their geometry programs. Results four years later showed that they had successfully done so. Interestingly, the schools also decided that probability was not a desirable topic for young students. So they used the test results to improve the attainment of the schools' own goals, but they did not change the program just to improve scores and "look better" in the area of probability.

While the intent of system-wide tests is to improve programs and instruction, often politicians and the media use the results mainly to "grade" schools and/or teachers, not taking into account the socioeconomic or language background of students. As a result, schools may focus mainly on what is tested. If so, these "high stakes" tests narrow the curriculum, downplaying the importance of the fine arts, foreign language study, and even social studies. Student motivation for learning may decrease. In some jurisdictions, student dropout rates have increased with the emphasis on testing. Often the tests take much class time to prepare students and to administer, taking away time from more varied instruction.

Furthermore, most of such tests make use of a multiple-choice format with its inherent limitations. This format prevents them from adequately measuring critical thinking, creativity, or the ability to express thought. Yet it is crucial that schools develop such important God-given gifts.

Word alert

Standardized tests are administered to large populations (e.g., all fourth-grade students in a state or province). A central agency develops, assesses, and evaluates them. When such tests are used to rank students or schools, or to determine whether a student can be promoted or can graduate, they are called high-stakes tests. Student tests are *reliable* if the results are consistent year after year. They are *valid* if they satisfactorily assess a program's intended learning outcomes (that is, the test content matches that of the curriculum). It is possible, for instance, for a test to be reliable but not valid when the results are consistent year after year but the text does not assess a representative sample of what students were to learn.

Also, the reliability of standardized tests is questionable, especially for younger students. Teachers' own grades are usually better predictors of later success in school than standardized achievement test results. This is true both because teacher assessment is continuous and because teachers base classroom tests on what they have actually taught.

In short, standardized tests should be administered and interpreted with care. The results should be used to improve programs and learning within the context of a school's vision and aims. Remember that everyday classroom assessment for learning and assessment as learning can be more productive for improving learning.

Government tests in specific subjects at or near the end of high school are defended because they maintain and improve "standards"—and they do. A difficulty, however, is that the standards are set by the government and may thus limit the scope of learning. They may also be at odds with the aims of Christian schools in subjects such as English, history, and biology. From this point of view, the more general American Scholastic Achievement Tests are less objectionable. They also suffer from the shortcomings outlined above. However, with inconsistent academic standards from one school to the next, they do provide a nationally normed benchmark.

Grading and reporting

The primary goal of grading and reporting is communication. You want to keep not only students but also parents informed. Parents have the primary responsibility for their children's nurture. Good communication helps them support you, and this parental support in turn helps student learning.

Communicate with parents more often than at report card time. As one teacher said to me, "Parents dislike having heard nothing before they read a report card with negative news. We need to get parents on board with us as soon as we know that a student is struggling. Then we can jointly support the student's learning." Therefore, contact parents about problems but also about special achievements. The latter kinds of contacts especially pay off for learning. Try to talk to or e-mail one or two parents a week with a specific positive observation. Also, send home school products and share general results through a class newsletter or on your classroom website.

Grades communicate less information than most parents assume. Grades (as well as single scores on major assignments) "average out" the assessment of very different qualities. In the process, those who see the composite mark get little idea of student achievement in specific elements, or even of the standards a teacher used to assign the grade. Moreover, grades are subjective. For example, a B given by two different teachers may mean quite different things. In fact, a B given by the same teacher on two different assignments or to two different students may not mean the same thing. Once I asked a group of principals who taught language arts to grade a photocopied seventh-grade student composition. Their assigned grades ranked from a D minus to a B!

However, if assigned with care, grades can provide a useful indicator to parents. Despite their limitations, grades provide quick, symbolic summaries of overall student achievement. They may help to give students a realistic concept of their own abilities in diverse areas. They can also be used to recognize excellence.

Grades are usually norm-referenced. That is, they compare students against one another. For instance, a B would mean that a student is somewhat but not exceptionally above average for his age group. Some schools use criterion-referenced grades. This method may give students and parents a detailed list of specific learning outcomes that students have successfully attained in each subject. Or it may define grades in terms of students' exceeding, meeting, or failing to meet all or most of the standards or stated expectations. The advantage of criterion-referenced grading is that teachers base assessment on set criteria. Students are not pitted against one another. In a strong class, most students could have all items on a list checked off as "meets" or "exceeds" the expected standards, with most receiving an A. The

> ## Word alert
>
> *Grades* are summaries of student achievement, often designated in terms of alphabet letters (e.g., an A indicating the highest grade, an I for "In progress," and an F the lowest). *Marks* are scores obtained on tests or assignments. These may be numerical scores (including percentages) or letter grades. Sometimes the terms are used interchangeably.

description of grades in the sample assessment policy earlier in this chapter is a criterion-referenced one.

Criterion-referenced assessment does not tell parents how their children are achieving in relation to other students. Yet most parents still want to know this, so many of them like norm-referenced grades, especially when the average class grade is also shown.

To minimize the pitfalls of grades, make clear to students and parents what the grades mean, and how they should be interpreted. Have established criteria, even if they are informal ones, for giving specific grades. Ensure that their use is relatively consistent throughout the school. Since grades present an incomplete picture, accompany them with comments on essays, projects, and report cards. Avoid giving grades in the first few years of schooling. Grades easily pigeonhole young students. If this pigeonholing happens, research shows that weaker students perform more poorly in the long run. Except for good students, grades do not motivate learning, so do not use them for that purpose.

If you use numerical percentages for assigning grades, do so flexibly. If a major test turns out to be too difficult (or easy), your preset scale has little validity. Further, if four or five students are all grouped right at the border of B and C, there is no defensible reason for giving some a B and some a C. While a scale may provide a basic guideline, use "natural breaks" between groups of scores as well as the difficulty of tests and assignments to adapt the scale to a specific situation.

For completing report cards, use your anecdotal notes, your checklists, and your grade book. Then you can be specific and give helpful feedback about significant aspects of student progress. Balance positive comments with constructive criticism. At parent-teacher interviews, have sample work available for parents. Point out specific strengths and weaknesses in students' work. Both your reports and your parent-teacher interviews should develop a "we-together" attitude of mutual cooperation.

Finally, remember that grading depends on a number of value judgments. As a teacher you decide the importance of what and how to teach and assess. You decide how to mark and give a weight to various assignments. Teaching and assessment are interpersonal activities, and judgments and feelings come into play. Try to be as fair as you can be, even as you recognize that giving grades is a subjective activity based on a multitude of decisions you make. Also remember that grading that is perceived to be faulty or unfair damages interpersonal relations and can have a detrimental effect on learning (O'Connor 2002).

5.13 Reflect and respond

Photocopy an unassessed student assignment. Ask each person in your group to assess and grade it. Discuss the results, drawing conclusions about the consistency of the criteria and the standards used. Then debate the pros and cons of grading assignments rather than just giving formative comments. How can grades be used in positive ways, if at all?

Using assessment to improve learning

Connie Clements' and Jim Vance's school staff decide to review their student assessment procedures. Connie and Jim become part of a committee that considers what a Christian approach to assessment and evaluation should involve. The committee does not find a large number of Bible texts with a direct bearing on evaluation. But they do conclude that a number of scriptural givens are relevant.

First, each child uniquely bears the image of God. Therefore, teachers use assessment to keep track of each student's progress and responses. They do not use it just to rank them. Ideally, assessment leads students to boost their learning, not to hinder it. Assessment is not always done by the teacher. Students learn to assess and evaluate their own work. They also learn to contribute to the learning of others through peer assessment.

Second, the fruit of the Spirit must be evident in student assessment. Ideally, teachers are motivated by love and fairness. They patiently reassure students and animate their learning as they assess and evaluate. They help their students strive for excellence. But excellence for the Christian does not mean being first or second academically. Rather, it means developing all one's gifts and abilities optimally for service to God and neighbor. That means that assessment takes into account student growth and achievement in a wide range of insights, abilities, and dispositions.

The committee shows that much of the school's assessment has focused on giving summative information to parents. Also, it points out inconsistencies. For instance, some teachers use mainly student work to grade students and give mostly Bs on report cards, while others put a heavy emphasis on tests and have a wide spectrum of grades.

After some initial discussion, the teachers write a coherent student assessment policy. They develop sample skill checklists, assignment and project-marking rubrics, and student profile charts. They discuss how they can maintain the motivation of weaker students while giving students and their parents realistic information about performance and growth. They consider how assessment for learning and assessment as learning can take place on a daily and weekly basis. They share ideas on giving corrective yet positive feedback on assignments. They discuss how assessment can be an integral part of classroom instruction and how they should use the results of teacher-made and standardized tests. They revise their report cards in order to give more specific and detailed information to parents, with the description of grades becoming more criterion referenced.

The teachers establish a common understanding. They seek out methods that help their students develop and use their abilities without becoming disheartened. They move away from allowing their teaching to be governed by their summative assessment. Instead, they consider how their intended learning outcomes can determine their assessment. They regularly ask themselves how their assessment strategies affect student attitudes and learning and whether they are in touch with students' needs. They try to maintain high but realistic expectations and to give much formative feedback. And they use a summative grading guideline that clearly spells out what each grade means. All of this is summarized in an assessment policy that is shared with students and parents.

Of course, the teachers' different personalities and varying grade levels still mean that each goes about assessment and evaluation somewhat differently. It is still difficult to interest and motivate students frustrated by years of lack of academic success, or to be patient with apathetic ones. However, the change of emphasis from summative to formative assessment and from judgment to encouragement will improve student learning and achievement as well as classroom relationships.

Chapter 5 enduring understandings

Assessment should ...

- Encourage and improve learning.
- Be a blessing for the students, a blessing that embraces grace, justice, and encouragement.
- Be an integral part of learning, closely related to specified learning outcomes.
- Foster excellence in all a student's gifts on the basis of the student's potential as a bearer of God's image.
- Emphasize assessment for learning and assessment as learning, and not just assessment of learning.
- Develop plans that enable teachers and students to interact frequently about student progress as well as learning challenges, with opportunities to refine or retry learning activities.
- Use a variety of meaningful tasks, products, and performances, with specific descriptive feedback to students.
- Use accurate descriptors for all grades based on the achievement of learning outcomes.

• Communicate meaningful and clear information to students, parents, and school authorities.

References

Aker, D. 1995. *Hitting the mark: Assessment tools for teachers.* Markham, ON: Pembroke.

British Columbia Primary Teachers' Association. 1992. *Evaluation: Techniques and resources,* Book 2. Vancouver: British Columbia Teachers' Association.

Brookhart, S. 2008. Feedback that fits. *Educational Leadership* 65, no. 4:54–59.

Brouwer, E. 2006. Assessment as gift: A vision. In *Educating toward wisdom,* edited by E. Brouwer and R. Koole. Langley, BC: Society of Christian Schools in British Columbia: 2.1–2.2.

Burke, K. 2005. *How to assess authentic learning.* 4th ed. Thousand Oaks, CA: Corwin.

Coil, C., and D. Merritt. 2001. *Solving the assessment puzzle piece by piece.* Marion, IL: Pieces of Learning.

Edlin, R. 2000. *The cause of Christian education.* 3rd ed. Blacktown, Australia: NICE. Also printed by and available from Association of Christian Schools International.

Fenwick, T., and J. Parsons. 2000. *The art of evaluation: A handbook for educators and trainers.* Toronto: Thompson.

Graham, D. 2003. *Teaching redemptively: Bringing grace and truth into your classroom.* Colorado Springs: Purposeful Design.

Harlan, W. 2007. Formative classroom assessment in science and mathematics. In *Formative classroom assessment,* edited by J. McMillan. New York: Columbia Univ., Teachers College Press: 116–135.

Herman, J., P. Aschbacher, and L. Winters. 1992. *A practical guide to alternative assessment.* Alexandria, VA: Association for Supervision and Curriculum Development.

Lewin, L., and B. Shoemaker. 1998. *Great performances: Creating classroom-based assessment tasks.* Alexandria, VA: Association for Supervision and Curriculum Development.

McMillan, J., ed. 2007. *Formative classroom assessment: Theory into practice.* New York: Columbia Univ., Teachers College Press.

Oakes, J., and M. Lipton. 2003. *Teaching to change the world.* 2nd ed. Boston, MA: McGraw-Hill.

O'Connor, K. 2002. *How to grade for learning: Linking grades to standards.* 2nd ed. Thousand Oaks, CA: Corwin.

Smalley, G., and J. Trent. 1986. *The blessing.* New York: Pocket Books.

Smith, D. 2001. The Bible and education: Ways of constructing the relationship. *Themelios* 26, no. 2:29–42.

Stiggins, R. 1997. *Student-centered classroom assessment.* 2nd ed. Upper Saddle River, NJ: Merrill.

Part Three

Creating Learning Communities

Schools are more than collections of students and teachers. To be effective, schools need to be communities of learning. They need to be environments where students and teachers take delight in working together, where everything that takes place is built on a common commitment, common values, and a common purpose. They are places where the board, parents, teachers, students, and support staff all build relationships on the basis of the Great Commandment, and where the Holy Spirit touches the hearts and lives of community members as they live and work together as the apostle Paul describes in Ephesians 4. Chapter 6 discusses how we can nurture our classrooms to be supportive learning communities. Chapter 7 considers how we can ensure that students with special needs become integral, valued, and supportive members of the classroom community. And chapter 8 looks at how the whole school can function as a Christian community.

How Do We Give Leadership that Fosters Classroom Communities?

6

Chapter 6 guiding questions

- How can classrooms function as supportive learning communities?
- How do we prevent and deal with disruptions that detract from community and from learning?
- How do we practice discipline that leads to discipleship?
- How can we group students for learning?

Marilyn Chung and Donna Van Dyke both teach second-grade classes of about twenty-five children. Both consider their teaching to be a vocation, one to which they give much time and effort. Both have the best interests of their students at heart. Both use the curriculum outlines that the school has developed for the various subject areas. Parents regularly express their satisfaction with both teachers to the principal, Marsha Hall. Yet, Marsha knows, second grade is quite a different learning experience for the children in each class.

Marilyn Chung's verbal and body language—even her clothing—set the tone for her teaching. She projects the idea that learning is serious business and that no one is going to waste time in her class. Her organization breathes efficiency. Learning materials are filed neatly in their designated spots. Classroom routines are well established. The children know exactly what she expects of them. The classroom has five rows of five desks each, with three small tables for carefully planned learning centers at the back. When Marilyn works with one of her reading groups, the other students follow the precise instructions on the chalkboard. They know that they may not interrupt the teacher or one another with questions. In all their work, from reading to art, neatness and accuracy are the foremost concern. In mathematics, each unit begins with hands-on material, but Marilyn quickly moves on to practice worksheets. Her class functions as a quiet, efficient machine.

The principal knows that students in Marilyn's class learn the "basics" well. Yet she has some questions. Does Marilyn's approach stifle her students' creativity and spontaneity? The projects, compositions, and artwork that are displayed all seem similar and regimented. Also, some students seem uptight and even fearful in Marilyn's class. Marsha knows that Marilyn is a loving person, but she can also be somewhat rigid and even unnecessarily sharp with her students, sometimes even when they try their best.

Donna Van Dyke, on the other hand, maintains a warm, loving classroom atmosphere. She greets each child personally at the door each morning. During her opening exercises and devotions, children share some of their experiences. They practice some mathematics skills informally using the daily calendar. Then they give input as they discuss the plans for the day. The room displays, put up by the students themselves under Donna's direction, are colorful and vibrant but not very well organized. The reading corner has a large number of books but looks messy. Donna says nothing when children put down their books almost anywhere as they exchange books for their personalized reading program. In language arts, Donna emphasizes "guided reading" where she supports a small group of learners as they learn various reading strategies. However, her students in the other small groups are not always on task. In mathematics, the children usually work at their desks in small groups of four. They move around for different types of activities. The students enjoy and get excited about their learning. Things get noisy from time to time, forcing Donna to flick the lights as a signal that the children must work more quietly.

When Principal Hall visits Donna's room, she sees a group of enthusiastic students engaged in stimulating learning activities. Yet here, too, she has questions. Shouldn't Donna put more emphasis on the focused learning of specific skills? The students' printing skills, for instance, are below par. Some activities seem to be done on the spur of the moment because they are interesting rather than because they fit planned intended learning outcomes. But, Marsha asks herself, can Donna tighten up her structure without losing precisely what makes her a good teacher? If she does, will her children continue to use their unique abilities in so many creative ways?

Marsha Hall reflects on how she can support both second-grade teachers. She wants them to use their personal strengths and overcome or at least cope with their weaknesses as they structure their classrooms as encouraging and successful learning communities. Yet she does not want either one to be cast into a mold that would not fit her personality.

Reflect and respond 6.1

Identify what you think are the positive and the negative aspects of Marilyn Chung's and Donna Van Dyke's classroom structures. Which of your personal tendencies can you use in teaching to build positive classroom structures? Which may detract from that goal? Think about how you can cope with the latter or channel those tendencies positively.

Classrooms as learning communities

Marsha Hall's school is blessed with two committed and skillful second-grade teachers. Children are learning in both classrooms even though improvements are possible. Yet, as may be seen from the above examples, good classrooms can vary a great deal. Teachers have their own personalities and gifts. They have also been molded by their experiences. Moreover, they face unique classes. The practice of sound pedagogy has common elements, but how a particular teacher applies these elements will differ. No two classrooms will ever look or feel quite the same. No two teachers will deal exactly the same way with similar situations. Teaching is not a mechanical act but a personal one. Teachers should use rather than suppress their personalities in carrying out their roles as stewards, priests, and guides. At the same time, as in the case of Marilyn Chung and Donna Van Dyke, they may have to learn to compensate for personal traits that detract from a good learning environment.

The Bible makes clear that God calls us to be a community in which we all contribute our special gifts (Romans 12:5–8, 1 Corinthians 12:12–30). As a Christian teacher, therefore, you consciously strive to forge your classroom into a learning *community* in which students experience the richness of living in a caring and supportive but also challenging environment. Ideally your classroom is a place where students learn to accept and use their abilities in relation to themselves and others. Here they experience the joys and difficulties of working together toward common goals. These are essential aspects of learning to live and work in the larger community. With technology taking over some of the repetitive tasks of life, it becomes even more important for people to relate well to others.

A classroom that is a learning community works and prays together. When one member fails or suffers, all feel the pain. When one rejoices, all rejoice. As much as possible, all members

> ### Word alert
>
> *Pedagogy* is sometimes defined as the art and science of using methods of instruction. It is a richer word than either *teaching* or *instruction*. It includes the notion that teachers are sensitive to the backgrounds, circumstances, and aptitudes of their students. The teachers then adapt their craftsmanship to the dynamics of the class as well as to the learning needs of individual students, so that the teachers are tutors, guides, and mentors.

contribute to the learning success of the others. As a teacher you structure your classrooms for meaningful learning. You convey trust and respect. Your enthusiasm, warmth, and humor not only motivate your students but show them you want to encourage and support them. You demonstrate that you are trustworthy and are committed to helping each student make a special contribution to the class community.

Your students, at the same time, are called to respond to your guidance to the best of their abilities; second best is unacceptable. They must realize that they have responsibilities beyond themselves. Their conduct affects how well others will be able to learn. They have direct obligations with respect to others when they work at collaborative learning tasks.

Another key to a classroom's functioning as a community is that the teacher engenders common motives and goals. If you allow students to have significant and successful roles and give them recognition for their work, they will more likely see themselves as your partners. Discuss and set rules together to create a sense of ownership. Ask students what they already know and what they would like to know about a topic in order to allow them meaningful input into unit planning. Require students to set personal learning goals. Discuss how they can achieve or have achieved them. Such a discussion lets them celebrate their successes and renew their determination to do well. Give each student special responsibilities ranging from setting up equipment to peer tutoring. That way they will realize that they contribute to the fulfillment of the community's goals. Appreciate student work for its merits in terms of each student's own abilities, not in comparison with that of others. Otherwise, student motives easily become competitive and self-centered, with potential disruptions of positive relationships.

Also, plan academic and social activities with your students that encourage them to interact and cooperate in a variety of settings. The more everyone in the class knows and accepts others and recognizes their special strengths and needs, the more the class works together as a cohesive group. Celebrate cultural differences, personal characteristics, diverse learning styles, and strengths in certain modes of knowing. Emphasize that God made all persons unique in order that they can contribute their gifts and experience and insight to the whole community. Collaborative learning methods, as described in the section on grouping for learning, help students respect and learn from one another. If carefully designed, these groups also improve achievement.

God created us to function as contributing members of communities. He calls us as followers of Christ to support one another in loving interaction. And He calls teachers to take the lead in enabling such interactions to happen in their classrooms. Teachers aim to enable all members of the classroom community to fulfill their responsibilities in a mutually supportive environment.

Reflect and respond 6.2

Discuss features of the classroom that affect its atmosphere as a learning community—both positively and negatively. Then make a list of ways in which you can bring about a positive sense of community in your classroom.

Personal relationships in the classroom

Classrooms cannot function as effective communities of learning unless harmonious relationships exist. Marilyn Chung's efficiency and pointed disapproval at times made some students afraid of her—to the point where it curtailed their learning. On the other hand, the fact that Donna Van Dyke did not set consistently high standards also affected her relationships with her students. They liked her as a person but intuitively sensed that they could get away with things. To an outside observer, the relationships in each classroom did not seem harmful. Nevertheless, they were not as wholesome as they might have been.

Teachers care about their students. That means that they not only create a warm and supportive tone in their classrooms ("love your neighbor as yourself"), but they also provide an environment in which students will develop their talents to make a positive contribution to the classroom and to their future life contexts. Caring has both interpersonal and curricular implications, and they must complement each other. As Nel Noddings put it, "As human beings, we care what happens to us. We wonder whether there is life after death, whether there is a deity who cares about us, whether we are loved by those we love, whether we belong anywhere; we wonder what we will become, who we are, how much control we have over our own fate" (1992, 20). Oakes and Lipton quote studies showing that "trusting, mutually satisfying relationships and a sense of community at school create conditions where all children—even those in quite desperate circumstances—can learn and develop well" (2003, 283). They point out that even simple but frequent relationship phrases such as "I'll help you" engender trust and lead to a respectful atmosphere that promotes both social and academic growth. And as Noddings suggests, teachers must be sensitive to the big questions about life that students wonder about.

In a sinful world harmonious relationships are not always easy to establish and maintain. Nevertheless, as a teacher you are strategically placed to do so. The types of relationships you nurture and establish have an immense impact on the success of your teaching. As teacher-priests and teacher-guides, listen carefully. Interact sensitively. Show personal interest. Teach enthusiastically. Praise genuinely, with respect to specific achievements or behaviors. Confront sensitively when necessary. And forgive freely (Ephesians 4:32). Treat your students as bearers of God's image. Each pair of eyes looking at you is created in God's image! That fact does not mean that you should not be firm. Demand that students treat you and one another with respect and responsibility. Speak the truth in love but also insist that your students speak the truth (Ephesians 4:15, 25). Firmness, however, needs to go hand-in-hand with fostering an atmosphere of openness, warmth, and care. God gives you authority as a teacher to serve your students and to enable them to be responsive disciples.

Vernon and Louise Jones (2006) give a number of suggestions for building sound relationships. They suggest that you maintain a high ratio of positive to negative statements. Respond as much as possible to positive student behavior. Communicate high expectations of all students. Call on and give as much feedback to the academically weaker as you do to the stronger. Create opportunities for personal discussions about students' activities. Demonstrate personal interest by having lunch with individual students, joining in playground games and community events, greeting students individually each morning, and similar actions. Moreover, plan activities that nurture group cohesiveness, especially at the start of the year. Such activities could include organizing and decorating the classroom together as a class, creating special days, maintaining a class photo album, and asking questions at the end of the day about what students liked and disliked about the day.

Confident and authentic communication is an essential ingredient of community. Such interaction requires being knowledgeable and prepared. You should transmit thoughts, feelings, instructions, and concepts calmly, smoothly, and clearly. Nervous, overpowering, loud, threatening, or uninterested communication through body or verbal language hampers your role in shaping community. Seeing yourself on a video recording may be a humbling experience. It may show you, however, that *how* you say things to your students can undermine *what* you say. You also should insist that students communicate with you and with one another with respect. They must listen as well as speak, and they must not interrupt others. If they are angry or frustrated, you can help them express those feelings in terms of "I feel ..." instead of loudly accusing others.

As a teacher, you need to be confident and constructively assertive without being aggressive or argumentative. Describe issues and concerns clearly. Maintain eye contact. Be unambiguous in your body language. Let your facial expression reflect what you are saying orally. Respond empathetically to your students. Listen carefully to their concerns. Try to see things from their perspective, paraphrasing their input. Respond so that you invite further discussion rather than cutting it off ("Tell me more" or "I'm interested in hearing your ideas about this"). When appropriate, work with students to develop future goals or plans for improvement or change (Evertson, Emmer, and Worsham 2006).

A safe and secure environment provides the setting for respectful and honest interchange. Pay close attention to students and remain open to what they say or write. Through active and careful listening (asking, for instance, "Are you saying that ...?"), draw out and clarify students' thinking. Create a climate in which students feel free to question, explore, discuss, and reach conclusions. When students express beliefs contrary to biblical teachings or values, ask probing, directed questions that help students reassess their views and behavior. However, accept that a diversity of views and insights is possible, even within a biblical framework. In your role as a guide and mentor, pray that you may influence your students to follow Jesus. Nevertheless, honor their views, if respectfully defended, even when you disagree with them.

Disruptions in community

A classroom never functions as a perfect community. Sin disrupts, and we need to deal with its reality. To build and maintain community, we must establish, teach, and enforce positive behavior. Students need the security of knowing what we expect and what we will enforce (see the section on expectations and limits later in this chapter). When students harm relationships or learning through word or deed, confront them with the need to repent and to heal the resulting brokenness. Ask from time to time how your own actions affect relationships and learning.

Students sometimes create a tension-filled tone in a class. Such a tone affects learning. Deal quickly and openly with momentary flare-ups. Discuss with your students their perceptions of more serious problems. Attempt to draw out the root causes. Ask how the conflict or problem may be alleviated. Encourage openness, admission of guilt, and forgiveness. Develop acceptance and commitment to improvement, and hold students accountable for their commitments. Seek the guidance of the Holy Spirit while working toward a solution. When a student becomes a "scapegoat," work with the class for greater acceptance. Sometimes you can use a "reaction story" that mirrors the existing problem in a slightly different form. By discussing and presenting possible solutions, students may be willing to commit themselves to a parallel solution for the classroom problem.

Occasionally, personality clashes do occur between a teacher and a student. When this happens, recognize that the problem exists. Then try to develop an attitude of acceptance between yourself and the student. Make a distinction between students and their behavior. Reject inappropriate behavior but *not* the person. Once forgiveness is obtained or given, grudges must not be held. Remember that we do not like all students equally. We may even find it hard to like a particular student. God calls us, however, to accept all our students in love, to reach out to all with understanding, and to guide them all into discipleship. Therefore, we strive to avoid communicating negative feelings by our tone of voice, posture, verbal responses, grouping of students, or informal or formal assessment strategies.

Walking with God in the classroom means expressing love and concern for all, without exception. Listen to the apostle Paul: "Love is patient, love is kind. It does not envy, it does not boast, it is not proud. It is not rude, it is not self-seeking, it is not easily angered, it keeps no record of wrongs. Love does not delight in evil but rejoices with the truth. It always protects, always trusts, always hopes, always perseveres" (1 Corinthians 13:4–7). But remember that, when necessary, love also involves discipline in order to produce "a harvest of righteousness and peace" (Hebrews 12:11).

Word alert

Some educators tend to think of student discipline in terms of punishment. But note that the words *disciple* and *discipline* come from the same root, meaning "to learn" and "to follow." So it is preferable to think of discipline in terms of educating and nurturing students to act and behave more and more in ways that contribute positively to the classroom learning community. It is important for teachers to set out procedures that inhibit inappropriate behavior. That is called *preventive discipline*. And even when teachers need to reprimand or penalize, they ought to do it in ways that will increase the likelihood of gradual voluntary observance of community standards. That is part of *corrective discipline*. Of course, when the safety or well-being of students is threatened, teachers must take immediate action and only afterwards may be able to consider how to redirect the perpetrators.

Reflect and respond 6.3

If you discuss this chapter with a group, role-play and analyze classroom situations such as these:

- A teacher sees two boys fighting when she comes into class after recess.
- When the teacher is introducing a unit on poetry, a class "leader" says loudly, "This stuff sucks."
- A teacher discusses class rules and routines at the beginning of a school year.
- A teacher discovers that three students are regularly copying one another's mathematics homework.
- A student is continually "off task" and not completing her work.
- A student, in tears, comes in after lunch saying that some older boys on the playground regularly bully her.

Keep notes on how you feel the situations can be best handled. Then, after you have read the whole chapter, revisit each situation and discuss whether you would change your approach.

Discipline unto discipleship

The purpose of discipline is to disciple students in the Lord's way. Discipline is an opportunity to redirect students. Discipline opposes sin. More than that, however, it strives to overcome shortcomings. It nurtures commitment to uprightness and reconciliation. It affirms change for the better. Through discipline, students may realize the grace of God (Hebrews 12:5–11). Discipline is not harsh retribution. It must not cause bitterness from a perceived lack of grace and forgiveness.

School boards give teachers *legal* authority to conduct their classes. Teachers can also rely on *traditional* authority, since most parents do communicate to their children the respect that the parents have for teachers. If the authority of teachers is based solely on formal appointment and tradition, however, teachers can maintain their position only through authoritarianism—that is, through rigid domination—which in turn leads to power struggles between students and teachers and breaks down a positive learning atmosphere. Teachers need to establish their *personal* authority. Personal authority results from the teachers' insight and ability to guide students, to unfold content, to structure classroom learning, and to enable students to develop and exercise their gifts. The proper exercise of these four interrelated aspects will allow teaching to take place in a personally authoritative way (Mark 1:22, Luke 4:32). We use such authority to serve our students, both through encouragement and, when necessary, through rebuke (Titus 2:15).

Ultimately, it is God who gives teachers authority to perform their task of guiding and enabling students. He endorses them in their calling as teachers and gives them the abilities that make it possible for them to establish personal authority. When teachers apply such authority through discipline, they do so not for the sake of exercising power over their students but to give understanding and wisdom about the "way to life" (Proverbs 3:12–13, 6:23). Godly discipline is always administered in love (Proverbs 13:24; Revelation 3:19).

As a teacher, you exercise discipline in at least four ways:

- Structure your classroom learning so that students can work productively and without constant interruptions and so that they have a measure of responsibility for their own learning decisions. Students who are engaged in well-planned, reasonably challenging, meaningful activities are less likely to disrupt and more likely to develop self-discipline.
- Be a role model for students, particularly in showing and demanding respect. Do not embarrass students.
- Establish and teach relevant rules that encourage a positive context for effective learning.
- Enforce the rules by setting and consistently upholding consequences that refocus students on their responsibilities as members of a classroom learning community.

Note that three of these four ways emphasize *preventive* rather than *corrective* discipline. That is, as much as possible we try to prevent disruptions. However, when they do occur, we act with firmness, fairness, and the possibility of forgiveness and grace.

Setting and maintaining expectations and limits

When I began teaching, I wondered whether my students would cooperate with me to create a good atmosphere for learning. And I had my challenges, especially with an unruly group of ninth-grade boys to whom I taught mathematics at the end of the day, right after physical education! What I learned that first year was that even more than creating engaging lessons, I had to foster caring and respectful relationships. Above all, I found out that good teachers practice preventive discipline by anticipating and forestalling problems.

Here are some suggested ways to practice preventive discipline:

- At the start of the year, let your students know immediately by word and deed that you are prepared and organized. Clearly convey that you will enforce procedures and routines. Explain why and how these procedures and routines will help everyone. Practice the procedures and routines, especially with young children. Hold students responsible for following them. Give them frequent feedback.

- Carefully plan the transitions between activities and between classes. Indicate when a transition is about to begin (for example, turn off some lights). Give clear directions, and tell students exactly when they are to follow your instructions. Praise students for following instructions and for encouraging others to do so as well.

- Keep a repertoire of "sponge" activities available that students may do when they have completed their assigned work (for example, puzzles, high-interest reading materials, a science discovery learning center).

- Use humor to defuse tension—and learn to laugh at yourself at times!

- Walk through the room and stand close to a distracted student while continuing to lead the discussion.

- Change your planned activities to alter the pace when students get restless or when attention falters (for example, on a hot afternoon).

- Build relationships with students who are the cause of frequent playground disputes and ask them to do some playground tasks that they like.

- Change your seating scheme when two or three students cannot stop talking to each other.

- Ignore students as much as possible when they seek attention in unacceptable ways, but talk to them and help them when they work quietly and conscientiously.

- Be calm but firm with a student's unacceptable behavior (for example, say, "We don't talk that way in our classroom. Now, begin again").

- When there is no specific problem but you sense that things are not going as well as they have been, hold a class meeting. Ask questions such as these: What can we do to make things better? How can we improve our classroom as a learning community, a place where we help one another? How can we commit ourselves to our agreed-upon course of action?

There is one aspect of preventive discipline that needs further discussion: setting and maintaining expectations and limits. God has created us to function within certain laws and norms (Psalm 19:7–11). A prerequisite for effective discipline, therefore, should be to set wise limits according to the expectations of the school, the maturity of the students, and the characteristics of the class and the teacher. A class adapts surprisingly easily to the different expectations of different teachers. Students quite accurately read your mood and adjust their responses accordingly. In high school, they do so from period to period as they change classes and teachers.

To create an optimal learning situation, indicate your expectations clearly. Monitor student activity and reinforce your expectations. God's law sets general guidelines (for example, to love God and neighbor), but provides freedom for rule differences from class to class. The specific regulations you and your class set and agree on are not as important as whether you discuss them fully, explain them clearly, teach them regularly, enforce them consistently, and monitor class compliance constantly. You provide fences within which you and your students live and learn and make decisions. The older your students, the farther the fences should be pushed out. At the same time, setting unrealistic expectations frustrates students, and discipline may become ineffective.

Wise teachers clearly define procedures, expectations, and rules. Instruct your students in them, and then see to it that they are met consistently. Post a set of clear, simple rules such as these:

- Be loving, polite, and helpful.
- Respect other people, their property, and their opportunities to learn.
- Don't interrupt the teacher or other students when they are speaking.
- Obey all school rules.

Setting rules and procedures enables you to give reasons for them (for instance, skill learning requires a quiet atmosphere in which students can concentrate) and to give examples. Such discussions make students more willing to live and learn within the limits. You also need to clearly indicate your expectations for activities that involve noise and moving around (for example, project research, hands-on science activities, artwork). Remember that for rules to be effective, you must actively teach and model positive behavior and relationships. You also need to complement the rules with efficient routines and a consistent emphasis on individual responsibility.

Monitor your students constantly and reflectively. Scan the room and let students know that you are aware of what is happening. Circulate randomly through the class. Move toward off-task students. When helping one student, keep an eye on the rest. Keep the momentum of your class going. Ensure that all students remain busy. When necessary, remind the whole class of your expectations ("I'm still waiting for two people to turn to page 23"). Use positive language (for example, "Remember that to concentrate, we need quiet" rather than, "Don't be so noisy"). Recognize and reinforce desired behavior ("I appreciate how quietly you walked to the music room today"). Provide varied and challenging work (Cruickshank et al. 2003).

Consequences must follow if students overstep the bounds. Most students want the security of knowing that you are committed enough to enforce the limits. They *will* test the limits! One of the most common weaknesses of beginning teachers is that they do not consistently enforce the established framework. For example, if you expect students not to talk to one another while you are working with a group or an individual, insist on it each minute, each hour, each day! A basic rule in establishing your personal authority is to be consistent in your expectations for appropriate behavior at all times and for all students. Only unavoidable extenuating circumstances may demand that you make an exception (for example, a medical emergency or an announced special "fun" activity).

Similarly, students should know that presentation and discussion time requires the participation and attention of all. They must be courteous and listen to the speaker. They must maintain acceptable habits of participation: do not interrupt other speakers, speak only when recognized, respect the opinions of others, don't put others down, and so on. You can often deal with those who break the rules in unobtrusive ways. Don't recognize students who speak out of turn. Glance at one whose face shows disdain for another student's opinion. While you require more severe measures only occasionally, you must take some action *every* time a student knowingly breaks the established framework. Otherwise the classroom atmosphere gradually deteriorates. Of course, if a rule seems not to be working, you may have to stand back and ask whether the rule is reasonable and enforceable. Then discuss with your students how it can be modified in order to have the intended result.

Above all, as I mentioned before, foster an atmosphere of respect in your classroom. Each person needs to demonstrate respect for the time, space, property, and integrity of all other persons. Help students to make their own decisions and to follow through. Help them see that they are responsible, that they have freedom to choose, and that they are accountable for their decisions about their behavior and work. The key to a respectful and caring learning community is that we hold one another accountable for our actions.

Reflect and respond 6.4

Construct a set of basic classroom rules for a specific grade level. To what extent would you seek student input when discussing these rules at the beginning of the school year?

Teaching dispute and conflict resolution

Because of frequent conflict among students, many schools teach students how they can deal positively with disputes and conflicts that they experience with other students. A dispute- and conflict-resolution process is most effective when a whole school adopts the same strategies.

Such programs recommend that a number of steps be carefully and regularly taught and practiced. Here is a suggested process for dispute and conflict resolution:

1. *What is the problem?* First, the students involved discuss and establish exactly what the issue is.

2. *How does it feel?* The students take turns describing how they feel about the situation. They are not allowed to interrupt one another.

3. *What can be done about it?* The students discuss how they can solve the problem. They brainstorm ideas and list options for resolving the situation. Each person comes up with possible solutions. At this point they do not criticize one another's solutions.

4. *Which solution is agreeable to both?* All persons must agree with the solution that is chosen.

5. *Did we apologize and forgive?* Students must apologize to one another when appropriate. This is a necessary "cleansing" for all involved—both the victims and the aggressors. And the victims must then forgive.

6. *Did the solution work?* Later, the students should evaluate whether the solution worked. If it didn't work, they must agree on another option from the ones in step 3 and implement it.

This approach has several advantages. First, students do not perceive teachers as "referees." That attitude is often troublesome for teachers. The accuser as often as not is also the aggressor, but students' roles in a conflict are often difficult to sort out. Second, students learn to solve their own problems in a positive way. If the above steps are taught thoroughly and practiced for a time, conflicts seldom escalate to the point at which teachers need to become involved. Third, problems resolve themselves much more easily and quickly, with both students and teachers feeling positive about the outcome. Fourth, students learn to appreciate one another's feelings and concerns, which builds community. Fifth, students become peacemakers, a change that God requires of us in Scripture (Romans 12:18, 1 Corinthians 7:15, 1 Thessalonians 5:13).

Consider these examples:

Friction had erupted on the playground several days in a row in a kindergarten class. The teacher suggested that the class should solve the problem. The problem, it turned out, was that groups of students had formed "gangs" that did things together for security but excluded other students from their activities. The students' own solution was to do away with gangs but, in order to still feel safe and secure on the playground, to have "teams" instead. This worked well for a week or so; then the same problems seemed to reoccur. Again, the class discussed their feelings about the situation and concluded that the problem was that even teams excluded some students. So they made the decision that anyone was able to join or leave a team at any time. They played happily until the end of the year, without any further major problems. They had solved the problem themselves. The teacher's involvement had been limited to suggesting that they should discuss the problem and find a solution.

A ten-year-old wrote a letter to our local newspaper: "I have a major problem that has to be solved. My problem happens when someone annoys me and calls me names, and I tell them to be quiet. Then that person will tell our teacher something like I cursed at them. They do this because I am bigger. The teacher always takes their side. What should I do?" (*The Vancouver Sun*, June 25, 1996).

Teachers who consistently teach and use the above conflict resolution approach in their classrooms tell me three things. First, this problem would seldom come to their attention because students would almost always solve it themselves without coming to their teacher. Second, when teachers do hear about the problem, they ask students to resolve it using the steps that they know, with the students almost always finding a solution. (I have seen kindergartners do this very successfully.) Third, when a teacher does need to become involved, the use of the six steps will still yield solutions that are more acceptable to both sides than a teacher-imposed solution. In short, this method prevents most problems from escalating or becoming long-term, nagging ones.

Reflect and respond 6.5

Describe a realistic student conflict at the grade level you teach or intend to teach. With one or two others, demonstrate how students at that level might resolve the conflict using the steps outlined in this section.

Corrective discipline

Despite your careful planning of preventive measures, sin will still cause derailments in classrooms. Students may seek attention, power, or even revenge. In such cases you need to administer corrective discipline. Don't become overly discouraged. Rather, use misbehavior as an opportunity for nurture and spiritual growth for students as well as for yourself (Romans 5:3–5; Fennema 1977). Corrective procedures should be fair and should be seen as fair. Corrective action should fit the severity of the misbehavior. Overreaction can make the problem worse. Also, when students need to be reprimanded, avoid doing so in a demeaning, belittling, or sarcastic manner that could strip them of the self-worth they are entitled to as persons made in God's image (Colossians 3:21). Quiet and firm action is more effective than anger or threats. Often eye contact, a walk up the aisle, or a quiet gesture is sufficient and takes place just between the teacher and student.

If further action needs to be taken, talk to students privately. Ask them *what* went wrong (not *why!*). Let them reflect on and analyze how they have affected the learning situation. Continue the conversation until the student describes the situation accurately. You might ask older students to write down their perceptions of what happened. Say, "I am disappointed that ... What can we do to ensure that it doesn't happen again?" Gradually try to find, from a consideration of various options, a mutually acceptable course of action to remedy the situation in the future. Get students to commit themselves to the proposed solution, then hold them fully accountable for their actions. An in-school suspension may be used to isolate a student who continues to refuse to cooperate. While schools may have to suspend students for dangerous behavior, with other out-of-school suspensions parents legitimately complain that such an action accomplishes exactly what such students want: they do not have to attend school. Some schools use teacher assistants to supervise (and mentor) students for in-school suspensions. The students' removal from peers is a punishment, but students are still monitored to do their school work.

A biblical approach to resolving a discipline problem

- First, *confront* the student, privately if possible, with the unacceptable situation. Ensure that love and truthfulness guide how the confrontation takes place. Ask questions such as these: What were you doing? What was the result?
- Second, try to bring the student to the point where he or she genuinely *confesses* that there is a problem that needs correction.
- Third, after exploring different options to overcome the problem, get the student to *commit* himself or herself to a plan. The plan should spell out the student's future expected behavior as well as the consequences should the student fail to uphold the agreement. You may want to ask older students to sign a written agreement for serious breaches of acceptable behavior.

In short, three steps to follow when grave problems arise are confrontation, confession, and commitment (Fennema 1977). Do remind the student of his or her commitment. Ask how things are going. Encourage the student. However, do not accept excuses for failure to follow the plan (Parkay et al. 2008). In all serious cases, of course, make sure that you inform the parents or guardians of the situation and solicit their help in resolving the problem.

Punishment for unacceptable behavior is a last resort, especially since often it does not allow you to try to rectify the underlying cause of the problem. To correct defiance or unresponsiveness, for instance, you need to get at the motives of the student. Punishment by itself will not give long-lasting results. Punishment is necessary, however, when there is deliberate and repeated flouting of the rules, but it should come only after warning, and it should be used sparingly.

If punishment is the only option, use logical consequences when you can. If students are still noisy after two warnings, remove them to a "time-out" chair until they decide that they will be able to work quietly in the regular setting. If students misbehave at a learning center, remove their privilege of working at a center for a day or two. If students look at photographs during silent reading time, quietly confiscate them. If students have not done their homework, have them come in at lunch or before or after school to do it. If they litter, get them to pick up garbage in the halls or on the playground. The more the consequence is related to the misbehavior, the more effective the punishment. But note that assigning extra schoolwork as punishment causes resentment and affects learning negatively. Lowering academic grades is not an acceptable punishment unless it is the logical consequence of an action such as cheating on an assignment or test.

As much as possible, administer your own punishment. For instance, if you assign a detention, students should serve it with you to reinforce your personal disappointment and disapproval. You may even be able to use such occasions to extend personal relationships that in the long run may benefit your classroom community. Be firm, but calm and loving! Even while administering punishment, continue to help students formulate courses of action to prevent future misbehavior.

In administering reprimands or punishment, you need to make sure that you are in full control of yourself. If you feel you are losing your temper, postpone the confrontation. Simply say, "I will deal with you later." If necessary, remove the student from the class, giving specific instructions about where the student is to go and what the student is to do. Disciplining in anger often leads to regret. Remind students at appropriate times that it is not your actions but theirs that cause punishment. They must realize that they are accountable for obeying the boundaries set for them. This principle is in harmony with the biblical view that humans are responsible for their own fallen state and behavior.

If constant breakdown of the learning situation occurs, you may use positive and negative reinforcement with good effect. Such methods, if carefully thought out and administered for relatively short periods of time, may help students break self-defeating patterns of behavior. If talking out of turn is a common problem in a seventh-grade class, for instance, write the names of students on the board when they do so. For each additional offense, put a checkmark behind the student's name. If a student hasn't spoken out of turn for a period of time, erase one or two checkmarks (and/or the student's name). Students with their names still on the board should expect to serve a detention, but forgiveness is possible! Do remember that positive reinforcement (such as assertive disciplining through which students earn points) is generally more effective than the negative kind. Also, with all punishment, both teachers and students should perceive that the punishment is fair. Note that in using such techniques your goal is to help students toward responsible self-discipline so that they no longer need extrinsic reinforcement.

One problem that occurs in schools is that some students taunt, threaten, or bully other students. Those being bullied feel unsafe and are at risk. Such behavior must therefore be dealt with right away. Bullies often belong to a group of students who intimidate others. They act aggressively to bolster their self-confidence. On the one hand, schools must enforce strict rules against bullying, supervising areas where it is likely to take place. On the other hand, teachers should try to develop personal relationships with bullies, giving them responsibilities in which they can be successful. Often bullies need positive adult role models and will respond to adults who care about them and who enable them to become respected members of the community in more appropriate ways (Cruickshank et al. 2003).

Reflect and respond 6.6

A middle school unexpectedly found itself with a group of ninth-grade skateboarders who intimidated and bullied other students, even using physical violence. The school's enrollment had jumped from 390 to 540. It faced overcrowded conditions and had many inexperienced new teachers. It found itself with little positive student leadership and many more at-risk students. To counter the bullying and violence, the school quickly adopted a zero-tolerance policy. It immediately suspended students involved in any violent act. This school suggests the following steps for schools in which bullying or violence becomes a problem:

• Be proactive in dealing with student violence. Have a clear policy in place. Notify students, parents, and the community about the policy.

• Use a multifaceted approach to dealing with student violence. Zero-tolerance policies are not enough. Teachers need to increase supervision, teach the values of tolerance and respect, increase student ownership of school policies, and build interpersonal relationships within the school.

• Form an advisory program. Advisory classes, often held at the start of the day, help the school to become a moral community. These classes focus on building relationships, fostering acceptance, and teaching positive values.

• Be aware of group dynamics. Students who are reasonable on a one-to-one basis may become dangerous to other students when they are part of a group. Consider the effects of group behavior.

• When in the middle of a crisis, take action. Don't philosophize! When faced with unexpected turmoil, swift action is necessary to ensure a safe and secure environment for your students. A crisis is not the time to seek to build consensus; it is time for action. (Litke 1996)

Do you agree with the suggestions this middle school makes for such a situation? Why or why not? Look back over the previous sections of this chapter and jot down some of the guidelines that would apply to a situation such as this. What other steps might a school take to deal with bullying or violence in a positive way?

Grouping for learning

During His ministry on earth, Jesus, the Master Teacher, taught large groups, small groups, and individuals. Sometimes He taught hundreds of people at a time. But He explained the parable of the sower to a small group of close followers. He addressed both the Samaritan woman and Nicodemus one-on-one. He sent out His twelve disciples with special tasks in groups of two. The point here is that there is no one ideal group size for teaching. Rather, the size of a teaching group depends on the aims and nature of the learning activity, as well as on the characteristics and receptivity of the learners. Teaching a whole class of twenty-five or thirty pupils is effective for some types of instructional situations but not for others. As a teacher you need to reflect on how you can group students effectively for different learning outcomes.

What is more important than specific methods of grouping is that teachers treat students with care and concern and allow them to exercise the abilities that are part of their personhood. You should structure learning to involve tasks and methods that, as much as possible, meet the needs of all your students. When appropriate, you should also encourage them to make choices about their learning, set personal goals, act on them, and bear a measure of responsibility for their own classroom decisions. In short, whatever methods of grouping you use, allow students to exercise their calling as God's image-bearers, helped and encouraged to make responsible choices and decisions.

Large-group instruction is an efficient way to disclose concepts that the whole class should know. Most teachers make extensive use of this mode of teaching— sometimes too much so. Large-group instruction is often (but not always) effective for the disclosure phase of learning described in chapter 4. Teacher presentation is appropriate, for instance, when you choose, organize, or interpret material in a way not available in another source, or when you want to clarify issues or consider different points of view. To be effective, presentations must be purposeful, clear, brief, engaging, and thought provoking.

To ensure that students learn concepts and can apply them, presentations need reformulation follow-up. This follow-up occurs through individual or small-group activities. You may give individual students or small groups several options to reinforce concepts, to examine some specific part of the topic under consideration, or to expand what they have already learned. I describe more ways to group for learning in the next two sections as well as in the section in chapter 7 on differentiated learning.

One way you may maintain personal contact and recognize the needs of individual students is to hold individual conferences. The purpose of these conferences is to assess students' progress. In reading conferences, for example, teachers discuss the content, ask students to read orally from a part they enjoyed, make notes, and come to an agreement about which skills the students will work on. Keep conferences short (five or six minutes) and ensure that the rest of the class is working quietly. Similarly, a personal conference about a unit project helps students to set goals and plan further learning.

Ability-based tracking

Putting students into ability-based classes has been controversial for several decades. Research consistently shows that such grouping or tracking seldom benefits students. Grouping by ability or achievement is particularly harmful for the academic and social development of students with weaker academic abilities. When grouped together, such students can no longer benefit from interaction with academically strong students. They easily become discouraged and even alienated. Teachers lower their expectations. They spend less time preparing, and they do not teach as well. Further, they end up having more discipline problems with such classes. In addition, when students are placed in a low track, they tend to stay there. Academically weak students achieve less in tracked classes than in the heterogeneous classes found in small high schools where tracking is not possible. Moreover, the majority of academically strong students do not advance appreciably more when grouped in separate classes (Oakes and Lipton 2003).

Tracking has negative implications. It labels students, often to their detriment both academically and socially. It prevents contact among students of diverse abilities and backgrounds. It also creates antagonism in schools, both between groups of students and between teachers and students. Preparing students for responsible discipleship means that we provide a setting for optimal personal development. By and large, tracking affects the learning community negatively. Therefore, as much as possible, we should avoid it.

Despite the negative effects of tracking, teachers find that teaching classes with students of a wide range of abilities is demanding. Planning is more complex and time-consuming, especially since teachers need to provide alternative activities and assignments regularly. It is harder to keep all students on task, even when a teacher balances whole-class instruction with small-group and individual tutoring.

In spite of these teacher challenges, for the sake of student learning, schools do well not to track students in different ability groups. The one exception might be at senior grades for sequential subjects such as mathematics and foreign languages. For other courses, instead of tracking students according to ability, schools might define a core for each topic that all students should learn, and then develop alternatives at varying levels of difficulty for smaller groups within the class.

At upper grade levels, of course, students self-select by choosing courses that suit their abilities and interests. Also, many high school students now take online courses to complement those offered by the school, enabling them to specialize and complete some courses at their own rate while continuing to be part of the school community.

Cooperative or collaborative learning

One popular method of in-class grouping is collaborative (or cooperative) learning. Collaborative learning can be an effective strategy when used judiciously. When carefully planned, it can improve time on task and develop social skills that not only enhance community but that are increasingly important in the workplace. It enhances a sense of mutual responsibility and a sharing of gifts ("all for one; one for all"). It counters self-centered individualism and promotes collaborative servanthood. Collaborative learning, however, is not just "group work." Here are some factors to keep in mind when grouping students for collaborative learning (Cruickshank et al. 2003; Good and Brophy 2008):

• *Group activities must have a clear purpose.* Students must know the expectations and procedures thoroughly: rules for behavior, standards for the work, and where and when to get help. While you work with one group, students from other groups should not interrupt.

• *Groups must be heterogeneous.* An important objective of a group (usually three to five students) is to encourage students to accept diversity in aptitude and background. Also, mixed groups benefit the students of low-level ability without holding back high-level ones. Moreover, groups of mixed abilities are more likely to function well together.

• *You must train students to work cooperatively.* Show students how to share responsibility, listen, and handle conflicts. Specify desired behaviors such as listening carefully, encouraging all to participate, and using personal names. Begin with a series of simple tasks so that you can focus on cooperative skills. Teach students how to take on specific assigned roles in the group (for instance, the encourager, the summarizer, the mover, the checker, the gopher, the recorder, the reporter, and the noise monitor). To ensure that students stay on task, always circulate. This allows you to monitor student behavior and learning, teach collaborative skills, and provide task assistance.

- *You must structure groups for positive interdependence.* What this means is that students must benefit from working together. Assign each student a specific role (see above) on a rotating basis. Each student may have to complete a specific part of a project or be responsible for a specific required resource.

- *You must hold group members accountable for their performance, both as a group and as individuals.* Collaborative groups might complete a summary of the main points of a topic and receive one group grade for this summary, no matter how much each individual contributes. But the students might take the test on the topic individually, with individual grades assigned.

- *You must use collaborative learning selectively.* Students do not have the pedagogical and content background for the active instruction needed for systematic development of key concepts and higher-level thinking. Such content and instruction are the responsibility of the teacher. Also, collaborative learning may not work well in primary grades. Moreover, tasks involving routine practice are better done individually. Effective collaborative learning tasks are those that allow a range of formulation and solution strategies, or tasks that benefit from collaborative planning.

Many widely used collaborative-learning activities are appropriate for your class. You may ask groups to work on applications of material that you have just presented. You may have groups put together a project requiring library research. You may ask them to design and produce a mural or skit that sums up a unit. You may use a jigsaw technique, by which each student learns about a concept or topic and then teaches it to her or his "home group." Depending on the class and subject, when collaborative learning is used 10 to 20 percent of the time, it appears that students accept greater responsibility, exercise positive social skills, and achieve academically as well as they do with other types of teaching strategies.

Reflect and respond 6.7

Choose a unit topic at a specific grade level. Brainstorm and discuss how you could use different types of groupings to enhance learning in community.

Providing for diversity

Classrooms today are diverse. Teachers have to be sensitive and must plan for diverse aptitudes and learning styles; for diverse special needs; for diverse cultural, ethnic, and religious backgrounds; for diverse parental expectations; and so on. God has created each child special. Each deserves to have fitting, optimal opportunities to learn. Chapter 4 addressed how to plan for the varied aptitudes and learning styles in a classroom; chapter 7 will consider how to take other types of diversity into consideration.

Arranging your classroom

Your classroom is a workshop for learning, and the physical layout and the uses you make of it will affect learning as well as student-student and student-teacher relationships.

Many different classroom arrangements are possible. A well-organized, attractive classroom leads to more receptive and positive students, as well as to improved learning. Classrooms should include space for individual, small-group, and large-group learning activities. You should be able to see and monitor students at all times. In turn, students should be able to see all instructional presentations and displays without difficulty. Keep careful watch for students with sight or hearing problems. Keep high-traffic areas—including bookshelves, storage areas, the pencil sharpener, and your desk—separate and easy to get to.

Classroom displays—or the lack of them—also influence the learning environment. They direct students' attention to topics under consideration. They allow students to exhibit and share their work. They also provide an aesthetically pleasing and stimulating learning environment. Your displays should challenge students to further thinking and learning. Let all students share and display their best work efforts with others. It is contrary to the concept of Christian community to display only the work of superior students. Teach your class to respect all classmates' contributions when these reflect genuine, productive efforts. Also, gradually involve students in planning and arranging classroom and hall displays, partly to teach them responsibility and cooperation and partly to teach them the principles of aesthetic display.

Designate special areas to which students take completed work during the day. At the elementary level, each student can have a cubbyhole (perhaps constructed of milk cartons or large tin cans) into which you place work that you have checked along with messages and newsletters for parents. Seemingly minor routines such as these can help a class function smoothly and thus prevent friction that might break down community.

Reflect and respond 6.8

Design a classroom for a specific grade level; the classroom should include several learning centers. If possible, first visit several classrooms that have effective learning centers. Note how the teacher and students can easily see and hear one another, how movements are easy and safe, how supplies are kept within easy reach, and other features. Then develop one or two suitable learning centers for a unit topic. In what ways and to what extent would you use learning centers in the unit?

Arranging time

A schedule or timetable is your guide for your daily instructional program. Timetables help you plan a balanced learning program, but use them flexibly. Most elementary teachers frequently integrate aspects of different subjects and thus combine time blocks and move them around. They may teach a social studies unit for a few weeks, followed by one focused on science. What is important is to spend sufficient time on each subject area, using school or government guidelines.

There is a natural rhythm to the day (as well as to the school year). Some activities are best done early in the morning. Many elementary teachers give focused skill instruction in the morning when students are fresh. Right after lunch, they may also plan some time for reading aloud to the class or for sustained silent reading (SSR). Good teachers are sensitive to when transition activities are needed before effective direct instruction can take place (for example, when students return from physical education). In high schools, the timetable is usually set. You will find, however, that student learning in a subject like mathematics is more efficient at 9:30 AM than at 2:30 PM.

In eighth and ninth grades there is an increasing move toward longer blocks of time, with one teacher for humanities and another for mathematics and science. That arrangement allows teachers to plan combined units and to use time in a flexible way. The longer time blocks, especially when combined with a homeroom period, help make the class into a close-knit learning community. At both the elementary and middle school levels, avoid the temptation to spend more than the allotted time on subjects you like!

Whatever your official time schedule, maximize the time on task, that is, the amount of time when students are actively engaged in learning. Develop efficient routines and procedures to take care of organizational matters and logistics. At the beginning of the year, spend time teaching, reteaching, and practicing routines so that later on these will become a matter of habit. Have materials and equipment planned and ready at the start of the day. Begin on time and maintain a brisk pace, keeping all students involved. Plan transitions carefully and make them routine so that you do not have to explain them each time. Use special signals such as ringing a bell or raising your hand to get everyone's attention. Establish clear beginning-of-day and end-of-day routines. Keeping the learning momentum going helps students recognize that schools are communities for *learning*.

Reflect and respond 6.9

For elementary grades, look up time requirements for the subject areas you are responsible for. Then discuss specific ways in which you can design your timetable to optimize learning.

In North America, the length of high school class periods can vary from 40 minutes to 100 minutes, depending on whether the school operates on a semester system and on how many times per week a subject is taught. For a subject of your specialization, discuss how you would use the time effectively, for both short and long periods.

Leadership for discipleship

This chapter has given many practical suggestions for giving classroom leadership—suggestions that are valid no matter what context you teach in. Many teachers in a variety of circumstances have found them to be effective for nurturing positive classroom communities in which students can learn in positive ways.

Schools exist for our students. Therefore, we must gear our classroom leadership to helping students learn. That is not to say that schools must be child-centered. Rather, they are God-centered, teacher-directed, and student-oriented. First, our teaching should be God-centered. As Christian teachers we let God's revelation in His creation and in His Word provide the framework for education. Also, our classrooms are teacher-directed. We guide and enable students because we believe that God calls them to live responsibly as His image-bearers and that our unfolding of knowledge can lead to truth and purposeful personal response. Our classrooms, finally, are student-oriented. We design our learning structures so that we encourage our students and assist them in taking on life's tasks in a faithful, responsive, and responsible way. Thus our classrooms strive to be learning communities in which all persons fulfill their God-given possibilities and responsibilities. The strategies suggested in this chapter are intended to help you make that goal a reality.

Chapter 6 enduring understandings

Christian teachers do all they can to ...

- Mold their classrooms into loving, supportive learning communities in which students are able to develop their God-given talents as they learn.
- Strive for harmonious relationships within their classrooms, built on authentic communication with their students.
- Discipline unto discipleship, putting an emphasis on setting and enforcing expectations and limits that prevent disruptions to the classroom community.
- Teach dispute and conflict resolution in harmony with biblical guidelines.
- Group their students for learning, organize their classrooms, and design their timetables so that they best meet their students' learning needs.

References

Cruickshank, D., D. Bainer Jenkins, and K. Metcalf. 2003. *The act of teaching.* 3rd ed. New York: McGraw-Hill.

Evertson, C., E. Emmer, and M. Worsham. 2006. *Classroom management for elementary teachers.* 7th ed. Boston, MA: Allyn and Bacon.

Fennema, J. 1977/1995. *Nurturing children in the Lord: A study guide for teachers on developing a biblical approach to discipline.* Sioux Center, IA: Dordt College Press.

Good, T., and J. Brophy. 2008. *Looking in classrooms.* 10th ed. Boston, MA: Allyn and Bacon.

Jones, V., and L. Jones. 2007. *Comprehensive classroom management: Creating communities of support and solving problems.* 8th ed. Boston, MA: Allyn and Bacon.

Litke, C. 1996. When violence came to our rural school. *Educational Leadership* 54, no. 1:77–80.

Noddings, N. 1992. *The challenge to care in schools: An alternative approach to education.* New York: Columbia Univ., Teachers College Press.

Oakes, J., and M. Lipton. 2003. *Teaching to change the world.* 2nd ed. New York: McGraw-Hill.

Parkay, F., B. Hardcastle Stanford, J. Vaillancourt, and H. Stephens. 2008. *Becoming a teacher.* 3rd Canadian ed. Toronto: Pearson.

How Do We Embrace and Support Diverse Learners?

7

Chapter 7 guiding questions

- What types of student diversities do we experience in classrooms?
- How do we provide for "exceptional" students?
- How do we foster cohesive classroom learning communities that encompass diverse cultural and socioeconomic backgrounds?
- What is differentiated learning, and how do we implement it?

Half an hour before her twenty-three sixth-grade students are scheduled to come in to start the school day, Megan looks over her day's plan. She wants to make sure that she will remember all the "special" items. There are more than usual.

The vice principal will take her class at ten o'clock, when she has a meeting with a psychologist, the school's special-education teacher, her aide, and the parents of one of her students to discuss how best to help that student, who is autistic. She still has to prepare some instructions for the vice principal. She also has to talk today with the learning-assistance teacher about an individualized educational plan (IEP) for a new Korean student whose English is very limited. In addition, she will have to make time to discuss with Olivia her special journal, in which she is drawing and describing how she feels about her parents' recent separation. And, she notes to herself, before she leaves school today, she has to prepare some differentiated assignments for the center work on her unit on China in social studies.

Megan has a number of students with "special needs" in her classroom. Some require extra help in developing basic literacy skills. She regularly needs to give others challenging learning activities to enable them to stay interested and involved. She is glad that she has a competent special-education assistant for her student with autism. Now that it is well into the school year, the assistant can also sometimes help her with some other tasks that benefit students with weak mathematics skills.

Megan considers each one of her students "special." But she is very conscientious about helping and encouraging students who face exceptional learning challenges. She carefully keeps track of their progress and works with other staff to ensure optimal learning. Doing so is time consuming, but Megan knows that intellectual as well as behavioral growth is crucial for students' future success.

Megan appreciates the opportunity God has given her to make a positive difference in the lives of "exceptional" children. At the same time, she always feels some tension. How can she take care of the exceptional needs and yet give all the children in her classroom the attention they need? What are the best ways to give additional support to children who need it and yet make them feel valued as regular, accepted members of her classroom community—and not have other students label them as unusual? How can she interact with parents of exceptional students in a positive way when sometimes they are unrealistic in their demands? How can she be sure that, overall, she is doing the best for all students, with no one falling through the cracks?

As the first bell rings, Megan prays that today she will have the insight, discernment, and stamina to treat each student as a very special child of God. She also prays that her servant leadership will help each student to be an accepted and appreciated member of the learning community.

Types of diversity

One of the themes of this book is that every student is a uniquely gifted person created in the image of God. Therefore, all students are able to contribute something to the classroom community as they unfold their particular gifts.

During His earthly life, Jesus made a point of seeking out and ministering to all kinds of people. He chose twelve disciples with very diverse personalities and gifts. He also reached out with compassion and restored those scorned by Jewish society. These included people of different ethnic and religious backgrounds, those with perceptual and hearing impairments, those unable to function normally in society, and those who were social outcasts. Christ's example makes clear that Christian teachers should not only accept but honor diversity in their classrooms.

Similarly, the apostle Paul makes very clear that all parts of the Body can contribute to the whole (Romans 12, 1 Corinthians 12, Ephesians 4). Parts that seem weaker are nevertheless very important. All persons can exercise their gifts for the benefit of others in our communities. Thus, we accept and enfold each student in our classroom as a gift from God. Our human interconnectedness and interdependence can then bring about unity and wholeness.

Students who do not fit what we consider the norm are God's gifts to us no less than any other students. That does not mean that diversity is easy to deal with. Quite the contrary! Providing for students with different aptitudes, different learning styles, and different preferred modes of knowing requires careful planning and extra effort in the classroom. Some students have special needs that cause emotional and social stress to themselves and others.

However, all students are special beings. God, in His wisdom, also entrusts those with special needs to our care, both for their benefit and for the benefit of our classroom communities. Moreover, God gives such students the ability to contribute, often in surprising ways. In His parable of the talents, Jesus expected the person with one talent to develop that gift "according to his ability" (Matthew 25:15). How particular students can be constructively involved depends, of course, on their backgrounds, circumstances, personalities, and aptitudes.

Writing about students with special needs, David Anderson argues that our classrooms must reflect God's reconciliation that He accomplished through the work of Christ. As teachers, we are agents of reconciliation. Acceptance and sensitivity need to characterize our relationships with all students—particularly, if we follow Jesus' example, with those who have special needs. We reconcile such students with their classroom peers as well as, at times, with their families, especially if they display emotional or behavioral volatility. That is, we make our classrooms inclusive communities in which we help students bond with their classmates as full human beings, no matter what their gifts or challenges. As teachers, we strive to reconcile students to the realization that despite their special needs they are created in the image of God and are therefore of great value, uniquely gifted and purposed. Anderson adds, "Some disabled individuals and/or their families may need to be reconciled with God, toward whom they may have much anger" (2003, 25).

Of course, we need to exercise reconciliation in our classrooms not only to students with disabilities. We must reconcile all students across barriers caused by different abilities, cultures, ethnicities, social classes, and genders. Accordingly, we strive for classrooms in which students deepen their relationships with God and with people around them as they gain the knowledge, abilities, and values they need to live positively in society.

Many types of diversity exist in classrooms. Teachers will experience most of the following in their career. All involve fostering reconciliation in a learning community in which everyone contributes freely to the needs of others.

Physical diversity. This type of diversity ranges from students who feel awkward about their height or weight to students who are permanently wheelchair-bound. Physical health needs may include diseases such as diabetes; sensory impairments in hearing, sight, or coordination; or severe allergies.

Emotional and social diversity. Some students fear life because of abuse or bullying; others cannot control themselves because of fetal alcohol syndrome or parental drug use during pregnancy. Some students are naturally outgoing, while others are withdrawn.

Intellectual diversity. Some students are "gifted" and need additional learning challenges; others have specific learning difficulties.

Cultural diversity. In some Christian schools in my community, students have roots in twenty or more different countries. Classrooms may have children from Caucasian, Asian, Middle Eastern, and aboriginal backgrounds.

Communication diversity. Students from different cultural or ethnic backgrounds may have varying degrees of facility in the main language used in a school. Even children whose first language is the school's main language will have diverse speech and language backgrounds and skills.

Economic diversity. Not all Christian school students come from well-to-do families. Some students may feel that they do not "fit" because their social class, clothes, and lifestyle do not match those of their classmates. When both parents or a single parent must work outside the home to make ends meet, there may be little time to read to the children or help them with homework.

Religious and ethical diversity. Children in Christian schools come from different religious backgrounds. Some parents' faith commitment directs everything in their lives; others may be nominal believers whose children attend because their parents believe the school is a "good" one. Parental views—and therefore those of older students—may also differ on topics such as baptism, war and peace, and the interpretation of Genesis 1.

You may be able think of other types of diversity. The starting point for dealing with classroom diversities is to be aware of them and to be sensitive to them. You want your classroom to be one in which all students feel accepted and secure. To deal appropriately with these many types of diversity requires not only attentiveness to differences but also insight and skill.

It is impossible in this chapter to discuss all possible types of diversity, let alone explain how to manage all the exceptionalities that may exist in your classroom. What makes things even more complex is that each child is unique not only with respect to how a special need manifests itself but also in personality, interests, aptitudes, and behavior. My wife has had children with autism in her kindergarten class for six of the past seven years. The children have done very well under her care. She has attended workshops, read a great deal about autism, and consulted with experts in order to understand and develop appropriate strategies. However, while that has been helpful, she has found that even children with this one exceptionality need different behavioral and learning strategies.

In this chapter, I will consider some general issues relating to "special education" and cultural diversity. I will conclude by describing how we can use differentiated learning to meet the needs of a broad spectrum of students. God calls us to love our neighbors as ourselves. As teachers, we therefore love our exceptional students as ourselves. My intent is to expose you to some of those special needs and to give you some initial ideas about what it means to love your neighbor as yourself as you support exceptional students.

Reflect and respond 7-1

Describe the types of diversity that you have observed or experienced in classrooms. In what ways do these types of diversity enrich the classroom? In what ways do they create demanding situations for the teacher? In light of the sovereignty of God, Ken Pudlas says that diversities, including disabilities, cannot simply be explained as some accident: "God is not capricious" (1997, 179). Do you agree? If so, does that mean that all children should be included in "regular" classrooms? Should Christian schools accept all children with disabilities?

Embracing exceptional students

The proportion of students needing special help in learning is significant. Students defined as exceptional usually make up about 10 to 14 percent of all students. In my jurisdiction of British Columbia, where both public and Christian schools receive special-needs funding from the government, the percentage of students with special needs in Christian schools is about 2 percent higher than it is in public schools. Overall, in North America about twice as many males as females receive special-education services. In addition, depending on the definition, about 2 to 5 percent of students are identified as gifted and talented.

Over the past decades, the trend has been to include exceptional students in regular classrooms as much as possible. We call this practice *inclusion* or *full inclusion*. Inclusion enables all students to benefit from being part of an ordinary classroom community. It assumes that having students with different abilities in the same classroom is desirable since it treats all students as worthy human beings created in the image of God. Moreover, it also helps students with disabilities to have the same kinds of experiences as all other students. This enhances the likelihood of their fitting confidently into society.

Full inclusion has not been without its challenges, however. To ensure that teachers can address the learning needs of all students, teachers need adequately trained special-education assistants. In addition, resource teachers and other experts need to be available to help teachers develop strategies for the disabilities represented in their classrooms. Even then, teachers find that time spent dealing with difficult behavioral and other issues may reduce time spent on teaching.

Inclusion also affects teachers' workloads. For instance, consulting about, preparing, and monitoring individual education plans (IEPs) is time-consuming. Making sure that teachers and their assistants work in harmony takes careful planning. For these reasons, the number of students identified with special needs should normally be limited to no more than three per classroom.

Some students face challenges in being part of a regular classroom community. Schools cannot meet their needs without extra and specific help from a special-education assistant or a learning-assistance teacher, either in the regular classroom or in a learning-resources space. For some severe disabilities, especially behavioral ones, it may be best to place students in a separate small class with a highly specialized teacher. This is the case when students are unable to function in a regular classroom without seriously affecting the learning of other students. However, this practice may increase the frequency of "regular" students labeling, ridiculing, or taunting students with disabilities. In an inclusive classroom, it is easier for teachers and schools to prevent and minimize such unacceptable behavior.

Despite the challenges of inclusion, students with disabilities should be included in regular classrooms as much as is workable. Christians have a responsibility to defend the cause of the weak and needy (for example, see Psalm 82:3–4)—including students with disabilities. Therefore, we must optimize learning opportunities for them; and, whenever possible, we must help them to be, and to feel like, integral members of an inclusive classroom.

An effective inclusive classroom is one that is secure and congenial. As a teacher, set an engaging and positive tone at the start of the year, welcoming each student. Tell your students that you want each one to have meaningful and successful learning experiences. At the same time, set a clear framework of expectations that you consistently enforce. Students with special needs require an environment with minimal disruptions—even when they may be the cause of the disturbances (Edmunds and Edmunds 2008).

It is important to appreciate students with special needs for who they are. Always look beyond their disabilities and teach them as whole persons. Studies suggest that 24 percent of such students feel unaccepted by their peers, compared with only 9 percent of other students. Their self-concepts are also significantly lower (Pudlas 2008). So discover and experience with them that special learning needs do not reflect their worth as persons. How you assign and assess learning tasks can affirm that serving God does not hinge on how well students read or add numbers, but on their effort and conduct. Help them identify, use, and celebrate their abilities.

You also need to ensure that exceptional students experience forgiveness and hope. Often they perceive that what they do and say is "wrong." Help them overcome feelings of frustration and failure so that they can deal with their uniqueness in healthy ways. Listen to them in order to meet their needs as they understand them. Encourage them to articulate when and why they feel they need a particular kind of assistance. When desirable, explain their learning needs to them, and explore with them how to meet those needs. Show all students how learning rates vary and how the learning assistance program helps all children and teachers. Stress the importance of treating all classmates with respect (Vanderhoek 1997).

Also, make a special point of teaching commonly accepted social skills to special needs students. They may not have experienced a stable family situation, sometimes because of the extra pressures their families face due to the disability. Special needs children who lack social skills that are normally taken for granted need help in developing those skills (Pudlas 2008).

Inclusive classrooms do not just happen. Here are some ideas to help you optimize the learning of special needs students in the regular classroom (Cushner, McLelland, and Safford 2003):

- Once you realize that a student is having particular learning or behavioral problems, adjust your learning and management strategies. If this action does not overcome the difficulties, refer the student to your school resource person. He or she will assess the student (or refer the student to a specialist for assessment). An IEP may be developed for the student. Work with the resource persons and parents (and students, where applicable) to implement the IEP.

Word alert

Exceptionality and *special education* are usually defined in terms of each other. Exceptional students are those needing special assistance to learn well. The most common exceptionalities, in order, are learning disabilities, behavioral disorders, autism, and physical disabilities. The interests, concerns, and needs of exceptional students are similar to those of other students. They are exceptional in the sense that learning or behavioral strategies for them need to differ significantly from those of the majority of students. For instance, they may need physical accommodation, modified programs, or behavioral intervention.

Some students with special needs are sometimes referred to as having *disabilities*. We need to be careful that we do not unduly label students with exceptionalities. Students who were several years below the norm for literacy achievement in the past were called retarded, for instance. Strictly speaking, the term is correct: these students reached reading fluency in a retarded or delayed period of time. However, the term is now viewed as pejorative because it grew to be a socially negative label. *Physical* and *learning disabilities* are legitimate terms, but they should also be used with care. While some disabilities can be clearly defined, most occur along a continuum (e.g., having speech difficulties; being diagnosed as dyslexic). Therefore, the identification of a disability is often a matter of informed but somewhat arbitrary judgment (Cushner, McClelland, and Safford 2003).

The IEP includes a statement of the extent to which the student will participate in your classroom. It sets out short-term and long-term measurable learning or behavioral goals. It also describes the overall special provisions and strategies that will be used to manage the special need. You will provide regular progress reports to the parents.

- Collaborate with the school's resource or learning-assistance teacher (LAT) to develop effective learning strategies. A learning assistance teacher will assess referred students and will help you modify the learning environment and activities for them. You may have an aide assigned to your class either part-time or full-time, or a student may be given individual LAT help inside or outside your classroom. If that help is given in a special learning resource area, work with your LAT to ensure that in-class and out-of-class learning fit and support each other. LATs are problem solvers and helpers. However, their time is limited, and the effect of suggested strategies may not be known for several months. While you work in partnership with an LAT, you are still ultimately responsible for determining how best to meet students' learning needs.

- Continue to plan to accommodate different learning styles and abilities (see, for example, the section on differentiated learning later in this chapter), taking particular note of special-needs students. As much as possible, place special-needs students in age-equivalent classrooms and let them follow the same schedule as their classmates. Involve them in extracurricular activities. Encourage special-needs and other children to help one another and to form friendships. Always focus on the child first and on the disability second. Remember that children with disabilities have far more similarities to than differences from their peers.

Students gifted in some outstanding way have received relatively little attention over the past decades. Special programs for those called "gifted and talented" have been few and far between. Educators have assumed that these students will do well on their own. Ornstein points out that this is a false assumption. Fifteen to twenty percent of gifted and talented students in the United States tend to drop out of high school, often because of boredom. Ornstein adds, "These are the same children and youth who have the most potential to shape our future world ... they represent a large portion of the future leadership for society, and they should be nurtured at the school level" (2003, 259).

Schools face several difficulties in meeting the needs of talented and gifted students. I a school of three hundred students has ten gifted and talented students, they will not only be in different grades, but they will also be talented in diverse areas. Some may excel in creative writing; others, in mathematics. What some Christian schools do to meet these needs is have "pull-out" programs in which a teacher works with a group of six or so students, setting up challenging individual and group learning activities. Sometimes those activities relate to classroom unit work. At other times, they may involve special topics. The sponsor teacher will plan activities suitable for the special giftedness of each student. In primary grades, schools sometimes accelerate gifted and talented students by letting them "skip" a grade. This can give students learning experiences more suited for their intellectual ability, but schools also need to take social "fit" into account.

Even if a school does not have the resources to provide special programs, other opportunities exist. When my son needed an academic challenge in seventh grade, his teacher arranged for him to take a correspondence course in the history of mathematics. This was the beginning of his being known today as an expert in the field. To meet my granddaughter's learning needs, her high school planned her schedule so that she could take her mathematics courses a year ahead of the regular schedule. In senior grades, some Christian high schools help gifted and talented students by offering Advanced Placement or International Baccalaureate courses. Sometimes students can take online college courses in twelfth grade. Under the guidance of classroom teachers, the Internet also offers many resources that will challenge gifted students to develop their insights and abilities. At the same time, gifted students must also learn to use their gifts for the benefit of the classroom community. For instance, they can help other students with their learning or take on leadership roles.

Embracing students with special needs is a question of justice. The Christian view of justice expresses this universal principle in terms of shalom—harmony, peace, and complete well-being throughout creation. Justice begins with treating all persons with dignity and respect. In the classroom, we therefore strive to enable all students to develop and use their God-given gifts in ways that contribute to personal and societal well-being. Teachers care especially for the "poor"—whether they be the intellectually poor, the poor in personality, the emotionally poor, the behaviorally poor, or the socioeconomically poor—and promote fairness for all (Groome 1998). At the same time, we help outstanding students use their gifts to become servant leaders.

We do our utmost to nurture an atmosphere of gratitude for whatever gifts God has given each student. In that way we contribute to an attitude of hope, that wellspring of motivation that exists deep within us, and help all students take on their calling as ambassadors of our Lord and Savior.

My wife, Wilma, had a child with autism in her kindergarten classroom. At the beginning of the year, he regularly fell on the floor limp, refusing to do anything. Wilma treated him with respect and much love, but also immediately set certain behavioral standards, telling him over and over again what she required. After a few days the boy did not want to return to kindergarten. Wilma told his mother not to keep him home, but to bring him even if he stayed only a little while at first. Soon the boy accepted what Wilma expected. In the meantime, Wilma read up on autism and watched some videotapes, following the suggestions that seemed to apply. She used a couple of other students who related well to the autistic child to do things with him. Gradually the boy voluntarily participated more and more in regular class activities. At the end of the year, the boy still had autism, but he participated in all class activities without question. On the last day he made a card that said, "Good-bye, Mrs. Van Brummelen, I love you," adding a heart and a happy face—an example of reaching out to another person in a way that is unusual for a child with autism. He had learned to function well in an environment that was loving and encouraging, but also one with specific, clearly defined, and consistently maintained expectations.

Reflect and respond 7-2

The quotations below are based on actual assertions. Taking into account the biblical emphasis on providing for the weak and needy, describe the context and situation under which you believe that the view expressed is legitimate, or why it is unacceptable.

• My K–6 school has only eighty students, so almost all our teachers have two grades in their classes. With the amount of preparation required, it is impossible for us to accommodate special-needs students.

• Our community recognizes our school for successfully including children with disabilities in our regular classrooms. As a result, the percentage of such students in our school is now above 15 percent. I love the challenge of helping such children, and our administration does its best to provide assistants and other resources. But I wonder whether it is fair to our other students to have three or four special needs students in each classroom. I think we should limit the number of special needs enrollments.

• Our school's mission is to prepare students for university and college. Our very high success rate is due in part to our strict entrance requirements for new students. We do not admit students who are unlikely to "make the grade." Therefore, we seldom enroll special-needs students, even if their siblings attend our school. Our parents expect quality education.

• All students deserve an education that suits their abilities. While all classrooms have students with a range of abilities, full inclusion is poorly thought out. Thrusting disabled students into a regular classroom is good neither for them nor for the other students. If we were truly sensitive to the needs of disabled students, we would offer many more classes that are specialized and schools with teachers who are experts in dealing with a particular kind of disability. This may cost more than full inclusion, but it will help such children gain the necessary self-respect and abilities to become productive members of society.

- Full inclusion may work at the elementary level. However, high school teachers just have too many different classes to be able to get to know the needs of students with disabilities and to prepare appropriate learning strategies for them.

Ethnic and cultural diversity

If you are a teacher in the Western world, you more than likely face cultural diversity in your classroom. Already the Old Testament books of God's law make very clear that we are to treat "aliens" with respect, justice, and love (Exodus 22:21, 23:9; Leviticus 19:34). It is significant that when God poured out His Holy Spirit on the believers, people from various regions heard the apostles speak in their own language. This was more than a translation: they could understand "the wonders of God" explained in their own linguistic and cultural context (Acts 2). And several chapters later God reemphasized the importance of accepting and relating to different cultures by giving Peter a vision and pouring His Spirit on an Italian family that the Jews considered to be "Gentiles" (Acts 10).

In what ways can we be just and compassionate in providing meaningful learning to students whose cultural backgrounds differ from the "mainstream" culture in our school—or from our own cultural background? It may first require a shift in our own attitudes. All too often Westerners (I include myself!) assume that Western culture is "civilized." We consider other cultures less advanced. Therefore, we implicitly want them to conform to our "superior" culture. Yet what we consider highly developed in our culture has built on the strengths of other cultures (e.g., Islamic mathematics in the Middle Ages). Moreover, some non-Western cultures have a much richer sense of community and have created a more sustainable way of life.

Western culture benefits from a justice system and a view of tolerance and respect that is rooted in the Protestant Christian tradition. However, the legacy of Western culture also includes war and violence, exploitation and neglect of the poor and disadvantaged, and repression and abuse of other peoples and nations. Westerners need to face the fact that often they have not taken the words and example of Jesus seriously. Moreover, God has not limited valuable insights and practices to any one culture. Thus, we can enrich our lives as we learn from cultural differences.

Our first responsibility is to reflect on what we consider "normal" in our own cultural heritage and how that perception may affect students from a different cultural background. Europeans and North Americans tend to view themselves as separate from nature and thus able to master and control their environment. They are action oriented, and they believe in ongoing progress. They have a strong sense of individuality and therefore are self-motivated (Cushner 2003). Western cultures teach children to value self-reliance and individual achievement. Schools expect students to stay in their own seats and to take personal responsibility for success at learning tasks.

Proverbs such as "Necessity is the mother of invention" and "God helps those who help themselves" exemplify European and North American cultural assumptions. The African proverb "It takes a village to raise a child" describes a different view of life. Similarly, Descartes' famous saying, *Cogito ergo sum* ("I think, therefore I am"), typifies Western culture. It is in sharp contrast to the African proverb *Ubunthu* ("We are, therefore I am"). The biblical emphasis on social justice and compassion ("To act justly and to love mercy and to walk humbly with your God," Micah 6:8) opposes the cultural outlook of European-American materialistic individualism that is spreading across the globe. It also differs, however, from the inclination of other cultures to relinquish all individual choice in favor of communal expectations. Christians have both communal and personal responsibilities to promote God's shalom.

About two-thirds of world cultures, including many aboriginal, Asian, African, and Latin American traditions, are collectivistic. That is, they value group helpfulness, solidarity, and cooperation above personal accomplishment and independence. Students from such cultures value working together cooperatively and interdependently. For them, it is important to engage socially in order to get a task done. Above all, they strive for group success. They generally favor group-oriented, collaborative learning. They are modest about their personal accomplishments and prefer private rather than public recognition. They may also feel that bothering teachers with questions is disrespectful (Rothstein-Fisch and Trumbull 2008).

What is clear is that learning styles can result from cultural patterns. Also, some children may have difficulty understanding their teacher's cognitive style. Moreover, sometimes parents from collective cultures are more concerned about their children's social behavior than about their academic progress. They may not want their children to contribute orally in class since quiet listening shows more respect. These generalizations, however, work themselves out in different ways for different groups. Besides, higher social class and parental educational background as well as an urban residence all tend to make families less collectivistic (Rothstein-Fisch and Trumbull 2008). Nevertheless, expectations in a student's home environment may differ considerably from those in the school. The bottom line is that we need to be reflective observers and listeners, sensitive to and understanding of students and parents with cultural backgrounds that differ from our own.

As a teacher, you need to become aware of how you respond to differences in behaviors, values, ways of communication, and appearance—and how your responses reflect your cultural biases. An inclusive Christian classroom community honors God's revealed truth. Within that framework, such a classroom is open to diversity and difference. It honors and draws on the deep mystery of personal and cultural uniqueness. It allows students to identify with their own cultural group. The whole class, at the same time, recognizes and experiences that cultural diversity enriches the quality of life.

> ## Word alert
>
> *Culture* refers to a shared set of beliefs, habits of the mind, customs, practices, and behaviors that characterize a group of people. A specific culture is rooted in the group's basic beliefs and assumptions about life. Usually those are implicitly understood and unconsciously practiced by members of a culture. Cushner (2003) compares culture to an iceberg. Culture includes small visible elements such as distinctive food, clothing, and mannerisms. However, a much larger invisible component beneath the surface consists of a set of complex beliefs, values, and attitudes. It is this deep dimension that most often causes intercultural misunderstanding, emotional reactions, and tension.

We teach in a multicultural situation even if only one or two students have a background that differs from that of the majority. How do we interact effectively in a cross-cultural classroom? Find out the essential features of cultures that differ from your own. Talk with students and their families. Respect their knowledge and conventions. Since it is easy to misread or ignore significant verbal and nonverbal cues, learn how to interpret your students' behavior. Remember that students may, at the same time, misread your behavior. Do not take unexpected behavior as an affront, but find out whether it reflects the student's culture.

Here are some specific suggestions (Cushner, McClelland, and Safford 2003; Sheets 2005; Rothstein-Fisch and Trumbull 2008):

- Recognize and deal considerately with strong emotional responses in students who differ culturally. These may include anxiety to "fit," reluctance to admit a lack of understanding, or feelings of real or perceived rejection. The stress of unfamiliar situations or tasks may cause students to withdraw into wariness and silence. Students with a different cultural background may not have understood you, or may feel that different behavior is expected. Treat all students fairly but not the same. For instance, aboriginal students may need time for reflection. Even when they want to tell you something, you may need to sit next to them while also being silent. This does not mean, of course, that you should not intervene when problems arise. You do have to insist on order, and in certain situations you must demand immediate obedience, especially if the well-being of other students is threatened.

- Try to understand behaviors that are uncommon to you. For instance, children from collectivist cultures may assume that helping classmates is more important than listening to the teacher or finishing their own work. They may look down or avoid eye contact in order to show respect. They may seek physical proximity to other students. They may naturally take on leadership activities, but they will do so to contribute to the group, not for individual recognition. Boys from some cultures may find it difficult to defer to the authority of a female teacher, especially if she is young. Some students may believe that paraphrasing rather than copying a reference word for word is showing dishonor to the author. Some cultures have a much more elastic sense of time than North American Caucasians and place little value on punctuality. Gather relevant information about such differences. Respond in nonjudgmental ways. Perceive and listen empathetically. You will need to solve problems and make decisions, but do so in a way that makes it clear that you honor the dignity and culture of the persons involved even when the decision may implement a course of action based on Western values.

• Provide a learning context in which students from diverse cultural groups feel safe and secure as they learn. Sheets (2005) suggests that you value home knowledge that students bring to learning events. Allow them to express aspects of their cultural identity in learning activities. For instance, you could discuss differences in physical traits, cultural practices, and language. Or you could allow two students with the same first language to help each other in math. Or you could respond to a book whose setting is in one of the minority cultures in your classroom. What is important is to affirm students' cultural heritages on a regular basis.

• Do not stereotype children because they come from a particular cultural background. While general cultural commonalities exist, students will show a wide spectrum of attitudes and behaviors both within and outside of a cultural "norm." Some cultural characteristics may also diminish over time as children adapt to the majority culture.

• Encourage and facilitate students' social interaction in various settings. Plan classroom events to help students from minority cultures develop a sense of being integral and valued members of the learning community. Assign diverse students to each group of desks. Assign buddies of different cultural backgrounds for activities such as field trips. Encourage students from minority cultures to participate in after-school activities. Discuss with your class the role of friendship and the importance of everyone's having friends.

• Use a variety of strategies as you plan learning. This practice, of course, will help motivation and achievement for all students. Note that collaborative learning strategies will especially benefit students from collectivist cultures. Also, build the confidence of such students by regularly giving them tasks at which they can be successful.

- Extend students' skills in the language used in the classroom, but also encourage them to maintain their first language because of its cultural and social value. Students who are not fluent in the common classroom language are likely to experience stress. I well remember entering sixth grade as an immigrant boy with little knowledge of English. The most nerve-racking times for me were twice a week when our principal taught us Shakespeare's *Hamlet*. On the first test, the only thing I knew was Shakespeare's birthplace. The principal made no accommodation. He just gave me my first-ever failing grade on my report card, without any comment. It took years for me to overcome my dislike of Shakespeare! Some students may need special modifications or assistance or pull-out services to learn the common classroom language. Give such students opportunities to demonstrate learning in a variety of ways, not just through writing and speaking. And remember that even when students all speak your classroom language, there still are differences in their language backgrounds (e.g., in the United States students may speak standard English, Appalachian Mountain English, or Black English—and "standard" English varies from region to region).

It may be easier to teach in classrooms in which all children come from either an individualistic or a collectivist culture. Even in such situations, however, we need to help students appreciate that they can learn from people with different cultural backgrounds. In addition, our global interconnectedness means that cultural diversity exists in more and more classrooms. To foster an inclusive and cohesive learning community in such classrooms, or to help students appreciate the diversity of people in the world, you might try some of the following learning activities:

- Tell how God's story of salvation included heroes of faith from various cultures (e.g., Rahab, Ruth), how Jesus reached out to the poor and to persons looked down on by the Jews, and how the book of Acts tells us that Paul deliberately interacted with people of a wide range of cultures.
- In kindergarten and first grade, use puppets to encourage children to express their feelings as they share the richness of their family traditions and cultural backgrounds.
- At the beginning of the year, have students interview one another about their cultural heritage and traditions and then introduce one another to the class.
- Build relationships with schools and classrooms in different cultural contexts.
- Develop a unit on the Olympic games that highlights the accomplishments of athletes from the cultures represented in the class.
- Study aboriginal or immigrant literature and discuss how students from different backgrounds experience the society in which they now live.
- When studying other cultures, discuss why most people prefer to continue to live in their original country even when they face difficult situations.

- In history or current events consider how people in different nations look at conflicts, and why. Consider the ethical issue of sharing resources equitably across the globe.
- Encourage family and community involvement in teaching and learning. Invite elders or community leaders of various cultural backgrounds to share their life stories, their cultures, and their values.
- Visit a community or an area of the city in which cultural groups represented in your classroom are living.
- Discuss how cultural diversity can enrich society as long as we all agree to uphold basic biblical values such as compassion, justice, and integrity.

You may wonder whether these suggestions and examples are specifically Christian ones. I believe that they are faithful to God's call to all believers. As Paul wrote, "Prepare God's people for works of service, so that the body of Christ may be built up.... From him the whole body, joined and held together by every supporting ligament, grows and builds itself up in love, as each part does its work.... Be kind and compassionate to one another, forgiving each other, just as in Christ God forgave you" (Ephesians 4:12–32). What I have described in this section will help our culturally distinct students grow in knowledge, wisdom, and skill. It will also strengthen the whole classroom and school community as we unfold our gifts in a supportive setting. We pray together; we learn together; we live together. And we do so in ways that help each person experience grace and peace from God and from one another.

Reflect and respond 7-3

Discuss how, as a teacher, you would respond to the following situations:

- A student from Hong Kong enrolls in your tenth-grade homeroom for one year. She is boarding with a family whose children have graduated from your school. You introduce her to your class. During the first few weeks you make sure that other students make her feel welcome, help her learn the routines, and ask her to join in various activities. The student appears to adjust. Generally she does well in her courses. However, after a few weeks she becomes increasingly withdrawn. She sits by herself during lunch. When this morning you ask her whether she is willing to share something of her life in Hong Kong with the class, she just says no without any explanation.
- Raymond, an aboriginal student, is an outstanding artist. He is knowledgeable about the work of other native artists. He uses some of their work as a model for the style of his paintings. When he submits one of his paintings to an art contest, he wins high accolades from the judges. The school mentions to him that they will honor him at an assembly.

When the day comes, however, Raymond is absent. When asked the next day where he was, he just says that he couldn't make it to school.

- This year you have two new Korean immigrants in your fifth-grade classroom. Their English skills are poor, but the school provides some special tutoring. You involve them as much as possible in classroom activities. One day the students come in after lunch, visibly upset. You ask the other students whether they know what happened. One says that several older boys on the playground called the Korean students names and taunted them. The students that stood around were embarrassed but did not come to their defense.

Differentiating learning

For optimal learning, an inclusive classroom requires differentiated learning strategies. Differentiation is not new, but it has come to the fore as teachers have realized that not all students think, learn, solve, and create in the same way or at the same rate. Sometimes it is appropriate and efficient to teach a whole class at once. However, this approach needs to be complemented with providing certain students with different learning activities or with two or three distinct levels of assignments. The essential understandings, concepts, abilities, and values that you want students to learn may be the same. However, you vary the type and complexity of learning activities. You challenge more able students. You prevent frustration for weaker students. And you give all students opportunities to use and display their personal strengths.

I have already described several ways of differentiating learning. Chapter 4 addressed how we can plan for varied learning styles and modes of knowing. Chapter 6 discussed collaborative learning, which is especially but not solely suited to students from a collectivist cultural background. This section will suggest some other ways to differentiate learning for students with diverse aptitudes and backgrounds.

One way to differentiate learning is to design activities and assignments at different levels of difficulty. Students learn best when they face high but achievable expectations. Tomlinson (1999, 89–90) gives an example of two fourth-grade poetry contracts. Each has twelve activities with almost identical headings, but at two different levels of difficulty. For instance, an activity for students weaker in language skills is to "Use good descriptive words in a poem that helps us know and understand something important about you." A more difficult but parallel activity is to "Use good description, figurative language, and images to write a poem that helps us understand something important about you."

Similarly, learning centers can include activities with a range of complexity, structures, and learning styles. You will need to keep track of the activities students choose and the quality of their work, and give them appropriate suggestions for their future center work choices. For project work, you can also provide a range of levels of difficulty (e.g., research sources or product expectations). In an eleventh-grade unit on the French Revolution, for instance, the project for one group might be to put together a simulated television newscast about the storming of the Bastille. A second group might put on a debate about the causes of the French Revolution, with the participants representing a nobleman, a Catholic clergyman, a shop owner, and a "citizen" leader during the reign of terror. Another group might prepare and show an audiovisual presentation on the decade of turmoil during the Revolution. And an advanced group could explore and make a presentation on the long-term effects of the French Revolution.

In mathematics you can assign more practice-type work to slower students and additional challenging problems to advanced ones. Sometimes we call this "tiered problem solving." Especially if you pretest students, you can "compact" the curriculum for those who already demonstrate a certain level of understanding and have them complete work at a more advanced level. When I taught high school mathematics, I developed a set of extra problems and small projects for each unit. The more advanced students worked on these on the condition that they would also help weaker students with the "regular" work. (I taught them how to help as peer tutors but not to do the work for those students.) As an incentive, I gave the advanced students some minor "extra credit" for solving advanced problems. This arrangement gave me the opportunity to help small groups of weaker students, who then had more time to comprehend and complete the essentials of a topic. Sometimes I would reteach abstract concepts using concrete examples. At other times I would ask focused questions so that the students would reflect on and improve upon the strategies they were using.

When differentiating, be open with your students, especially older ones, explaining why at times they will work on different tasks. Explain that sometimes you will group students on the basis of their interests, sometimes on modality strengths or preferences, and sometimes on aptitude for certain types of activities. Unless you do so, your students may feel that setting different expectations is unfair. Discuss why fair is not always equal. Students will be more comfortable when you candidly recognize differences. Usually you just confirm what they already know. However, a discussion helps to foster an accepting community.

Use different groupings and allow students to move between groups from time to time. You want to avoid students' being labeled—and possibly living down to their labels! Remember also that students who are weak in one subject or topic may be strong in others. Moreover, strengths and weaknesses may be fluid and not fixed over time.

We saw in chapter 5 that teaching and assessment are inseparable. Therefore, in differentiated classrooms you vary the ways you assess students. For different tasks, you use different assessment strategies and different rubrics. Portfolios and work folders can be particularly helpful in that they empower your students to show what they have learned in a self-reflective way.

While it is important to introduce differentiated instruction, you should begin in small ways. Initially, limit adaptations to the most vital ones. For example, you could use differentiated tasks for only a short period of time, you could design just one differentiated lesson or product in a unit, or you might introduce some options for students at the end of a unit. You will be gaining skill in diagnosing learning needs and in finding ways to modify lessons to meet diverse needs. You also need to explore when it is most effective to teach the class as a whole and when it is best to work with small groups or individuals. If you start small and gradually increase your repertoire of differentiated learning strategies, you will not be overwhelmed. In the long run, you will then be more successful in meeting your students' needs.

Research suggests that all students benefit from varied teaching and learning strategies. At first you may differentiate mainly to meet the needs of exceptional learners. However, in the end all your students will benefit from improved achievement.

> ### Word alert
>
> *Differentiated instruction* or *differentiation* is a process by which teachers adapt teaching and learning to meet the needs of diverse students. For each topic taught, teachers take into account their students' varying needs, strengths, and abilities. They provide different types and levels of learning activities, both across and within lessons. They do so to assist students in grasping enduring understandings and attaining skills in ways and to levels that suit them. Differentiated instruction incorporates differences in content, process, and student products.

Reflect and respond 7-4

Choose a unit topic at a grade level you teach or want to teach. Develop one or two "differentiated" lessons that take into account the diverse learning needs of your class or a class with which you are familiar.

Welcoming all students

All three synoptic Gospels report Jesus saying, "Let the little children come to me, and do not hinder them" (Matthew 19:14, Mark 10:14, Luke 18:16). In Matthew 18:5 Jesus adds that whoever welcomes a little child welcomes Jesus Himself. If we walk with God in our classrooms, we will welcome ("well-come") all children and young people, no matter what their special needs and disabilities, their cultural and economic backgrounds, or their personalities and aptitudes. At times, implementing the strategies of this chapter will be challenging, perhaps even arduous. But it is part of welcoming all students in the name of Jesus our Lord.

Chapter 7 enduring understandings

- As much as possible, we welcome all children and young people into inclusive classroom learning communities.
- We treat special-needs students with dignity and respect, striving to help them develop and use their God-given gifts in ways that contribute to personal and societal well-being.
- Responsive teachers are sensitive to, and adapt their instruction for, children whose cultural and socioeconomic background differs from that of the school's majority population.
- Optimal student learning requires timely differentiated learning strategies with respect to content, process, and level of difficulty.

References

Anderson, D. 2003. Special education as reconciliation. *Journal of Education and Christian Belief* 7, no. 1:23–35.

Cushner, K. 2003. *Human diversity in action: Developing multicultural competencies for the classroom.* 2nd ed. New York: McGraw-Hill.

Cushner, K., A. McClelland, and P. Safford. 2003. *Human diversity in education: An integrative approach.* 4th ed. New York: McGraw-Hill.

Edmunds, A., and G. Edmunds. 2008. *Special education in Canada.* Toronto: McGraw-Hill Ryerson.

Groome, T. 1998. *Educating for life: A spiritual vision for every teacher and parent.* New York: Crossroad.

Ornstein, A. 2003. *Pushing the envelope: Critical issues in education.* Upper Saddle River, NJ: Merrill Prentice Hall.

Pudlas, K. 1997. Exceptionality in a communal context. In *The crumbling walls of certainty: Towards a Christian critique of postmodernity and education,* ed. I. Lambert and S. Mitchell. Macquarie Centre, NSW, Australia: Centre for the Study of Australian Christianity.

———. 2007. Head and heart and hands: Necessary elements of inclusive praxis. *ICCTE Journal* 3, no. 1. www.icctejournal.org.

———. 2008. Head and heart and hands: Searching for inclusive education. Inaugural full-professor lecture, Trinity Western University.

Rothstein-Fisch, C., and E. Trumbull. 2008. *Managing diverse classrooms: How to build on students' cultural strengths.* Alexandria, VA: Association for Supervision and Curriculum Development.

Sheets, R. 2005. *Diversity pedagogy: Examining the role of culture in the teaching-learning process.* Boston, MA: Allyn and Bacon.

Tomlinson, C. 1999. *The differentiated classroom: Responding to the needs of all learners.* Alexandria, VA: Association for Supervision and Curriculum Development.

Vanderhoek, J., ed. 1997. *Learning assistance and special education resource.* Langley, BC: Society of Christian Schools in British Columbia.

How Can We Develop Schools that Are Supportive Learning Communities? 8

Chapter 8 guiding questions

- What are the attributes of supportive learning communities?
- How do we foster supportive learning communities?
- How do we develop teacher collegiality?
- What is the role of parents and other supporters in schools?

The first bell of Faith Christian Community School rings at 8:25 AM. Students flock to the doors. Teachers greet them with a cheery "Good morning!" while making sure that they enter in orderly fashion. The custodian, broom in hand, congratulates some fourth graders on the hall display based on their science unit. The school secretary helps several students. She says to one boy, "Kevin, I appreciate that you came in to tell me right away. But I am disappointed that you forgot to return your uniform again. Let's think of a way you will be sure to remember tomorrow."

Principal Hall is the last person to come in. As usual, she has spent the previous fifteen minutes circulating through the school and playground. She talks with and gives words of encouragement to teachers, students, volunteers, and parents. She makes a mental note to speak with two teachers. One of Ms. Brown's fifth-grade students is troubled about the accidental death of an aunt. And she wants to compliment Mr. Wood. His eighth-grade students are excited about an innovative model they have made of an "ideal" community. Ms. Hall quickly delivers birthday cards to the two rooms where students have birthdays. She also stops in the third-grade class to thank the students and teacher for organizing yesterday's chapel. There she finds students sharing prayer requests. She stays a few minutes for devotions.

Later in the day, she speaks with a prospective parent who has spent some time in the school. The parent remarks on the warm atmosphere of the school. "Everyone here seems to feel part of a close-knit community. People care for one another."

Ms. Hall replies that the school consciously works at this. She says, "All of us stand in relation to God as well as to one another. Our school tries to be a community that provides a supportive setting for developing everyone's gifts. That includes students, teachers, volunteers, secretaries, janitors, and, yes, our parents and board members too. We want to help all members of our school community live as disciples of Jesus Christ."

"But other schools also try to be welcoming communities," the parent says. "What, specifically, makes you different?"

"Well, we work together to develop an atmosphere of respect and responsibility. Everyone must experience that he or she plays an important part in making the school a pleasant and meaningful place. Our parents helped us develop a school covenant. It applies to everyone. A key statement is that we treat people with love, respect, and compassion.

"As teachers we make this code part of our school's daily life. At the start of the year, we explain the covenant. Then our students help develop three or four general classroom rules that reflect the covenant. 'Be on time and prepared,' for example. Students also help in setting classroom procedures. The class reviews and practices the rules and procedures, both to give students a sense of security and to develop good habits."

"What does that have to do with being a Christian school? Don't many schools do this kind of thing?"

"Yes, they do," agrees Ms. Hall. "But our sense of community is rooted in our faith commitment. Our school covenant reflects God's covenant of grace with us, as described in Psalm 111. We are neither teacher-centered nor child-centered, but Christ-centered. Jesus offers redemption to each person in the school and allows each of us to use God's creation for His glory. That is why we work at developing a spiritual context that fosters personal and communal commitment. You've seen our prayer bulletin board in the hall and attended our weekly chapels that always involve students. On Monday mornings parents are encouraged to join our staff devotions in the school foyer. On Friday afternoons teachers and students review the week and pray specifically for personal and class needs for the following week. After school on Fridays, our teachers share joys and concerns, and pray for one another and their students."

"I noticed some students in the hall working out some kind of disagreement," says the parent, "What is that all about?"

"Well, we have implemented a schoolwide program of problem and conflict resolution. From kindergarten on, students learn and implement the steps of resolving problems themselves in a peaceful and loving way. Our trained student mediators help prevent problems, especially on the playground. We also team up younger classes with older ones to plan weekly 'buddy' activities. At each grade level, some units address

aspects of what it means to live as followers of Christ in community. And students put these principles into practice not only in their academic learning but also in service learning opportunities."

"But with all this going on, do you have time to teach all the academics?"

"When schools are places where people really care for one another, research shows that students like school more. Attendance improves. Students interact better socially, with fewer behavior problems. Not only that, but students are more motivated to learn. They work harder and achieve more. We have a sound curriculum and set high expectations for our students. But more than that, our school works hard at implementing what Paul says in his letters about living as a Christian community. That helps us be a place where students learn well. Moreover, we also help students to develop biblical dispositions and to use them and their emotions in socially effective ways. That is as important for how they will function in life as their academic achievement."

"What else should I know before I decide whether to enroll my child?"

"We believe that open communication is a key to making the school a community. We listen carefully to all students—our school exists for them! We try to be loving and positive. At the same time, we set high expectations for students to do likewise. We want our parents to have regular and open contact with our staff. I will give you a copy of our school information package. Then, if you have any more questions, give me a call."

The importance of school culture

Schools are significant agents for enculturating children. However, our students live in a society in which biblically based values are frequently ignored and even derided. Children and adolescents often endure serious emotional, social, and ethical problems. These may be brought about by factors such as little parental time for children, family breakdown, increased mobility, hedonistic individualism, waning of religious beliefs, and abuse of various kinds. Moreover, the media are "a corrosive phenomenon that comes between parents and children, threatens nonmaterial human relationships, and undermines democratic values" (Molnar 1997, 164).

Children throughout the world today show increasing anxiety, depression, overdependence, inability to concentrate, loss of temper, aggression, disobedience, and moral insensitivity. Daniel Goleman calls this slide "a new kind of toxicity seeping into and poisoning the very experience of childhood, signifying sweeping deficits in emotional competencies" (1995, 233). He adds that within this context, schools have to go beyond their traditional mission. They must help children develop and live with emotional, social, and moral proficiency so that they become compassionate, just, and dependable.

Effective schools are much more than collections of individuals going about their own tasks. Rather, they are communities for learning. School communities are united in common ideals and purposes. They share with those in need, are faithful in prayer, and live in harmony with one another (Romans 12). They commit themselves to making learning purposeful and effective for all. Teachers and students appreciate one another's gifts and allow them to flourish. They encourage their use and development for service.

Whether schools function as supportive learning communities depends a great deal on their culture—their beliefs, values, attitudes, ethos, traditions, and celebrations. School culture affects student and teacher attitudes and achievements. If a school culture is negative, it can undermine relationships as well as learning. So schools strive to establish and maintain a culture in which

- Teachers are passionate about implementing the school's vision while remaining open to God's leading in a prayerful, humble way.
- The principal and teachers promote shared values and an atmosphere of shalom. Students feel physically, emotionally, and intellectually secure. The staff treats the students respectfully and fairly.
- The school focuses on purposeful, meaningful, and interesting learning in an orderly environment. Teachers believe that all students can achieve. Teachers and students experience joy as they learn and live together in community. Students have opportunities to share their knowledge and gifts with others, both inside and outside the school.
- The school values individual contributions while encouraging collaborative teamwork. Both focus on efforts to improve all aspects of the school.
- The school community regularly examines whether its vision and stated values agree with those lived in the school. What are the positive and negative aspects of its culture? What do teachers see, hear, and experience in the school? What don't they see, hear, and experience? What things are celebrated? reprimanded? What things are "nondiscussables" that need to be discussed? Is there open and caring communication, relational trust, support for staff and students, interest in learning, and shared decision making? Are restorative practices in place to manage conflicts and tensions? Is the negative confronted head-on, and is the positive celebrated frequently?

No school community is perfect. The power of sin affects both teachers and students. That is why building school communities requires commitment and work. The school's structures must encourage respect and responsibility. School policies must promote the welfare of students, not just administrative convenience. Community members must strive to create a positive atmosphere throughout the school. Teachers model and insist on courtesy and respect. They teach skills for resolving conflicts. They pay attention to the emotional, social, and ethical dimensions of learning.

While teachers are caring and supportive, they do not make learning painless. They allow students to tackle new topics, overcome challenges, take risks, venture opinions, and make mistakes without feeling threatened or judged. They encourage students to help and collaborate with classmates. Teachers give students a genuine say in the life of the classroom. They also hold them responsible for the community they help to shape.

Roland Barth writes, "The vision is, first, that the school will be a *community*, a place full of adults and students who care about, look after, and root for one another and who work together for the good of the whole, in times of need and in times of celebration" (2002, 11). This chapter considers how schools can develop as communities in which students and teachers can thrive as valued persons created in the image of God. The first aim for school leaders, write Barry and Tye, is "to develop, in the school, a caring community, exercising concern and respect for the welfare of others, and emphasising the overriding importance of good human relations, based upon sensitivity, tolerance and good will" (1972, 44). That aim highlights how obedience to the Great Commandment is fundamental for schools that are considerate and productive learning communities.

Reflect and respond 8-1

Describe your understanding of the term *learning community*. Make a list of four or five characteristics that you believe to be particularly important. Compare this list with the points mentioned by Ms. Hall at the beginning of this chapter in describing her school, and with lists made by two or three other persons. Can you reach a consensus?

Spirituality and school culture

"Teach me your way, O Lord, and ... give me an undivided heart," the psalmist prays (Psalm 86:11). It is our spiritual heart that sets the direction of our lives and enables us to walk in God's truth. It is our spiritual heart that makes it possible for us to bring glory to God's name in our work and studies. It is our undivided spiritual heart that leads to action for our own good and for the good of those around us (Psalm 86:8–13, Jeremiah 32:39).

Even in public schooling more educators are once again recognizing the importance of spirituality (e.g., Anderson 2004; Garner 2007). They understand that the meaning of life transcends the material and the self. Regrettably, spirituality is often defined superficially. Garner, for instance, defines spirit as the "life force that creates, learns, changes." Classroom strategies then include to "Recognize that students listen more with their hearts than with their heads," and "Reflect on personal values, beliefs, and feelings about spiritual matters" (137, 146, 147). Teachers do these things mainly by encouraging quiet reflective times when students get in touch with themselves. This practice leads to a spirituality in which God may or may not have a place, depending on personal student choice. Christian schools have a more solid spiritual foundation.

Board members, administrators, teachers, and a good proportion of parents and students in Christian schools share the bond of biblically informed faith in the triune God. That bond is the basis for schools' being supportive learning communities that honor God. We do have to remember, however, that Christian schools are not churches. In churches, worshipping God and learning about the faith dimension of life are central. In Christian schools, the focus is broader: to prepare students to function in society in competent, trustworthy, and loving ways. So devotional times, worship, and Bible study are not the singular focus of schools. Nevertheless, they are part of the Christian school's total learning experience. They lead students and teachers to share faith insights and to reflect on the meaning of learning. They help students understand their place in God's story of salvation. Also, they foster community through fellowship with God and other community members.

Prayer in Christian schools unites the community. Staff and student prayer is meaningful in one-on-one meetings between students and their teachers. The need for prayer often stems from a concern or problem that a student shares with a teacher. Some teachers pray for several students each day before school. They make it a point to pray for each of their students every week or so. Besides personal prayer for their own teaching and learning situations, teachers may also pray with fellow staff members from time to time. I have experienced meaningful prayer on the phone with a colleague when the tasks God had placed before me overwhelmed me. In addition, a staff as a whole also bring praises and requests to God several times a week. Prayer not only changes individuals and situations, it affects the tone of a school and its culture.

Regular chapel services balance daily classroom devotions. The whole school community needs to worship God. Chapels may include biblically based, interesting, and sometimes provocative presentations. These will challenge students to dedicate and rededicate themselves to serve their Savior and Lord as they learn and study. Enthusiastic singing also strengthens community.

In middle schools and high schools, student committees can plan the chapel schedule in consultation with a teacher. In some schools, different classes are responsible for chapels each week. Student-led chapels require teacher guidance as the students develop leadership skills. Tuned-out fellow students often sit up and notice when they hear a peer attesting to the reality of Jesus Christ in his or her life. Students who feel awkward about speaking may read a written devotion or an excerpt from their own work. Classes may also plan chapels to sum up their thematic units or to celebrate special occasions. Guest speakers may need reminders to address special needs in the school—and to keep things short, especially with younger children.

The Bible rejects a dichotomy between sacred and secular activities. In Bible times, even the cooking pots and the bells of the horses were to be holy to the Lord (Zechariah 14:20–21)! If a school emphasizes mainly the need to get good grades but forgets to study the Bible or praise God in word and song in its classrooms, it lacks full spirituality. However, if we pray a lot but are indifferent to applying the guidelines of Scripture to structure classrooms and plan curriculum, we also lack full spirituality. If we worship God in devotions and chapel but our worship does not penetrate our teaching and learning in the classroom, our school lacks the holiness that God demands.

Spirituality must be an integral part of our curriculum. We need to explore life's big questions with our students (Van Brummelen, Koole, and Franklin 2004):

- Who am I? What is the purpose and meaning of my life? How can I experience fulfillment?
- What should I believe? How do I know that God exists? What is my relationship with God?
- How do I deal with loneliness, suffering, and death? What happens after death? How does that affect how I learn and live?
- How should we live together? How can I connect meaningfully with others? What values should bind us together? How can we build a more compassionate, peaceful, and just world?
- What is the origin of the world? What is the meaning of creation for my life?

As teachers we ask such questions to awaken students' consciousness about the purpose and meaning of life. We want them to think about what was, what is, and what might be, whether that involves ethical issues, justice, suffering, violence, poverty, or ecological challenges. We explore such questions not just in Bible study but also in literature, social studies, and science. In literature we discuss what is good or evil and the source of morality, values, and worldviews. In social studies we consider how ideals and beliefs have influenced cultural development.

Word alert

Spirituality is "the developing relationship of the individual, within community and tradition, to that which is—or is perceived to be—of ultimate concern, ultimate value and ultimate truth" (Wright 1998, 88). Spirituality encompasses, but is broader than, religion. It aims to illumine life's meaning and larger purpose, putting humans in touch with the "beyond" of everyday existence.

Education anchored in spirituality rejects the modernist approach to education that is performance oriented but neglects the human quest for faith, values, and the transcendent. It also rejects the postmodern notion that there is no universal truth and that no ultimate values are essential for society to flourish. Rather, education must connect students with their deepest selves as they explore how faith has answers for the larger questions of human life in an awe-inspiring cosmos.

In science we investigate how God created each species of animal and plant to fit a certain niche and how we can unfold His creation because we can depend on His created order and its scientific laws.

Spirituality and holiness are direct results of the work of the Holy Spirit in us. Spirituality depends on commitment and trust in God, and on faith, hope, and love. We cannot force spiritual commitment onto our students. But schools can provide an atmosphere that encourages faith commitment and a deep sense of spirituality. They can model a spiritual lifestyle and nurture spiritual maturity. Spirituality must not be an "add-on" that provides a Christian veneer. Rather, spirituality ought to direct, pervade, and support everything that is planned in a Christian school. That includes its policies, its learning structures and activities, and its efforts to foster moral, emotional, and social development. Only then will a school be a true learning community where teachers and students learn to walk with God.

Reflect and respond 8-2

Revisit the goals of Christian schooling outlined in chapter 1. Do these goals reflect the claim of this section that spirituality ought to direct, pervade, and support everything that is planned in a Christian school? Why or why not?

Teaching virtue

Educating for virtue or fundamental values is nothing new. The Greek philosopher Aristotle argued that communities will be strong only if children are habituated into appropriate virtues and then later learn the rationale for them. Strong communities acquaint children with their traditions and value systems. God instructed the Israelites to do so (Deuteronomy 6:4–9, Psalm 78:1–8). Paul encouraged leaders to teach not only the basics of faith but also values such as temperance, self-control, love, respect, endurance, honesty, soundness in speech, peacefulness, obedience, humility, and doing good (Titus 2 and 3).

Teaching ethical principles and conduct is sometimes called character education. It promotes the virtues that Paul mentions in Titus as well as the fruit of the

Spirit: love, joy, peace, patience, kindness, goodness, faithfulness, gentleness, and self-control (Galatians 5:22–23). Character education virtues overlap with these: respect, responsibility, integrity, empathy, and compassion. All these traits are more than personal ones. They also affect a community's understanding of social justice and equality. They relate, for instance, to treatment of visible minorities and the economically disadvantaged. Thus character education goes beyond striving for improved personal morality. It helps students participate in creating a just and loving society. It also addresses, for example, communal economic greed, ecological devastation, and the cruelty of armed conflict. Character education affects individuals as they, in turn, affect their communities. "To do what is right and just is more acceptable to the Lord than sacrifice" (Proverbs 21:3).

In view of our current societal context, it is little wonder that character education has once again come to the fore. Since schools do influence students' values, dispositions, and behaviors, character education proponents teach morals and values directly and systematically. However, values clarification and Kohlberg's moral reasoning, popular in the late twentieth century, fell short. Values clarification rejected universal moral standards. It allowed students to choose their own values, leading to individualism and ethical relativism. Kohlberg's approach taught moral reasoning but did not consider actual behavior, God-given standards, or relationships in community.

Character education can have a positive impact both on individual students and on the school. Students like school better when their schools deliberately and carefully implement a program with clear goals and values. They have better attendance records, more constructive behavior, and higher academic achievement (including in low-income locales). The schools have a better learning climate and experience less bullying. Effective character education promotes positive personal growth and learning (Dovre 2007).

Christian schools are, on the whole, fairly homogeneous-value communities. Therefore, they are able to teach biblical virtues. The school community, including parents, can explicitly and collaboratively affirm the core values that should be taught. The school can then give teachers adequate support and time to develop and implement ways of teaching those values throughout its program. Teachers and students together can explore the implications of biblical values. Students have opportunities to cooperate, resolve conflicts, set goals, make decisions, and solve ethical problems. Teachers and other adults in the school model the values in their work with one another and with students.

The strategies described below have proven to be effective (Dovre 2007; Howard, Berkowitz, and Schaeffer 2004; Lickona in Molnar 1997; Ryan and Bohlin 1999; Van Brummelen, Franklin, and Hilder 2005; Wolterstorff 1980):

- Teachers are caring ethical models and mentors. They love, respect, and support their students. They demonstrate moral sensitivity and responsibility. Each student is personally connected with at least one adult in the school.
- Teachers create a caring classroom community. They help students know, respect, affirm, and care about one another. Also, they make their students feel that they are valued and accountable members of the class. Teachers combine high expectations with high levels of support for student work. They promote shared decision making that increases responsibility for the classroom climate. They teach conflict resolution. They consistently prohibit disrespect and gossip while recognizing and celebrating positive conduct and accomplishments, especially character-oriented ones.
- The school community creates a positive moral ethos throughout and beyond the school. This includes an emphasis on showing mutual respect, acting responsibly and justly, completing work conscientiously, resolving conflicts peacefully, doing community service work, and being involved in activities that promote social justice. Teachers train students to mediate peer conflicts from kindergarten on. High school assemblies may bring in speakers who address end-of-life issues or the values embedded in computer games. Sports programs emphasize participation and good sportsmanship.
- Teachers help students develop ethical reflection and reasoning. They encourage students to apply general ethical principles to concrete situations and moral dilemmas. Some issues become part of the planned curriculum. Others arise in the daily life of the school. Teachers give moral guidance through explanation, storytelling, discussion, encouraging positive behavior, and feedback. Students learn to apply value-based norms and to respect the rights and needs of others. Schools become communities of ethical inquiry within a biblical framework.
- Teachers teach values through the curriculum. They deliberately choose curriculum content that encourages students to examine questions of morality and social justice. Teachers can do so, for instance, by carefully choosing literature selections that are rich with meaning and imagery (ranging from *Charlotte's Web* to *Lord of the Flies*). They can investigate challenging historical topics such as the Holocaust. They can raise the ethical aspects of science issues. They can teach units on friendship or heroes. Teachers can also implement learning strategies that implicitly teach values (e.g., collaborative learning activities; writing thank-you notes and other thoughtful letters).
- Schools recruit parents and other supporters as partners in character education. Parents are the primary nurturers of children. Schools need their input and support. Home-based activities, whether initiated by schools or parents, are important for character education. Some schools send home short case studies

or poems involving ethical issue or dilemmas; parents are asked to discuss the handouts with their children before they are analyzed at school.

With respect to the use of literature, we are always teaching students how to live, and therefore we cannot afford to neglect the teaching of enduring values such as hope, courage, and justice (Monika Hilder in Van Brummelen, Franklin, and Hilder 2005). Life-shaping ethical education using literature, Hilder says, must engage students' imaginations, offering them imaginative experiences of encouragement and hope in which we honor students' voices.

Hilder describes how students need to explore moral courage and goodness in ways that are neither moralizing nor boring. Teachers highlight life as an ethical journey on which we grow stronger or weaker as we make ethical choices. Moral imagination, according to Hilder, is powerful when students explore heroic reversals in which the so-called weak or foolish subvert the powerful. In responding to the problem of evil and suffering as it arises in literature, teachers strive to engage students with an attitude of nurture, discussing how possible healing may come about. Such teaching helps students explore new insights and meanings. It helps to connect them to a deeper level of awareness of what happens around and within them.

> ### Word alert
>
> *Character education* is often used interchangeably with *moral education* and *values education*. Character education is intended to help students become ethically responsible, self-disciplined, and community-oriented persons who understand, accept, and act on values such as respect, empathy, compassion, integrity, self-control, responsibility, justice, stewardship, humility, patience, and prudential courage.
>
> Teaching of such values and morals stresses the importance of students' recognizing what is valuable and what to do—what it means to live by ethical principles. It promotes habits of the mind, habits of the heart, and habits of action. Teachers not only model value principles but also explain why they uphold those principles and how and why they apply them to specific situations.

One keystone for developing character is to foster a passion for justice. The Judeo-Christian view of justice embodies shalom—harmony, peace, and complete well-being throughout creation. This vision of justice begins with all persons being treated with dignity and having the responsibility to treat others the same. More than that, justice demands "participation in struggles to transform sociocultural arrangements that cause people to be hungry or homeless, oppressed or victimized" (Groome 1998, 363). Inside the classroom, Groome adds, teachers must promote fairness for all. They must also encourage students to ask, Who is suffering due to injustice? Why? What went wrong? How can brokenness be restored? How do I respond and why? Teachers carefully design curricula and pedagogical practices to ensure that they do not contribute to oppression. Where feasible, they also have students do some direct work with the poor or oppressed, and they carefully debrief such work. The search for personal meaning must include a search for the promotion of justice in personal relationships, in our communities, and throughout the world.

Finally, a value that is important, though seldom mentioned in character education, is gratitude. To live in gratitude is to appreciate, delight in, and be thankful for the positive experiences, realities, and possibilities of life that God offers us. Philosopher Nicholas Wolterstorff (2002) writes that gratitude lies at the foundation of a meaningful existence. Teachers and schools must model and breathe a spirit of gratitude to God. With their students, they find its manifestation in the appreciative use of things around them, in joyful delight and delighted joy. They ought to cultivate reflection on the immense richness of the wisdom, justice, and goodness that God's common grace exhibits around us. They help students exercise acts of gratitude. Nurturing an atmosphere of gratitude contributes to an attitude of hope made possible through the redemptive power of Christ's resurrection (Van Brummelen, Franklin, and Hilder 2005).

The Bible is clear that God calls communities to enculturate in their youth a way of life that upholds God's values. Schools cannot avoid teaching values. Even when public schools try to avoid teaching values explicitly, they still implicitly teach respect for others and the importance of being honest. But they may also implicitly teach that students can choose whatever values they themselves justify, without reference to universal values that hold for everyone. While not all Christians agree on how biblical values apply to specific situations, Christian schools do have a common commitment based on God's Word. That commitment requires them to foster the development of students' character on the basis of biblical standards.

Reflect and respond 8-3

Develop some classroom activities for two or three of the strategies outlined in this section. (If possible, brainstorm your ideas in a small group.) Are all strategies effective for all age levels? Are there any strategies that you would add, delete, or revise?

Thomas Lickona, whose 1991 book created momentum for character education, has been criticized for emphasizing personal virtues while neglecting social justice issues. David Purpel (in Molnar 1997) believes that the type of character education proposed by Lickona "is very much in the line of Puritan traditions of obedience, hierarchy, and hard work, values which overlap nicely with the requirements of an economic system that values a compliant and industrious workforce, and a social system that demands stability and order" (145–146). Does Purpel's criticism apply to the foregoing section? Why or why not?

Emotional and social health

In his book *Emotional Intelligence* (1995), Daniel Goleman argues that emotional (and social) "intelligence" is more closely linked to success later in life than is academic achievement. He describes a study of four-year-olds who were given a marshmallow. A researcher told the children that they could eat the marshmallow right away. If they waited until the researcher returned, however, they could have two marshmallows. About one-third ate the marshmallow right away. Another third waited a little longer. The remainder waited for the full fifteen to twenty minutes until the researcher returned. When these same children were tracked down as adolescents, those who had been able to wait were more self-assertive and better able to cope with school and with life. Those who had eaten the marshmallow right away were not as well liked by their peers. They were easily frustrated and provoked more arguments and fights. Also, they scored an average of 210 points lower on the Scholastic Aptitude Test than the ones who had waited. Goleman claims that, particularly when children are young, we can teach them emotional skills such as how to control impulses and how to read social situations accurately. These, he adds, will have positive payoffs for life.

It is not clear whether emotional intelligence is actually a type of intelligence or whether it is competence resulting from other personal traits. What is clear, however, is that students' emotional and social development affects their learning. That is why some schools purposely deal with self-awareness and relationship awareness in their curriculum. Most effective, according to Goleman, are small but telling lessons delivered regularly over a sustained period. An example is a fifth-grade lesson on identifying and distinguishing between feelings from pictures of a person's face. The students imitate and describe six basic emotions. Connecting facial expressions with feelings is particularly important for argumentative students, who often misinterpret neutral expressions as hostile ones (Goleman 1995).

There appear to be two crucial periods for emotional and social development: ages five and six, and the onset of adolescence. The school context discourages and frustrates young children who come to school without the social and emotional understandings needed to cope with the classroom situation. Teachers can help these children understand their own and others' motivations and intentions. Early adolescence is also a crucial time for learning emotional skills. During these years teens often suffer rejection or begin to experience depression. For intellectually able girls at this age, pressure to conform faces them with a serious conflict between their identity as achievers and their identity as females. Often schools give them little help in developing self-awareness, appropriate life goals, or a meaningful philosophy of life (Porath and Matthews 1997).

Students, as persons created in the image of God, are holistic beings. Their emotional and social states and competencies affect their ability to cope with school tasks and with life. They benefit from recognizing and reading feelings with sensitivity and with empathy as well as from learning to manage emotions and relationships productively. Teachers can be proactive in a number of ways. Not the least of these is to be sensitive and responsive to their students' feelings. Teachers can address emotional and social development in courses such as health, guidance, and personal planning. They can also discuss literary selections that involve feelings and social interactions.

What is significant is that many of the strategies suggested for emotional and social growth are similar to those promoting character education. Both areas include teaching conflict resolution and using peer mediators. Both use stories such as *Frog and Toad Are Friends* or *Charlotte's Web* to discuss feelings, perspective taking, caring, and the qualities of a good friend. Both use discipline "problems" as potential learning situations. Both employ class meetings to teach students to get along in respectful ways. Both ask students to role-play difficult situations. Both promote service learning with follow-up seminars in which students discuss feelings and positive social strategies.

The reason for this intersection is that character education and emotional and social development are closely intertwined. Many primary emotions are closely related to biblical commands. Love is part of the Great Commandment. Anger can lead to breaking the sixth commandment. Envy and jealousy are forbidden in the tenth commandment. Disgust, shame, fear, and sadness may arise from perceived, threatened, or actual sinful acts. Emotions such as surprise and enjoyment are less directly linked to biblical injunctions, as are emotional disorders. But those, too, affect people's dispositions and behaviors. Thus character education overlaps with emotional and social development.

Research in character education as well as in social and emotional learning shows that both are important ingredients in enabling young people to take on responsible roles in the school and in their broader communities. Students who do not act on sound ethical principles or whose emotional or social insights and skills are lacking will have difficulty functioning positively. They will break covenant with other persons and, ultimately, with God. Nevertheless, God still extends His grace to them. So if we as teachers walk with God in the classroom, we will show—especially to those students who lack positive moral commitments or emotional or social skills—all the love and support we can muster, wearying as that can sometimes be.

Reflect and respond 8-4

Find some credible Internet sources that deal with emotional intelligence and its implications for learning. Report on and discuss recommendations made for the classroom, as well as critiques of Goleman's views. To what extent would you implement the recommended strategies in your classroom?

Service learning

The Bible makes clear that knowledge is more than concepts and skills. Faith, knowledge, and deeds are all intertwined (James 2–3). A Christian worldview is not just a theoretical notion; it must also guide action. Schools therefore provide service learning opportunities as one way for students to exercise their knowledge and deepen their commitment. Service learning allows students to follow Jesus' footsteps: "Now that I, your Lord and Teacher, have washed your feet, you also should wash one another's feet" (John 13:14).

In well-designed service learning programs, "students do more than ladle out soup to the homeless or pick up trash.... They apply what they've learned in the classroom, develop leadership and communication skills, become more caring and responsible citizens—and help community needs in the process" (Willis 1993, 4). Good projects involve direct experiences that connect students with their communities. They also stimulate reflective thought about the meaning of these experiences, possibly in monthly "reflection sessions," to discuss the experiences and to explore related questions. Some projects may combine service and research. For instance, students may combine a renovation of a homeless shelter with research on poverty in the community.

Service learning provides students with hands-on experiences. Many students learn especially well from this type of experience. Service learning is most effective when it is an integral part of the curriculum. Kindergartners can prepare programs for senior citizens while studying a unit on All People Are Special. Sixth-grade students can plant small trees along an eroding riverbank as part of a unit on water and its effects. Ninth-grade students can use what they have learned in a unit on statistics to design and conduct a neighborhood survey on recreational needs in the community. Eleventh-grade students can set up recreational programs for young offenders while studying crime and justice. In all such cases the community benefits and the students' learning is motivated and enriched.

Pacific Academy, a large Christian school close to my home, involves all students from kindergarten to twelfth grade in service learning. The purposes of its program are as follows:

- To "open students' eyes" to the needs of others in their community and around the world.
- To recognize that each of us has God-given abilities and to provide opportunities for students to use them outside the classroom.
- To acknowledge that God has created us as part of the Body of Christ and to use our gifts and abilities to bring glory to God in community with others.
- To experience and appreciate the responsibility of world evangelism and to have opportunities to respond in obedience to Christ's call on their lives.

A large variety of service learning activities are possible to attain such goals. Here are some that teachers have shared with me:

Helping in the classroom. Students help set up audiovisual equipment or science experiments, arrange bulletin boards, or take charge of a learning center. Older students help younger ones by writing out stories told by younger ones and reading them back. First- and second-grade classes make ABC or thematic "big books" that are shared with kindergarten classes. Students tutor their peers or mentor younger students.

Helping around the school. Students volunteer in the school library or office. They are trained as peer mediators and counselors or as "kindersitters" during recess. Students organize and referee games and sports activities. For special projects, they organize special events such as a grandparents day or a fund-raising effort. A class takes responsibility for the school's recycling program, the food bank support program, or for beautifying the school grounds.

Presentations. Students present drama and music productions in senior residences or group homes. High school students write children's plays or songs and present these to preschool groups, children's wards in hospitals, or public libraries.

Service in the community. Students "adopt" grandparents at a senior citizen's home. They pay them regular visits, clean their apartments, read to them, and shop for them. Students set up maintenance programs for halfway houses or youth emergency shelters. Students maintain a bird sanctuary in a nearby park or become engaged in environmental activities. An art class makes a mural or other pieces of artwork for a homeless shelter. High school students set up a social justice club that prepares positions on issues and presents them to community leaders. Students volunteer in a soup kitchen for the "down-and-out" in their community.

Some schools make a certain amount of service work compulsory for graduation. They believe that all students should benefit from the joy of serving. They claim that students who would not volunteer benefit most from such experiences. Other educators caution, however, that forcing students to "volunteer" devalues the experience and that community agencies will not want to use resentful students who are there just to fulfill a requirement. Some high schools allow unwilling students to complete an alternative but related project.

Reflect and respond 8-5

Design a service learning program for an elementary, middle, or high school. Keep in mind the aims of such a program. Ask, Are the activities suitable for students' maturity level and life experiences? Do the activities provide for differences in abilities and interests? Do the activities encourage students to reflect on societal needs and to want to serve such needs? Is the program manageable for the teachers? Can students carry out the activities with modest supervision? Would you make the program a compulsory one for all students? Why or why not?

Schoolwide activities

Some Christian educators shy away from the phrase *school spirit* because they associate it with the superficiality of cheerleading and winning the "big game." Enthusiasm and pride in a school, however, do positively influence school morale and classroom learning. A vibrant atmosphere gives students the sense that they belong to a worthwhile learning community. The root of the word *enthusiasm*, significantly, means "God-inspired" or "God-possessed." Here are some example activities for fostering a sound community spirit with the Holy Spirit enabling all of us to live as God's children (Romans 8):

- Middle schools and high schools have active and meaningful homeroom systems, with students staying with the same "advisory" group for several years. Such homerooms allow teachers to form bonds with a specific group of students. Together they have devotions and also have discussions about school and personal concerns. They plan occasional special events together. They have class meetings about school-related issues. Homerooms can also work together on projects such as writing a class song or doing a service learning activity. The homeroom sharing and caring become the basis of the sense of community in the whole school.
- Students have meaningful audiences for projects through displays, visits by other classes, and exhibitions in the gymnasium.
- Schools have regular schoolwide celebrations. These can include school-community breakfasts, fine arts festivals, pajama reading sessions in the school library, special assemblies, swimming and skating excursions, science fairs, and track meets in which cross-grade teams collect points together.

- Cross-grade units or exploratory minicourses are excellent opportunities for students and teachers to interact in different ways and in different environments. This effort might involve a special school theme week or an exploration of a topic for several grades over two or three weeks (e.g., studying communities in different parts of the world; exploring a Christian approach to work and leisure; holding a mini-Olympics; investigating ethnic and religious diversity in the community). The school benefits both from teachers' planning collaboratively with students and from students' interacting in meaningful ways with teachers and with students from other grades.
- Extracurricular activities can foster a sense of belonging to the school community. The student council can sponsor various clubs and can organize special events. It may hold a snow sculpture contest after a heavy snowfall or a short pep rally before a school team goes away for a game. A school newspaper, a yearbook, intramural sport activities, and mathematics contests can also bind students together. Interschool sport teams should emphasize building team relationships, cooperation, and sportsmanship. A winning-at-all-costs attitude has no place in a Christian school.
- Schools consciously and consistently nurture student leadership skills. Teachers coach students in order to develop specific leadership goals. Depending on their age and maturity, students can serve on committees that help organize safety patrols, choose school jackets, plan chapels, organize band trips, or revise the school handbook. Student councils can plan special events, help organize hot lunches, and arrange sponsorships of Third World orphans or schools. They can also address problems such as messy hallways or name-calling, develop welcome programs for new students, or provide child care during parent-teacher interviews. Meaningful student leadership calls for some teachers to foster leadership skills, and to help students set goals and priorities.

School policies

School policies can enhance but can also detract from the school as a learning community. God gave us the Ten Commandments to enable us to flourish personally and communally within a framework of love for God and for our fellow human beings. Similarly, school policies describe agreed-on expectations that enable community members to live in and contribute to a supportive learning environment.

Policies, including codes of conduct, do not in themselves create spiritual or ethical maturity in teachers and students. However, biblically based guidelines do provide a scaffold within which all can exercise their responsibilities and become mature in accord with God's precepts for life. Very detailed and specific rules, however, may cause resentment. It is important, especially with adolescents, to discuss the school's community standards and the reasons for them. Schools may require older students to sign a statement that they will support the school's standards of conduct.

All those involved in formulating or revising school policies should keep in mind that effective communities thrive on trust. If policies are based on a shared understanding of the school's mission and aims, board members, administrators, teachers, students, and parents can collectively support them and commit to their implementation. However, sometimes policies undermine teachers' or students' responsibility as persons created in the image of God. If students perceive policies as picky, unfair, or superfluous, they may feel hassled. Such policies lead to legalism and may destroy trust. Then teachers and students all too easily withdraw from meaningful relationships with one another or with the school administration. Joint commitment and trust grow weaker, and eventually student achievement as well as school morale and vitality suffer (Hargreaves and Fink 2006).

Let me give an example. We installed a new computer lab in our education department. Because of a recent after-hours equipment theft in our building, we implemented strict rules. We kept the door locked at all times. Students could use the lab only when a staff member was present. Students had to sign in and out. Though well intentioned, the rules created problems. Staff were not always available, and they often went for lunch just when students had time to use the computers. Students felt slighted and thought the professors did not trust them. The faculty recognized that the rules were affecting relationships, so after a year or so they decided to revise the policy. The door would be open during regular working hours, whether or not a staff member was present. The sign-in requirement was scrapped. Students would need permission to use the lab only if they stayed after normal school hours. Then the last student was responsible for locking the door. The new policy improved relationships and enhanced trust, and it did not lead to thefts or other irresponsible behavior. The health of the learning community had outweighed the slightly increased possibility of immature conduct or theft.

Schools cannot function without policies. There are many repetitive circumstances that require established procedures—for example, inclement weather during recess, school assemblies, field trips, absenteeism, and student records. Policies lead to economy of time and effort, continuity, and stability. They ensure that details are not overlooked under the pressure of events.

Policies must be reasonable, however, and they must demonstrate an appropriate level of trust in teachers and students. New or revised policies need consultation and discussion. Once decisions are made, they need to be announced, explained, and made readily available in written form. Schools should also obtain input from older students when the school considers policy changes that will affect them. Almost always, students make sensible suggestions when they recognize and understand a problem. Generally they will be more committed to a new policy when they have been consulted. Thus, involving them contributes to a healthier sense of community. The point of having policies is to provide a context that encourages members of the school community to willingly and collaboratively implement the school's vision.

Reflect and respond 8-6

Describe, with reasons, your views of the following school policies in terms of how they will affect the school as a learning community:

- An admissions policy for a Christian school that accepts only students who are committed Christians or who have at least one parent who is a Christian.
- A policy that requires all teachers to submit their biweekly parent newsletters to the principal for approval prior to distribution.
- A policy that all volunteers in classrooms, including parents, must submit to criminal record checks.
- An attendance policy for high school students that suspends students after three unexcused absences.
- A dress code that prescribes school uniforms for a middle school.
- A mandate for a student council that makes all council decisions subject to review by the principal or his or her designate.
- A sports program that emphasizes the involvement of a large proportion of its students in intramural sports and participates in interschool sports only for occasional tournaments.

The school's physical environment and size

A school's physical environment also affects learning. Unless you are involved in planning a new school building, you need to work within the walls and structure of your building. However, teachers and principals can still make the learning space pleasant and agreeable. Is the facility well cared for? Are the classroom and hall displays appealing? Do they promote learning? Are communal spaces inviting for students and teachers, and do they encourage interaction? Are the hallways and classrooms kept tidy? Are repairs dealt with quickly? At the high school level a lounge area adjacent to the office area (for unobtrusive but constant supervision) can be a worthwhile gathering place. An attractive guidance area, a library designed to welcome students, a corner for table tennis—all these help students feel that the school cares about them and for them. A well-kept, attractive school creates pride of belonging.

It is easier to build a sense of community in schools that are small in size. In small schools, all community members sense that their contributions are important. Student participation in activities is much greater. Teachers and students have a greater voice in decision making, and decisions are made more easily. Friendships are more flexible and less exclusive. Students develop fewer self-interested social groups and cliques. Students feel a stronger sense of belonging. While teachers have a heavier preparation load, they feel more collegiality and support. The more personalized approaches used by teachers are helpful, especially to students who are at risk. Also, parents are more willing to become involved. Some large schools create distinct "schools within schools" to capture the advantages of small schools.

Of course, foremost in an enthusiastic ("God-inspired!") school is that all persons are treated with respect and have meaningful and rewarding tasks. Do teachers advance students' personal welfare and engage them deeply in learning? A general ethos of love and care, no matter what the school's physical context and size, will enhance the spirit of the school because the Spirit's presence will be felt.

The role of teacher collegiality in fostering a learning community

Ms. Hall recognizes that as principal she has a leading role in forging the teachers into a unified team. While the teachers must concur with the school's vision and values, they have much flexibility within that framework. Ms. Hall respects each staff member's insights and abilities. She encourages teachers to take initiative while she provides support. She is open to suggestions. She has an open-door policy. As much as possible, she tries to reach decisions by consensus. Ms. Hall delegates tasks according to teachers' expertise and preferences. Sometimes she relieves teachers so that they have the time to carry out special tasks. She also teaches several times a week in order to stay in close touch with students and teachers.

Ms. Hall and her teachers recognize the importance of joint worship, prayer, and reflection. They get together for brief devotions each morning. They also hold an annual midyear retreat to get away from urgent concerns and to focus on their spiritual growth. Such retreats include worship and praise, Bible study, and reflection on God's will for the school.

Ms. Hall and her staff also plan regular "sharing sessions." Teachers share their successes and frustrations. Some sessions have a specific focus. How can we improve parent-teacher communication? How is the art program going? Some sharing sessions are inconclusive, but others lead to proposed changes. Ms. Hall consults teachers about policy changes. As a result, teachers feel they are stakeholders, and they take pride in their school.

However, devotions, sharing sessions, and consultations are not enough. Ms. Hall wants to help teachers develop their insights and abilities. Each year, she solicits input from her staff about the school's in-service programs. The sessions, held a week before the start of the new school year, allow teachers to discuss the vision of the school and to review its implementation.

The teachers of Faith Christian Community School have different abilities and insights. Several are gifted musicians. One has a special interest in athletics. Another provides leadership in curriculum planning. Some have expertise in specific subject areas. One teacher enjoys organizing special events. Two or three are willing to mentor new teachers. Before the start of the school year, the teachers discuss how they can best use their gifts and interests to benefit the school community without anyone's becoming overloaded.

Ms. Hall uses frequent short classroom visits for support and encouragement. For longer visits, she usually has a brief conference with the teacher beforehand to discuss what things will be useful to observe. Ms. Hall asks teachers to evaluate themselves. Post-visit conferences become forums for sharing feelings and insights and for setting mutual goals. Ms. Hall's annual evaluation reports describe these goals and to what extent they were achieved. Ms. Hall's approach shows that she uses her authority as principal to assist her teachers.

All this does not mean that Ms. Hall's relations with her teachers are always smooth. Her teachers have different personalities and teaching styles, as well as diverse views and expectations. Some are more receptive to new ideas than are others. Ms. Hall builds community, but not uniformity. She encourages open discussion about differences. Nevertheless, she insists that everyone work within the framework of the school's vision and aims.

When hiring teachers, Ms. Hall assesses whether prospective teachers will model what it means to be a member of a Christian community. Do they display a naturalness and openness about their relationship with God and how God acts in their lives? Do they study and use their Bibles to determine their lifestyle, to choose their involvement in Christian and other groups, and to make decisions? Have they witnessed for Christ in various spheres of life? Do they model a neat and modest appearance? Ms. Hall knows that her teachers' personal qualities are important to the school. As a unit, her staff must model Christian love, integrity, and thoughtfulness. They must be sensitive to diverse views within the community supporting the school. They must have an esprit de corps that supports the tone and culture of the school.

Ms. Hall also investigates how teachers have treated students in the past. Did they deal respectfully with their students? Have they shown genuine concern for their students' personal and academic growth? Did they follow up on students' questions and concerns? Were they loving but punctual and firm? Above all, did they demonstrate to the students their commitment to Jesus Christ? Ms. Hall also introduces promising candidates to her teachers for feedback as to how the applicant will fit into the "team." Once they have been hired, Ms. Hall holds meetings with them to discuss the philosophy and goals of the school and how the school tries to implement them. The school requires teachers who lack a background in Christian approaches in teaching and learning to take courses to ensure that they know how to implement the school's vision.

In any school, staff collegiality is important. It is important that teachers are congenial and that they pray for one another. More than that, however, collegiality also means that teachers support one another in their teaching responsibilities and that they collaborate to build a professional learning community. Collegiality exists where the whole staff eagerly and collectively focuses on improvements that benefit student learning. Teachers openly discuss successes and frustrations. They do so in order to do what is best for their students within the contours of the school's aims. They complement caring relationships with mutual and supportive efforts to improve teaching and learning. Principals may take occasional classes to give grade-level or subject teachers time for joint planning. They also make time available for teachers to visit each other's classes in order to consider and discuss effective teaching and learning strategies. The faculty uses time during professional development days to review and revise programs and to plan units.

Robert Koole (2006) describes a number of challenges that may detract from a collegial professional learning community. First, teachers may be overloaded with teaching responsibilities, student diversity, and demands for accountability. Second, they may be isolated from their colleagues since they teach by themselves and have little interaction with other teachers, or because there are tensions within the staff. Third, teachers' gifts that could contribute to the school as a whole may be overlooked or not appreciated. Koole then points out how through God's grace we can regain interdependence, and all members of the body can do their part while building up others in love by the following actions:

- For the sake of their students, teachers commit themselves to teach in exemplary ways, reflecting on their practices and trying out new ideas.
- Teachers freely help and advise one another. They also gain insight from other teachers' stories about their experiences in particular situations.
- Teachers voluntarily share teaching strategies and resources with one another.

- Teachers work jointly to put into action a common direction. Together they benefit from one another's insights, and plan school-related tasks and specific teaching and learning initiatives.
- Teachers affirm one another's gifts, model honest and open communication, and resolve and reconcile conflicts within a context of understanding and forgiveness.

While any school will sometimes fall short of these ideals, Koole concludes that "a body in which teachers are bonded together in a covenant given by God in His Son Jesus Christ and through the Spirit learns that each one has a place in the body and that no one is better than another" (p. 2–37).

Reflect and respond 8-7

Read the following quotations and discuss how they describe situations that either enhance or detract from building a collegial professional learning community:

"Teaching in our school is stimulating! Our staff members, both individually and collectively, are always looking for more effective teaching strategies. We get ideas from one another, in the staff room, or in informal discussions after school. Our principal encourages us to try new ideas and follows up by asking how things went. We share the ideas that work well in our monthly staff newsletter or report them in our division meetings."

"Our staff meetings usually deal with business items and announcements that could be sent to us just as well by e-mail. I know that our administration needs to make day-to-day policy decisions without always consulting us. But even decisions that greatly affect our students or us are usually announced with little opportunity for input. At staff meetings teachers do not want to oppose what the administration has already decided. They don't want to be seen as challenging authority, and they feel it won't make a difference in any case. Most teachers just do their own classroom work as well as possible but avoid becoming involved in any controversies."

"I teach in a dynamic school. Our principal works closely with us to raise expectations and to improve student learning. Almost every month she sends me a note giving me some positive feedback. Professional development days focus on providing a program that meets our stated aims. They're interesting and worthwhile. At the same time, I constantly feel pressured to improve, and I wonder whether I can keep up the pace that is expected. A couple of teachers regularly complain that they find it hard to balance family, school, and community responsibilities."

The role of parents and supporters

The school is part of a larger community. That larger community plays a role in the school. The government's responsibility, for instance, is to ensure that children receive schooling in a safe environment that teaches the "basics" so that children can function in society. Nonetheless, the primary responsibility of children's nurture rests with parents (Deuteronomy 6:7, Ephesians 6:4). The home inculcates basic attitudes toward God, other people, self, authority, and learning. Parents thus have a major effect on their children's experience in schools. They have the right to choose the type of school their children attend. The United Nations Universal Declaration of Human Rights guarantees this, for instance. Also, to be Christian communities of learning, schools need parental support and involvement. A school is a community school only to the extent that parents have a meaningful role in its operation.

Parents and teachers together need to set out a basic direction for learning and discuss crucial issues in the operation of the school. Many Christian schools involve parents in decision making as members of the board, board committees, or parent advisory councils. Most schools also hold orientation meetings for new parents as well as parent-teacher meetings that discuss educational topics. They also invite parents to shape and participate in social events.

When families and schools work together to promote learning, student learning and attitudes improve. Parental support and encouragement matter. Schools need parents to be involved with their children's schooling (Arends 2004; Oakes and Lipton 2003). For example, teachers may ask families to discuss questions or problems before they do so in school. For instance, they may ask parents to read with their children a story of an eleven-year-old boy who shoplifts a DVD, and then discuss with their children what a friend who sees this should do. Or the school may ask students to interview their parents about an ethical issue. Teachers may also ask parents to read with their children or practice numeracy skills.

Most parents, especially at the elementary levels, enjoy and appreciate giving concrete help at the discretion of classroom teachers. Not all parents can participate in this way. Low-income families in particular, although interested in the success of their children, may have little or no time to be actively involved in their children's education. Don't assume too quickly that the failure of parents to attend events or respond to volunteer opportunities means that they are not interested in how well their children do in school! Most parents today work outside the home. When they do, parental time is scarce for involvement in school-related activities.

While parental support and assistance have many benefits, some parents may make demands that create burdens for teachers and interfere with the teachers' professional judgment. In such cases, teachers may have to insist on setting boundaries. I spoke with one experienced teacher who had to tell a parent, after considering her concerns, "I am the one charged with making the best decisions for all the students in my class, including your child. I want to be responsive to your concerns. However, I do not believe that your suggestions are in the best interest of your child in the context of the whole class. Please accept my considered judgment. I do promise that I will do whatever I can to help your child be successful." New teachers are wise to seek the advice of a senior colleague or their principal in cases where they feel that parents are unduly insistent on particular approaches.

Most schools have policies about dealing with parental concerns or with complaints about library books or literature selections. Schools need to be sensitive to parents' critiques and should listen carefully to parental misgivings. At the same time, they may have to help parents find the balance between recognizing their own responsibility for their children's education and the authority and expertise of the teachers implementing the school's aims. The school as a learning community has a tradition and practices that its supporters have developed and accepted over time. Those ought to be honored. Parents cannot expect all things to be done their way. At the same time, teachers need to realize that they are not the parents. They do not have responsibility for the complete nurture of students. In some instances, if the school's vision and aims differ considerably from a parent's expectations, a parting of the ways may be necessary (Edlin 1999).

An important aspect of preserving a positive parent-teacher relationship is to report frequently and regularly to parents. A school staff can keep parents fully informed of what is happening in the school through after-school informal contact, phone calls, newsletters, websites, open houses, and parent-teacher meetings. A community informed of the school's joys and struggles is a community that is more likely to support the school. Honest communication develops mutual respect and trust.

Besides the regular parent-teacher conferences and report cards, some teachers make a point of phoning several parents each week, especially to report learning successes. Particularly at the elementary level, it is a good idea for teachers to interact informally with parents before and after school when they bring or pick up their children. Weekly or monthly newsletters (also posted on your classroom website) are important. They may include what the class is studying, new routines and expectations, upcoming projects and events, and so on. It is worthwhile to include samples of student work, making sure that the work of each student is included sometime during the year. And newsletters offer another way to celebrate special student accomplishments and volunteer contributions!

Parents, grandparents, pre-service teachers, and other volunteers can provide invaluable service to schools. Volunteers do many tasks for which teachers do not have time. Some can assist individual or small groups of students with special tasks. Many are willing to prepare learning materials for students or to put up hall displays. Some are willing to organize escorts and transportation for field trips or to help with the school's hot lunch program. Some may teach short optional courses for middle grades. Others will pray for specific school concerns. Still others help the whole school through fund-raising activities.

The presence of volunteers provides students with opportunities to relate to other adults. Students, especially those from disadvantaged homes, benefit from having other adult role models. Adult volunteers enrich students' school experience and make them realize that adults are interested in their learning and well-being. They experience a community at work. In turn, volunteers usually become more committed to the school and its programs. Parent volunteers gain a deeper understanding of what school is like for the children. Schools do well to show volunteers regular appreciation for their work, perhaps during an annual tea.

Schools can observe several cautions to ensure that volunteers contribute to and become part of the school community. They may hold an in-service session for volunteers at the start of the year. Such a session might discuss expectations, set out schedules, and emphasize that teachers count on volunteers during the designated times. Volunteers work under the direction of teachers, who provide guidelines and training and also review the expectations. Sometimes volunteers intimidate students, do their work for them, or are sloppy in carrying out tasks. In such instances the school may try to find more suitable tasks for them. If necessary, the principal may have to talk to a volunteer gently but firmly, difficult as this is when people are giving generously of their time.

Reflect and respond 8-8

Make a list of ways in which parents can contribute positively to the school as a learning community—at primary, intermediate, middle school, and high school levels. Why do you think that parents more readily volunteer at the primary level than at any other?

Then for each contribution, indicate how volunteers could also disturb the learning community. How can schools prevent or deal with such pitfalls?

Chapter 8 enduring understandings

Each of the following helps make a school a purposeful, supportive, and caring community of learning:

- A school culture in which learning is focused and meaningful, where students feel secure and respected, and where teachers are passionate about the school's vision

- A unified spiritual commitment that directs, pervades, and supports what takes place in the school
- A commitment to biblical values such as the fruit of the Spirit
- Learning in ways that enable students to be and to become emotionally and socially healthy
- Service learning and school activities that encourage students to love God and neighbor as they develop their gifts
- Policies that enhance trust throughout the learning community
- A welcoming physical environment that facilitates learning
- Purposeful collegiality that binds the staff together as they support one another in their teaching and learning responsibilities
- A climate in which everyone's voice is appreciated and in which parents and other supporters feel an integral part of the learning community

References

Anderson, R. 2004. *Religion and spirituality in the public school curriculum.* New York: Peter Lang.

Arends, R. 2004. *Learning to teach.* 6th ed. New York: McGraw-Hill.

Barry, C., and F. Tye. 1972. *Running a school.* London: Temple Smith.

Barth, R. 2002. The culture builder. *Educational Leadership* 59, no. 8:6–11.

Dovre, P. 2007. From Aristotle to Angelou: Best practices in character education. *Education Next* 7, no. 2:38–45.

Edlin. R. 2000. *The cause of Christian education.* 3rd ed. Colorado Springs, CO: Association of Christian Schools International.

Garner, B. 2007. *Getting to "Got it!" Helping struggling students learn how to learn.* Alexandria, VA: Association for Supervision and Curriculum Development.

Goleman, D. 1995. *Emotional intelligence.* New York: Bantam.

Groome, T. 1998. *Educating for life: A spiritual vision for every teacher and parent.* New York: Crossroad.

Hargreaves, A., and D. Fink. 2006. *Sustainable leadership.* San Francisco, CA: Jossey-Bass.

Howard, R., M. Berkowitz, and E. Schaeffer. 2004. Politics of character education. *Educational Policy* 18, no. 1:188–215.

Koole, R. 2006. Teachers as colleagues: Problematic ideal or genuine reality? In *Educating toward wisdom,* edited by E. Brouwer and R. Koole. Langley, BC: Society of Christian Schools in British Columbia, 2.31–2.38.

Lickona, T. 1991. *Educating for character: How our schools can teach respect and responsibility.* New York: Bantam.

Molnar, A., ed. 1997. *The construction of children's character.* 96th Yearbook, Part 2. Chicago: National Society for the Study of Education.

Oakes, J., and M. Lipton. 2003. *Teaching to change the world.* 2nd ed. New York: McGraw-Hill.

Porath, M., and D. Matthews. 1997. Development in the social/emotional domain: Critical periods and educational facilitation. Unpublished paper presented at the Canadian Society for Studies in Education. St. John's, Newfoundland, Canada.

Ryan, K., and K. Bohlin. 1999. *Building character in schools: Practical ways to bring moral instruction to life.* San Francisco, CA: Jossey-Bass.

Van Brummelen, H., K. Franklin, M. Hilder. 2005. Creating space for personal meaning in schooling. *ICCTE Journal: Journal of the International Community of Christians in Teacher Education* 1, no. 1. http://www.icctejournal.org/ICCTEJournal/past-issues/volume-1-issue-1.

Van Brummelen, H., R. Koole, and K. Franklin. 2004. Transcending the commonplace: Spirituality in the curriculum. *Journal of Educational Thought* 38, no. 3:237–254.

Willis, S. 1993. Learning through service. *ASCD Education Update* 35, no. 6:1–8.

Wolterstorff, N. 1980. *Educating for responsible action.* Grand Rapids, MI: Eerdmans.

———. 2002. *Educating for life: Reflections on Christian teaching and learning.* Grand Rapids, MI: Baker.

Wright, A. 1998. *Spiritual Pedagogy: A survey, critique and reconstruction of contemporary spiritual education in England and Wales.* Abingdon, UK: Culham College Institute.

Part Four

Serving in Public Education

A ll teachers have worldviews that influence their way of life, their thinking, their actions, and also their teaching. Therefore, a Christian worldview, all-embracing as it is, will inevitably affect a Christian teacher's approaches to teaching and learning, even in a public school setting. However, in a public school you may not promote your own faith commitment. It would not only be illegal but also improper to promote your own beliefs. Christian parents would object to a Muslim public school teacher persuading their child of the superiority of Islam. The converse is just as true. So this chapter considers the difficult issue of how you can be true to your faith while honoring the reality that public school classrooms may not favor one religious view above any other.

How Does Commitment to Jesus Christ Affect Teaching in Public Schools?

9

Chapter 9 guiding questions

- How do Christians respond to the diversity and ideological pluralism in society as it affects public schooling?
- How can Christian teachers promote joy, peace, compassion, integrity, and justice in a public school learning context?
- What is a responsible framework for teaching and learning about religion in public schools?

Patricia needs time out to think and pray about her teaching vocation. Finding a seat on a park bench, she begins to contemplate her situation: "I want to bring my faith to my vocation. But how? Can I weave the Bible into my lessons? Can I insert relevant Christian values into my units of study? Can I bring Christian books into my class? What about guest speakers I know who are Christians? May I drop an appropriate word outside of class? Will saying anything about my Christian faith to students get me into trouble? Can I speak about my faith to fellow teachers in the staff room? There certainly are opportunities, but which ones are appropriate? How can I act with integrity? I have far more questions than answers."

Patricia has used all of the above strategies since she began teaching eight years ago. Lately she has been sensing, however, that some strategies are contrived or objectionable to persons of other convictions. Her principal takes a cautious line about religion in the school. Once he told Patricia to keep her religious views to herself. He vetoed her idea of developing an elective course on world religions. The school's "Holiday Concert" may not include religious carols.

Patricia reflects, "I think the principal respected my stand when I told him my first loyalty is to Christ, then to my family, and then to my work. Still, no day goes by without my questioning how I should think about things that happen in the course of my work.

"My pastor asked me to talk about the spiritual challenges of teaching in a public school. I talked freely about the incredible privilege of shaping young lives and of being a role model. I love the chance to bring a little sunshine into the lives of needy and mixed-up children. But I wasn't sure how to answer the really puzzling questions.

"To what extent can I restrict student access to what I consider objectionable websites? How should I approach students from other cultures whose values differ from those generally accepted by Canadian society? How do I support a student who is struggling with her sexual identity? What should I do with the government science guide that requires discussion of views based on native spirituality but does not allow me to mention the possibility of intelligent design when discussing the origin of the universe? Or the social studies curriculum that plays down the role of religion in the lives of people in history? And what is my role in our curriculum committee when it considers how to weave social justice into all our courses?"

Patricia teaches social studies in a middle school in a suburb of a large city. Her 450-student school opened twelve years ago. Located in a middle-class neighborhood, it has recently received an influx of immigrants, mostly from India. A close-by aboriginal band also sends some of its children to the school.

Patricia's experience will sound familiar to many Christians. Canada and the United States, for instance, have seen a dramatic increase of people with different ethnic origins and different religious beliefs. At the same time, long-term residents, while often still believing in God, have taken on varied lifestyles and commitments. The impact of this diversity will undoubtedly continue, especially in our school systems.

Many Christian teachers look at this cultural, religious, and ideological diversity and look for direction in a situation so different from the one in which they were educated. They ask, "How can I respond in a Christian manner to this diversity?"

This chapter is a revision of parts of two documents that I coauthored. The introduction, the next three sections, and the dream in the conclusion are an edited version of *Diversity and Faithfulness: Reflections for Christian Teachers on Plurality and Pluralism in Canadian Public Schools* (Evangelical Fellowship of Canada 1996). The authors were members of the Task Force on Education of the Evangelical Fellowship of Canada. The sections on promising curriculum approaches and a framework for teaching about religion in public schools are an edited version of sections of the paper by Van Brummelen, Koole, and Franklin (1996) listed in the references. I appreciate receiving permission to use these documents. I take full responsibility for the content and its editing.

Diversity and ideological pluralism in public schooling

As she rides home on the bus, Patricia sighs when she remembers Roger, one of her eighth-grade students, telling her yesterday, "Well, my opinions are just as good as yours!"

Patricia had given a test question in which she tried to elicit how society can be supportive and just in dealing with the problems facing Canada's aboriginal people. Roger said, without giving reasons, that all people in society have equal opportunity to advance themselves and that any special provisions discriminate against "us." He had been upset that she had not given him full marks.

But, Patricia thinks, while I have failed to convince Roger of what I consider to be a more considerate and just approach, to what extent can my teaching promote my biblical values of compassion, mercy, and justice? In a democratic society, we don't always agree on the values we should uphold. To what extent should I tolerate Roger's views? To what extent may I oppose them?

As she reflects, Patricia opens a reference book the librarian has asked her to review. It is a comparative-religions text titled Worldviews: The Challenge of Choice. *She almost dozes off when her eyes flicker on the word* tolerance. *It jerks her back to reality. "That's it!" she says out loud. The startled woman sitting beside her darts a puzzled look at her. Patricia apologizes, then goes back to the beginning of the paragraph. She reads,*

> Living ethically requires that individuals and whole societies distinguish clearly those things that should be tolerated and those that should be celebrated. Today, many Canadians tend to think that tolerance is a virtue in itself, as if tolerating all differences is admirable. Yet, most of us do not want a society in which beating up people we disagree with or the ancient Chinese tradition of foot binding is tolerated. As well, too much talk of tolerance undermines the sense that some of our differences are worthy of celebration. Racial difference might inspire celebration—not merely tolerance—once we pause to wonder that there are so many unique kinds of people in the world. (Badley 1996, 28)

The author outlines a continuum of responses to cultural, religious, and ethical diversity. The continuum ranges from what can be celebrated *in a pluralist society (such as personal and racial diversity), what can be* respected *(such as differing religious holidays), and what can be* tolerated *(such as inconveniences due to linguistic differences) to what requires* assimilation *(such as obeying the same set of traffic laws) or outright* annihilation *(such as child abuse).*

"That's the problem," Patricia thinks. "My convictions seem to sound disrespectful because I do not accept all differences, especially differences of opinions, as equally valid and not open to discussion. Badley's continuum seems to be a helpful way to distinguish things. Now I just have to figure out what issue fits into what category...." She begins to make notes.

Patricia's student Roger reflects a prevalent attitude in today's society. This view encourages us to be "tolerant" of all viewpoints and values. It urges us to recognize that there are equally valid different ways to believe and to behave. Some years ago a Canadian survey asked, "Is what is right and wrong a matter of personal opinion?" More than half the respondents in every age group said yes. Even 49 per cent of weekly church attenders agreed!

When more than half the population holds that values are just a matter of personal choice, it is no wonder that Patricia feels tension. If the people she deals with in school hold to ideological pluralism, then her attempts to answer difficult questions will seem no better than anyone else's answers. If she openly bases her response to an issue on her beliefs, she may well be met with, "What gives you a corner on the truth?"

Yet Patricia has to do much more in her classroom than teach basic skills. She has to bring meaning to all kinds of topics and issues related to life. She has to prepare children from a wide diversity of backgrounds to become contributing members of society. Indeed, in a very real sense, the battle for how people will view life is being played out every day in all classrooms.

During the last half of the twentieth century, many philosophers critiqued the modern world. Faith in reason and science had led to irresolvable problems. These scholars no longer saw any hope for unique, external, transcendent truth. They concluded that nothing can be known with certainty. Truth is elusive, subjective, and relative. Quests for universal truth must be abandoned. For those who hold to the philosophy of ideological pluralism, this approach to truth is both desirable and normative. It allows for all views found within a multicultural and multireligious society to be accepted as equally valid.

Many Christian teachers today are faced with students who come from a wide range of cultural and religious backgrounds. Moreover, ideological pluralism shapes the thinking of many colleagues, students, and parents. So how do Christian teachers respond in this context?

The Bible describes how God's people dealt with diversity under different circumstances. In Old Testament Israel, neither cultural nor religious pluralism was to be tolerated. However, God's people found themselves in a totally different situation when living in exile. So the prophet Jeremiah suggested a surprisingly different approach: "Seek the peace and prosperity of the city to which I have carried you into exile. Pray to the Lord for it, because if it prospers, you too will prosper" (Jeremiah 29:7). God's intent was to rebuild Israel into a people who could remain faithful in the midst of a culture that upheld religious views and values hostile to those of the Jews.

Similarly, Christian believers in New Testament times had no part in the political or the religious establishment. They could not establish cultural and religious uniformity, nor did God instruct them to do so. Jesus Himself showed tolerance and respect for those of other cultures. The Gospels include many stories of His interaction with non-Jews. This shocked even His disciples. For Paul also, cultural diversity was not an issue. He related to those of other cultures and beliefs. Paul's defense of the faith before Festus and Agrippa, two dominant political leaders of his day, shows us how he understood his role in the diversity of public life in the first century.

The situation faced by Christian teachers in public schools is more similar to that of the Jews in exile and the early Christians in the Roman Empire than it is to the nation of Israel. We do not have a social consensus based on shared belief in Jesus Christ. We are not able to model all institutions on biblical principles. Yet, we must find ways of living and teaching in faithfulness to God in a diverse society in which ideological pluralism is a major force.

We celebrate cultural and ethnic diversity in our schools as a gift, even when it complicates our teaching task. At the same time, seeking the "peace and prosperity" of our schools does not mean that we surrender our faith. Rather, we strive to prosper our students, our schools, and our society while we respectfully uphold our religious and ethical beliefs. Before we consider suitable classroom strategies, let us discuss more fully how we can respond to ideological pluralism.

Reflect and respond 9-1

Think of situations and views on issues involving diversity that arise in public school settings. In which situations should you respond with (a) celebration, (b) respect, (c) tolerance, (d) assimilation, and (e) annihilation? Compare your list with that of others. Can you suggest some criteria for placing a situation or view into each category?

Responding to ideological pluralism

When Patricia returns Badley's book to the school librarian, her eye catches a clipped newspaper column. The columnist, Michael Valpy, writes, "Religion in a liberal society belongs in private culture, in the family, and the house of faith. It does not belong in the public school system, which is our most important instrument of socialization, citizenship and community for all."

"Well," Patricia thinks out loud, "Doesn't Valpy recognize that his view to completely exclude religion from public education is an ideology or religion in its own right? Can't he see that his ultimate commitment is to a secularism that *purposely excludes religious considerations from life in society? How can he suppose that we can separate our beliefs and our worldview from who we are as teachers and from how and what we teach? Does he really think that any teaching can be 'neutral'? Can't he see that his worldview would exclude those from public schools who want children to deal with how they make sense of this world and the purpose and meaning of their lives? Doesn't he realize that questions of ultimate importance are inherently religious and value-based, and that their exclusion reduces education to training?"*

The school librarian has come in. "Oh, yes, Patricia, our science department head gave me that Valpy column when he realized that I was adding books on religion to our collection. How do you think I should answer him? And what did you think of the Badley book?"

Patricia says, "The Badley book deals with worldviews and religions in a fair way. It will deepen students' insight into how we can live together in a diverse society without giving up our own views. It gets into some really important questions about life. In fact, if you can order a few more copies, I'd like to use it later this year as a resource in my eighth-grade social studies class."

She continues, "Let's invite our science department head to have a coffee with us. He thinks that all of us should take off our religious hats when we enter the school. But I'd like to explain how no one can delete their basic views every time they step into their classrooms. I think I can show that he, like me, lives out his life and his teaching on the basis of what he believes to be of ultimate importance. Maybe we can discuss how I can deal with the role of religion in cultures around the world in a respectful and responsible way."

As we saw, religious diversity is a reality in Western countries. It includes an increasing number of people who no longer adhere to any institutional religion. However, that does not mean that the public arena is or can be religiously neutral, or that religion is only a private matter. Religion or ideology is the underlying commitment that provides personal and communal direction to life. It comprises what is of ultimate importance to a person, a community, or an institution. It shapes the worldview bases for human enterprise.

Christians cannot accept how ideological pluralism views religion: *Society must accept all religious points of view as equally valid. All religions can lead persons to God or to spiritual contentment. But religious views may not affect our actions in the public arena, including public schools.* This philosophy of life discards the clear identity and relevance of faith in Christ. It also takes great liberty in reducing all religious traditions to privately held points of view. It trivializes religion when it claims that religions can be excluded from public life or that all religions share a common core. Thus, it saps the vitality of faith from civilization. It is no accident, for instance, that nations with a positive human rights record generally have Christian roots, or that persons with a religious faith commitment donate most to the poor and dispossessed in the world.

The inability of ideological pluralism to deal with ethical issues may well lead to a growing realization that Christian faith has something to offer to public life after all. Recent history—the end of the twentieth and the start of the twenty-first century—has certainly seen an increased interest in teaching about spirituality and ethics in North American public schools. That means that Christian teachers have an increased opportunity to show themselves to be committed to the common good while living to honor God and His creation. They can explore the importance of religious commitment with their students and can demonstrate how religious belief is relevant to public life.

Christian educators ought to articulate the nucleus of values and the crucial institutions that are the glue for social coherence and for a civil and just society. They will uphold values such as mutual respect, responsibility, economic equity, social justice, and environmental integrity. The game rules for society must include civility and a respect for minorities, as well as a desire for integrity and compassion.

Christian teachers will also want to enter into dialogue with educational partners whose beliefs reflect society's diversity. That means participating in genuine, serious interaction among competing claims of truth. Tolerance does not mean accepting all points of view as valid. Rather, it means that we respect the right of people to hold and assert views that differ fundamentally from our own. As Stephen Webb (2000, 55) says, "Teachers with a strong faith frequently are the ones who are most sensitive to the various religious beliefs of their students."

Paul's second and third missionary journeys took him into cities whose citizens had worldviews very different from his. On numerous occasions Luke describes how Paul dialogued with his listeners, sometimes for several years. Paul explained his premises by opening people's minds to his ideas (Acts 17–19, 25–26). He gave them reasons to accept his point of view (Acts 17–18, 26). He treated them with respect (Acts 17:22, 26:25).

Our interaction with students and colleagues about faith commitments should similarly develop full and mutual understanding and should respect cultural and religious differences. This applies particularly to the diverse "lived values" within the culture of all ethnic and religious groups. Exchange of ideas develops attitudes and mentalities that welcome various cultures and lifestyles within a society. Such understanding will also see this variety as an enrichment of human life. At the same time, dialogue is not merely a tolerant, intellectual assent of shared opinions. Rather, it is a process whereby respectful exchange about differences results in deeper mutual understanding. We learn how we can live together without hiding or compromising our own beliefs.

Reflect and respond 9-2

Patricia's seventh-grade class was studying Pacific Coast First Nations (Indian) society. One group made a presentation on totem poles, and the subject of religion came up. The students seemed to feel that First Nations religion could be freely discussed and admired but that it was somehow out of place to consider and discuss their own religious beliefs.

Patricia pointed out that the same Charter of Human Rights that protects the rights of and freedoms of others also protected the rights of each student to explain his or her religious faith. "And the teacher," said a student, and then added, "What religion are you?"

How would you as a public school teacher use this opportunity? To what extent and in what ways does your answer depend on the age of the students?

Christian teachers in the public school classroom

So how can Christians teach within the ideological diversity of public school classrooms? What can they do in a context in which the meaning of life is uncertain and in flux—a context in which many students think that nothing can be known for certain and that truth is relative? How can Christians teach with integrity in an ever-changing pluralism? How can they contribute to the development of public culture?

Part of the answer begins with how you react to differences in the school and in the classroom. It is important that you discern the difference between what people do and say and who they are. Do not reject anyone because of that person's belief system or actions. Far too often, fear comes from a lack of understanding. In that case, one's identity rests on gender, race, language, class, religion, or even one's region of origin. Then differences may become inherently threatening.

You could spend some time in the community around the school and get to know the people who live there. You might also have someone come and describe the experiences of those who come from different cultural communities. This would provide a good opportunity for you to see how your students react to diversity. You may find it easier to preserve your own Christian identity if you realize how solid your identity appears to others.

Furthermore, you could expose your students to diverse settings, such as a Sikh temple or a local First Nations longhouse or a Christian church. This creates opportunities to discuss the development of the common public culture. You can also ask questions: What are the rights and responsibilities of minorities in the culture? Do we have a utopian view of other cultures? What are our stereotypes?

In this context you can build bridges. Don't assume that you really know the individual who is different. Instead, ask good questions. Be an active listener. Invite yourself into the home of a person with whom you are developing a relationship. Live with integrity, operating from a set of principles that come from God's perspective. Try to approach situations in the same way that Jesus dealt with His real-world situations—with compassion and integrity.

Bring into your curriculum the discussion of the role of religion in the lives of individuals and cultures around the world. Lead your students to the questions that deal with ultimate meaning and purpose in life. Without indoctrinating students into your own beliefs, look for opportunities to share with them how you answer those questions. Always respect the ways in which your students answer those questions for themselves.

Above all, live in such a way that you put to the lie the idea that religious belief makes no difference in your public life. And, by God's grace, do so in confidence and joy, remaining faithful to the God who created you, sustains you, and calls you into loving service.

Promising curriculum approaches

A number of public school boards have developed explicit policies on the inclusion of religion in their classrooms.

One of the largest public school boards in Canada has decided that since religion is an integral part of human life, it must be discussed when relevant to the curriculum (Dirks 2007). Teachers must help students understand human religious impulse as an ongoing quest for truth. They must nurture an appreciation of the spiritual and religious history of humanity. So its high schools offer courses in world religions and religious meaning. The elementary school curriculum explores

266 of the Classroom

the role of religion and how it affects our identity. A character education program encourages students to act ethically. While parents overwhelmingly favor the policy, what is disappointing that it also prohibits teachers from describing their own beliefs, even at higher grade levels.

The First Amendment Center in the United States, backed by a broad array of educational, civic, and religious stakeholders, also promotes the teaching about religion in an objective way (Haynes and Thomas 2001). A number of helpful publications are available for download on the First Amendment Center website. The center recommends that religion be taught for awareness and insight into a diversity of religions. It adds that this should not be done for the practice of or adherence to any religion. Nor may it promote or denigrate the ideals of any religion.

You cannot avoid, however, the fact that religion is a matter of both mind and heart. Therefore, be careful not to despiritualize religion by teaching it in a purely cognitive, rational way. Stimulate an understanding of what motivates humans. Encourage explorations of spiritual meaning.

As Nord and Haynes (1998) show, you can meaningfully weave the study of worldviews and religions into almost all subject areas. In history, you can explore how the ideals and beliefs of people have affected cultures, both positively and negatively. Students cannot understand history without considering religion as a powerful and ever-present force. For instance, William Wilberforce's strong commitment to evangelical Christian faith was the basis for his successful fight to abolish slavery in the British Empire. The California State Board of Education (1991) stresses that since religion has been a decisive factor in history, the curriculum must include its study (including biblical literature since it is essential for understanding Western history and values). The history of art and music also often manifests the role of religion in shaping culture. And students cannot comprehend secularization and its effects, a major theme of modern history, without studying religious worldviews.

Literature helps students grow in their personal insight about reality and meaning. Books as diverse as *The Lion, the Witch and the Wardrobe* and *Brave New World* lead to discussions of what is good or evil and the source of morality, values, and views of life. You can choose and teach literature selections to nurture students' moral imagination (Van Brummelen, Franklin, and Hilder 2005). Even the meaninglessness of life expressed in some modern literature can lead to significant discussions about basic beliefs. Anderson (2004) suggests that teachers can also involve families in consideration of crucial existential issues raised in literature studied in class. Indeed, "properly considered, the study of family, community, various cultures, the nation, and other key themes and topics important in the early grades all require some discussion of religion" (Nord and Haynes 1998, 63).

Teaching of religion is also important since adherents of particular religions—as well as adherents of no religion—often have stereotypical views of other faiths. The Islamic scholar Susan Douglass (2002, 33) argues that "learning about the history, cultures, and belief systems of peoples who share the globe engenders respect and understanding."

Make sure, however, that the study is not so superficial that it creates caricatures. Give historical and current coverage of major religions in a fair and balanced way. Also, take into account your local context and the diversity of religious views held by families in your school community. Promote the search for truth while not favoring any particular religious or ideological position. Encourage your students to weigh alternative points of view.

Incorporating life's "big questions" is another promising approach. Neglecting such big questions in school classrooms will not make them disappear. Indeed, disregard may contribute to students' living a shallow, consumer-oriented life. Or it may convince them that school has little relevance for life's real issues and questions. So explore questions such as these:

- Who am I? What is the purpose and meaning of my life? How can I experience fulfillment?
- What should I believe? Does a God exist? How do I know?
- How do I deal with loneliness, suffering, and death?
- How can I connect meaningfully with others and reach out to them with compassion and justice?

Plan to pose such questions in your curriculum. But also invite and stimulate students to raise questions. In mathematics, they may ask, "How can we be sure of anything?" In science, they may wonder, "What is the origin of the universe? What is life?" In the arts, encourage them to express their thoughts and inmost feelings and how these affect and transform them. In social studies, explore how justice can help us deal with compassion for other humans and with responsibility for the common good. In literature, help your students delve into themselves. Wonder with them about ultimate ethical and spiritual concerns in life, about their deepest convictions, and about their hopes and fears.

In all this, do not impose your own views. Rather, help students pose and answer "questions that are worth asking because they are worth living, questions worth wrapping one's life around" (Palmer 1999, 8). Life cannot be lived with true vitality and worth without a consideration of such questions. They touch the heart of our existence, including our spiritual selves.

One way to structure your units so that you deal with life's deeper issues is to use a revision of the questions of Chapter 3 as a basis for planning:

- If the area of reality or culture we are studying were perfect, what would it be like?
- What has happened to make it flawed? How have humans contributed to its imperfection?
- How can we respond so that things may be set right again, at least in part?
- How can we look forward with courage and hope?

These questions do not apply to all topics that you teach. But often your students' answers will provide a deeper perspective than what is presented in your textbooks or other resources.

Reflect and respond 9-3

Think about a curriculum topic with which you are familiar (e.g., a novel study, a history unit, or a science topic). How could you incorporate some of the foregoing promising practices in your teaching?

A framework for teaching about religion in public schools

As a teacher you can include spirituality and religion in your curriculum in meaningful and nonindoctrinating ways. However, this will not be without difficulty or controversy. Learning outcomes in government curriculum guides generally steer clear of the spiritual dimension of life. You may feel pressures to narrowly focus your program on the content of high-stakes standardized tests.

As soon as spirituality or religion is taught in the curriculum, some people will be concerned about bias. Parents for whom religion is important may fear that teachers, especially those without religious faith, will promote the view that any one religious commitment—or no commitment—is as good as any other. Or they worry that teachers will promote Valpy's view that religion should be limited to the private part of life. Still others may be concerned about bias, whether that is for native spirituality or against Christian or Islamic beliefs. Yet if schools steer clear of any mention of religion, they promote its irrelevance in life. The basic difficulty of teaching spirituality in the curriculum is that there is no one widely accepted approach.

Worldviews—whether religious, areligious, or antireligious—give rival comprehensive visions of life. Aspects of these are mutually exclusive. Some people feel so strongly about their own faith and values that they do not want their children exposed to any contradictory views. Yet avoiding the study of religion and spirituality in public education has led to the indoctrination of a secular, materialistic worldview. Then meaning is often implicitly defined in terms of efficiency in achieving standards and skills that, by themselves, impoverish the human spirit.

Within a pluralistic society, public education cannot promote one particular religious or areligious point of view. So explain diverse views without favoring any. Avoid coercing students implicitly or explicitly to accept any particular view. Do not present or advance a position unfairly vis-à-vis other positions. At the same time, do not curtail your students' growth toward rational autonomy. Your students must feel free to express their views openly, without real or perceived repercussions.

It is neither possible nor desirable for you to remain entirely neutral. Yet you must be as fair as possible to all positions examined in class. You "need to allow for real discussions about personal issues—in ways that are suitable to the students' level of development and interest," responding responsibly and appropriately "to the religious lives of [your] students and the specific nature of faith itself" (Webb 2000, 61–62). Pedagogically it is wise not to present your own views on issues and the reasons for them until students have fully investigated and conveyed their personal response. Still, as philosopher Mary Warnock (1996) has argued, it is important for you to show how you have reached personal conclusions. Your students need to see how you, as an adult role model, have come to grips with basic and controversial questions about life. If you neglect to reveal that you have a position, students may well interpret your attempts at remaining totally neutral as indifference.

You need to take into account children's ages. You can easily influence young children. Particularly with them, you need to be careful to honor the rights of parents to nurture children in a particular faith tradition. Also, remember that some school boards have a policy that does not allow you to express your own religious beliefs. Such a policy may not be easy to interpret (e.g., can you then not say that you believe that we should love our neighbor as ourselves?). Nonetheless, teaching for a public school board means that you agree to abide by its policies.

Here are some guidelines for the teaching of religion and spirituality in public schools:

- *Respect students as individuals of worth and dignity.* Earnestly consider and give sensitive response to students' insights into questions of existence and the transcendent. Ask probing questions, but allow freedom of response and respect diverse positions.
- *Offer elective courses in religious meaning and world religions in middle and high school.* If your school does not offer such courses, ask whether you may develop and teach one.

- *Introduce students to a diversity of religions and worldviews.* Present them, as well as tensions within and between them, in fair and respectful ways. Provide "critical access to alternative traditions so that informed insight and wisdom may flourish through the development of spiritual literacy" (Wright 1998, 97). Teach your students about different worldview and religious traditions when studying history, cultures, the impact of science and technology, and literature.

- *Have students consider how the transcendent can and does lead to transformation for many people.* All major religious traditions except Buddhism believe that a "Transcendental Reality" or God is the essence of the Being whom they worship; Buddhism neither affirms nor denies the presence of God (Ashraf 1997).

- *Help your students see that particular values common to most traditions contribute to the good of humankind.* Values held in common by most traditions include truth, justice, loving-kindness, forgiveness, compassion, peace, responsibility, and prudent care of reality (Lewis 1947).

- *Permeate your curriculum with a sense of mystery, imagination, and awe.* Align development of spirituality with imaginative and inspired opportunities for glimpses of the transcendent and the mysterious.

Within these contours, help students realize how religious traditions define an all-encompassing way of life. Allow them to respond in a personal but justified way. Inspire an ongoing commitment to the creative pursuit and expression of truth in the face of life's ultimate mysteries. In short, while you may not promote your own beliefs, help students recognize that the religious dimension of life is a significant and evocative one. Also challenge them to develop an awareness of and responsiveness to the need for respect, compassion, hospitality, and justice, both within their personal networks and within the global village.

Obeying God's calling in public education

That night Patricia had a dream. She dreamt that her principal was recuperating from a car accident. She went to visit him in the hospital. They reminisced for a while about the school, and then the principal started saying surprising things:

"You Christians bring a distinctive flavor into our school, and I want to thank you. Your attitude goes beyond being a good professional. You genuinely look out for the well-being of others, both staff and students. Others come first for you.

"You don't let the negativism of the staff room bury you. You model a spirit of joy and hope. Even when you're frustrated, you don't explode. It's not a stoical, grit-your-teeth sort of thing; you have a nice blend of realism and serenity. No matter how crazy it gets around here, you seem confident that everything's okay. Some of the rest of us don't cope with stress quite so well. Your patience has a hidden source or resource

within you somewhere.

"Because you are kind to others, you seem to bring out the goodness in them. In your words and actions there's a gentleness that is not weak or pathetic, but confident and authoritative.

"I know I can always rely on you. Not that you'll always agree with me! But you'll be truthful and straight with me. Students and parents have said the same thing; so has the secretary. Last week—the day before my accident—in our difficult interview with Roger and his mother, you were honest and direct, but you were also amazingly courteous and restrained.

"I've enjoyed every minute I've spent sitting in your classroom. You're not afraid to handle sensitive ethical issues or questions of religious significance. Some of us would be too unsure of ourselves to handle the differences of opinion that come up in these situations, but you respect the students' opinions and aren't afraid to share your own without pushing them.

"Your kids really respond well to your willingness to share what moves you, what gives your life meaning. Not all of us share your Christian beliefs. But we all could take lessons from you about how to teach about religion without indoctrinating at the same time.

"You know what strikes me? You're able to celebrate the differences among us that contribute to the richness of our school experience. You respect other opinions even when they clash with yours. Where you're convinced that differences will cause harm or injury to others, you're ready to step in and ask for assimilation into healthier ways of doing things. And you're not afraid to demand annihilation of harmful ways of thinking or acting. I remember, for instance, when you marched those students who were using racist and sexist language down to my office.

"It's funny, you know, I wouldn't use the word tolerant *to describe your attitude. You're always respectful, but you're not afraid to ask for change when it's needed.*

"If these things come out of your religious convictions, you have my permission to exercise that in your classroom. I couldn't restrict these things even if I wanted to. But why would I want to? We need more of what you bring, not less!"

Patricia had little to say in response. It was evident that her principal had had lots of time to think. They went on to talk about more personal matters, and Patricia was able to end her visit with a short time of prayer.

When she woke the next morning, Patricia read something that gave her a fresh sense of purpose about her role in the school. Her devotional reading included a passage from Jeremiah 6:16: "This is what the Lord says: 'Stand at the crossroads and look; ask for the ancient paths, ask where the good way is, and walk in it, and you will find rest for your souls.' "

"Okay, Lord," she said, "It's a crossroads out there where You've placed me. Sometimes I don't know which way to turn. Help me to experience Your rest in my soul and to be a crossing guard for those at school who are searching for direction."

Teaching about religion is only one way to "seek the peace and prosperity" of the public school where you teach. The prophet Jeremiah, in fact, immediately adds that we must pray for our city (that is, our *school!*) "because if it prospers, you too will prosper" (Jeremiah 29:7). We pray for our students, our colleagues, our administration, and our board.

There are many more ways in which we can seek the peace and prosperity of our schools. The principal in Patricia's dream mentions some. We model a Christian lifestyle by supporting our students and partner teachers. We develop relationships and exhibit servant leadership based on the example of Jesus Christ. We teach to the best of our ability. We demonstrate both justice and mercy in dealing with difficult student issues.

Further, as we gain teaching experience, we can become involved with and contribute to developing curriculum initiatives. We can also try to overcome the divisive polarization that often characterizes union and management relations (Edlin 2000).

Above all, as a public school teacher you work at creating a warm and supportive learning community in which students feel secure and accepted. You want your students to feel respected and appreciated as humans who are created in the image of God. You want your students to feel free to share their burdens as well as their successes in a supportive setting. You do this because you want your students to develop their insights, abilities, and dispositions in optimal ways.

You help your students become positive and contributing members of society. You want them to recognize and experience the importance of a purposeful and value-based life. You help them see beyond the individualistic materialism and the relativism of modern society. You want them to sense the importance of seeing life as a quest for truth. And then you pray that Truth may at some point in their life take hold of them.

In doing this, you obey God's calling, and He will prosper you.

Reflect and respond 9-4

You can walk with God in your classroom no matter where it is located. Think back to the three injunctions that God gives us as believers: the Creation Mandate, the Great Commandment, and the Great Commission. How does each of these affect you when you teach in a public school classroom?

Chapter 9 enduring understandings

• Cultural and religious diversity is a fact of life in Western nations. Christian teachers welcome cultural diversity and respect students of all backgrounds—the way Jesus did.

• Ideological pluralism, on the other hand, holds that all beliefs and values are equally valid. This in itself is a "religious" faith, one that runs counter to Christian beliefs. It also leads to the view that religious views must be excluded from public life.

• Christian teachers in public schools have the right to lead students to questions that deal with ultimate meaning and purpose in life. They may teach about religion and spiritual issues. However, they may not promote their own beliefs, and they must respect the diverse views of their students.

• God calls Christian teachers to contribute to the well-being of their students and their schools, no matter what their context. They do so by striving to develop classroom and school communities of respect, peace, trust, justice, and mercy within which people can develop their abilities for the common good.

References

Anderson, R. 2004. *Religion and spirituality in the public school curriculum*. New York: Peter Lang.

Ashraf, S. 1997. The Islamic response: Faith-based education in a multifaith multicultural country. In *Agenda for educational change*, ed. J. Shortt and T. Cooling. Leicester, UK: Apollos, 269–79.

Badley, K. 1996. *Worldviews: The challenge of choice*. Toronto: Irwin Publishing.

California State Board of Education. 1991. *Moral and civic education and teaching about religion*. Rev. ed. Sacramento, CA: California Department of Education.

Dirks, G. 2007. Religion and public schooling at the Calgary Board of Education: A case study. Session 5-1 in *The Cooperation of Church and State Conference*. Video recording. Ottawa, ON: The Centre for Cultural Renewal.

Douglass, S. 2002. Teaching about religion. *Educational Leadership*, 60, no. 2:32–36.

Edlin, R. 2000. *The cause of Christian education*. 3rd ed. Colorado Springs, CO: Association of Christian Schools International.

Evangelical Fellowship of Canada. 1996. *Diversity and faithfulness: Reflections for Christian teachers on plurality and pluralism in Canadian public schools*. Markham, ON: Evangelical Fellowship of Canada.

First Amendment Center. http://www.firstamendmentcenter.org.

Ghosh, R., and A. Abdi. 2004. *Education and the politics of difference: Canadian perspectives*. Toronto, ON: Canadian Scholars' Press.

Haynes, C., and O. Thomas. 2001. Finding common ground: A guide to religious liberty in public schools. Nashville, TN: First Amendment Center. (Also available at
http://www.mediastudies.org/templates/document.asp?documentID=3979.)

Lewis, C. S. 1943. *The abolition of man*. New York: Macmillan. (Full text available at
http://www.columbia.edu/cu/augustine/arch/lewis/abolition1.htm).

Nord, W., and C. Haynes. 1998. *Taking religion seriously across the curriculum*. Alexandria, VA: Association for Supervision and Curriculum Development.

Palmer, P. 1999. Evoking the spirit in public education. *Educational Leadership* 56, no.
4:6–11.

Van Brummelen, H., K. Franklin, M. Hilder. 2005. Creating space for personal meaning
in schooling. *ICCTE Journal: Journal of the International Community of Christians
in Teacher Education* 1, no. 1. http://www.icctejournal.org/ICCTEJournal/past-
issues/volume-1-issue-1.

Van Brummelen, H., R. Koole, and K. Franklin. 2004. Transcending the commonplace:
Spirituality in the curriculum. *The Journal of Educational Thought* 38, no. 3:237–54.

Warnock, M. 1996. The neutral teacher. In *Philosophy of education: Introductory readings*,
ed. W. Hare and J. Portelli. 2nd ed. Calgary: Detselig Enterprises, 139–48.

Webb, S. 2000. *Taking religion to school: Christian theology and secular education*. Grand
Rapids, MI: Brazos Press.

Wright, A. 1998. *Spiritual pedagogy: A survey, critique and reconstruction of contemporary
spiritual education in England and Wales*. Abingdon, UK: Culham College Institute.

Epilogue: Teaching as a Journey

If you've chosen to be a teacher, you've chosen a noble vocation. Once you have become a teacher, however, you have not reached a destination. Rather, you've reached the start of a journey. At times it will be a thrilling journey. At times it will be quietly rewarding. At times, it will be a trying journey. After some years, you will be able to reflect on what your journey has been. I pray that then you will see it as a fulfilling journey. What will have made your journey fulfilling is that you felt the Spirit of the Lord resting on and guiding you and your students: "the Spirit of wisdom and of understanding, the Spirit of counsel and of power, and the Spirit of knowledge and of the fear of the Lord" (Isaiah 11:2). May the joy of the Lord be your strength as you and your students journey in concert.

Rising above the frustrations of teaching

Teaching is a rewarding calling, but it is not without frustration and stress. The irritating behavior of some students may sometimes be too much. Demands for curriculum changes or extracurricular activities on top of your regular teaching and preparation may overwhelm you. It may bother you that not all students or parents like you or agree with your approaches. There are days when your students or you yourself would rather be anywhere but in the classroom. You may develop a case of February doldrums. At times, you may even become somewhat bored with your own teaching. You think you have prepared a great lesson; then it bombs, and you feel deflated. The legal obligation to report suspected abuse gnaws at you since you cannot be fully certain that it is occurring.

Such aggravations and the resulting stress are a natural part of teaching. Accept that they will occur. Learn to cope with them. First, take time for personal devotions and reflections. Speak to God and speak with a trusted colleague about your frustrations. Ponder why those frustrating events are occurring and how you may be able to overcome them.

Do you need to improve your competence in certain areas of teaching? If so, get some advice and help. Are you overtired? See whether you can change your schedule to make sure you get enough sleep. Find some time for relaxation. Do you feel defeated or overwhelmed? Think about ways to cope with your responsibilities. Talk to someone about your situation. Learn to present your views positively to parents. Listen carefully to parents, but accept that not all will see things your way.

Accept that all good teachers have lessons that fail. Perhaps the only ones who don't, in fact, are those who play it so safe that little excitement about learning exists in their classrooms—an approach that brings its own stress! Keep your students and yourself interested by changing your strategies. Sometimes tell your students how you feel, and, yes, ask them to keep that in mind during that day.

As a teacher, you need a support group. If you are a new teacher, it is helpful to be teamed up with an experienced mentor. If you don't have one now, seek one out. Help build a group of teachers in your school who care for and support one another. Help create an atmosphere in which teachers can share their joys and their difficulties. Teaching can become lonely when you isolate yourself.

I made the mistake when I began teaching of assuming that it was a sign of weakness not to solve problems by myself. I had one very difficult ninth-grade class. I did have to come to grips with the situation, of course. However, I would have benefited a great deal from discussing it with and being mentored by one or two experienced colleagues.

When you face difficulties or ethical dilemmas, discuss them with someone you trust. God did not create us just as individuals. Christ has apportioned grace to each of us not only to carry out our God-given role with our students but also to support and build up one another in love (Ephesians 4:7).

Being a guide on the journey of teaching

Teaching is a journey, a journey to which the Master calls you. During the journey, He wants you to help those He has put in your care to be and become responsive disciples. He gives you guidelines for the journey. Here are some of them:

- Act justly, love mercy, and walk humbly with God (Micah 6:8).
- Look not only to your own interests, but also to the interests of others (Philippians 2:4).
- Let the little children come to Jesus, and do not hinder them (Matthew 19:14).
- Tell the next generation the praiseworthy deeds of the Lord, His power, and the wonders He has done (Psalm 78:4).

- Teach the children to obey everything that God has commanded (Matthew 28:20).
- Set an example by doing what is good; in your teaching show integrity, seriousness, and soundness of speech (Titus 2:7–8).

But the Master leaves specific decision making up to you. He also wants *you* to be responsive and responsible. Which highways, roads, or trails do you take? Which turns do you make at crossroads? Which means do you use to make progress? Where do you linger? Whom do you keep with your group, and whom do you send forward or hold back?

The journey of teaching is a peculiar one, however. You usually make more progress toward your destination by walking or riding a bicycle than by taking an express train or a jet. A successful journey allows your group, under your guidance, time to explore the byways. You deliberately seek out some barriers that your group has to overcome. You help them sample and make use of the resources along the way, not so much to speed up the journey as to improve it.

You do not allow your group members to be passengers who just give one another an impersonal greeting at the beginning and end of the journey. Instead, you have them interact so that they become a company of travelers whose various abilities contribute to the communal goals. You guide your company so that the travelers can cope with personal and group failures and frustrations. Then you stand back to rejoice in success. In the end, you have not traveled as far as you might have. Yet, you have brought your group—and yourself—much closer to your destination than you would have done had you sped from one point to another. In the process, you have enriched each member of the company. You yourself have become a wiser, more insightful, more loving travel guide and companion.

However, not all journeys are successful ones. Some are unhappy. Perhaps the chemistry of your group constantly undermines progress. Perhaps your group members have little or no interest in the journey. Perhaps you do not have a clear vision of the aim of your journey, and your group makes little headway. Perhaps you do not know enough about the terrain, or the landscape has little that is worth exploring. Perhaps you do not have the patience or the ability to deal with the human dynamics in your group. Perhaps you set out to be a friend but forget that you are first of all a guide. Perhaps you cannot relate well to children at your group's age level. Perhaps your comments and reactions cut down members of the company rather than building them up.

Whether or not any of these possibilities apply to you, ask yourself why you want to set out on the journey of teaching. A requirement for a successful journey is that you have ideals, a vision of how the journey should impact the members of your company. If you have never before embarked on a journey of teaching, spend some time with groups of children and teenagers—if not in a school, then in a church, a camp, or a recreational setting. Do you enjoy being with and leading groups? (That experience differs from working with individual children!) Do you relate well with children of certain age groups? Are there some groups that make you feel uncomfortable or impatient? Do you respect children and teens even when they have values that differ from yours or when they belong to different socioeconomic or ethnic groups or when they declare a homosexual orientation? Do you enjoy working with children with special needs? Are you flexible enough not to be unduly baffled by unexpected situations—and able to deal decisively with them? Are you strong enough to set high expectations, and to enforce rules in a loving but firm way? Above all, are you able to love the people whom God has called you to work with—to love them as you love yourself?

Teachers and learners are on a pilgrimage together, a pilgrimage that focuses on the kingdom of God. To embark on such a pilgrimage, Christian teachers must have clear goals, as described earlier in this book. But more than that, they must ask themselves whether God has called them to go on this particular pilgrimage. "To each one of us grace has been given as Christ has apportioned it" (Ephesians 4:7). If Christ in His grace has given you the primary gifts needed to become a teacher, be grateful and rejoice in a worthy and fulfilling calling. You may still find some classes difficult; in the end, however, the journey will gratify both your students and you. Many experienced teachers say, "I actually get paid for doing what I love doing most!" Their journeys have had an indelible and praiseworthy impact on many of their students, both for this life and for eternity.

If, however, self-analysis or advice from others shows that in one way or another Christ has not given you the grace to be a teacher, be thankful for other gifts. Rejoice in embarking on a different worthwhile and fulfilling vocation. Airline reservation clerks unhappy in their position may affect individual passengers for a few moments. But teachers not suited for teaching often not only become unhappy themselves but each year affect the lives of many students in unpleasant and even harmful ways. They may exasperate children—something Paul warned against (Ephesians 6:4). If you find yourself in such a situation, find another calling—for their sake and for yours.

On your journey of teaching, seek to discover, recognize, understand, and appreciate truth with your pilgrims (Colossians 2:2–8). Practicing obedience to the Truth who holds all creation together (Colossians 1:17) is what ultimately makes teaching such an exceptionally rewarding vocation.

For further reading

An insightful book about the biblical foundations of teaching is David Smith and John Shortt's *The Bible and the Task of Teaching* (Nottingham, UK: The Stapleford Centre, 2002).

Albert E. Greene deals with the foundations of Christian schooling in his *Reclaiming the Future of Christian Education: A Transforming Vision* (Colorado Springs: Purposeful Design, 1998).

Richard Edlin presents a rationale for Christian schooling that highlights the impossibility of religious neutrality in education in *The Cause of Christian Education*, 3rd ed. (Colorado Springs, CO, 2000).

Two books that directly address Christian teaching are John Van Dyk's *The Craft of Christian Teaching* (Sioux Center, IA: Dordt College Press, 2000) and Donovan Graham's *Teaching Redemptively: Bringing Grace and Truth into Your Classroom* (Colorado Springs: Purposeful Design, 2003).

Nicholas Wolterstorff, Professor Emeritus at Yale University, is one of the foremost North American Christian philosophers. A collection of many of his writings and presentations on Christian schooling was published by Baker Books in 2002 under the title *Educating for Life*. Thomas Groome published a volume under the same title (New York: Crossroad Publishing, 1998). Groome discusses schooling within a Catholic theological framework, but he intersects with Wolterstorff when he discusses what it means to teach for biblical justice.

The Association of Christian Schools International has published an edited volume on the biblical, philosophical, psychological, social, and cultural foundations of Christian school education: *Foundations of Christian Education* (2002).

Steppingstones to Curriculum: A Biblical Path, 2nd ed. (Colorado Springs: Purposeful Design, 2002), a companion volume to *Walking with God in the Classroom*, develops the foundation and practice of curriculum in much more depth than does this book.

A book of interest to Christian teachers in public schools is Ronald Anderson's *Religion and Spirituality in the Public School Curriculum* (New York: Peter Lang, 2004).

Parker Palmer has written a bestseller that is rooted in his Quaker faith but is not explicitly Christian: *The Courage to Teach* (San Francisco: Jossey-Bass, 1998). He offers guidelines for creating communities of learning and suggests that only when we know ourselves can we help students develop into whole people who will become lifelong learners.

Magazines for Christian school teachers include *Christian School Education* and *Christian Early Education* (both published quarterly by the Association of

Christian Schools International), *Christian School Teacher* (published three times a year by Christian Schools International), and *Christian Educators Journal* (published quarterly; see www.cejonline.com). *The Journal of Education and Christian Belief* features in-depth articles and is published twice annually (www.jecb.org). *The Journal of Research on Christian Education* provides a forum for research findings about Christian education (www.andrews.edu/jrce).

Bibliography

Aker, D. 1995. *Hitting the mark: Assessment tools for teachers.* Markham, ON: Pembroke.

Anderson, D. 2003. Special education as reconciliation. *Journal of Education and Christian Belief* 7, no. 1:23–35.

Anderson, R. 2004. *Religion and spirituality in the public school curriculum.* New York: Peter Lang.

Angrist, J., and V. Lavy. 2002. New evidence on classroom computers and pupil learning. *The Economic Journal* 112, no. 482:735–65.

Arends, R. 2004. *Learning to teach.* 6th ed. New York: McGraw-Hill.

Armstrong, T. 1987. *In their own way: Discovering and encouraging your child's personal learning style.* Los Angeles: J. P. Tarcher.

Ashraf, S. 1997. The Islamic response: Faith-based education in a multifaith multicultural country. In *Agenda for educational change,* ed. J. Shortt and T. Cooling. Leicester, UK: Apollos, 269–79.

Badley, K. 1996. *Worldviews: The challenge of choice.* Toronto: Irwin Publishing.

Baker, D., and M. Piburn. 1997. *Constructing science in middle and secondary school classrooms.* Boston: Allyn and Bacon.

Barry, C., and F. Tye. 1972. *Running a school.* London: Temple Smith.

Barth, R. 2002. The culture builder. *Educational Leadership* 59, no. 8:6–11.

Blomberg, D. 2007. *Wisdom and curriculum: Christian schooling after postmodernity.* Sioux Center, IA: Dordt College Press.

Bolt, J. 1993. *The Christian story and the Christian school.* Grand Rapids, MI: Christian Schools International.

British Columbia Primary Teachers' Association. 1992. *Evaluation: Techniques and resources,* Book 2. Vancouver: British Columbia Teachers' Association.

British Columbia Teachers' Federation. 2007. *Members' guide to the BC Teachers' Federation 2007–2008.* Vancouver, BC.

Brookhart, S. 2008. Feedback that fits. *Educational Leadership* 65, no. 4:54–59.

Brouwer, E. 2006. Assessment as gift: A vision. In *Educating toward wisdom*, edited by E. Brouwer and R. Koole. Langley, BC: Society of Christian Schools in British Columbia: 2.1–2.2.

Brueggemann. W. 1982. *The creative word: Canon as a model for biblical education*. Philadelphia, PA: Fortress Press.

Burke, K. 2005. *How to assess authentic learning*. 4th ed. Thousand Oaks, CA: Corwin.

California State Board of Education. 1991. *Moral and civic education and teaching about religion*. Rev. ed. Sacramento, CA: California Department of Education.

Coffield, F., D. Moseley, E. Hall, and K. Ecclestone. 2004. *Should we be using learning styles? What research says to practice*. London: Learning and Skills Research Centre.

Coil, C. and D. Merritt. 2001. *Solving the assessment puzzle piece by piece*. Marion, IL: Pieces of Learning.

Cotton, K. 1999. *Research you can use to improve results*. Alexandria, VA: Association for Supervision and Curriculum Development.

Cruickshank, D., D. Bainer Jenkins, and K. Metcalf. 2003. *The act of teaching*. 3rd ed. New York: McGraw-Hill.

Cushner, K. 2003. *Human diversity in action: Developing multicultural competencies for the classroom*. 2nd ed. New York: McGraw-Hill.

Cushner, K., A. McClelland, and P. Safford. 2003. *Human diversity in education: An integrative approach*. 4th ed. New York: McGraw-Hill.

Damon, W. 1993. Teaching as a moral craft and developmental expedition. In *Effective and responsible teaching: The new synthesis*, edited by F. Oser, A. Dick, and J. Patry. San Francisco, CA: Jossey-Bass.

Denig, S. 2004. Multiple intelligences and learning styles: Two complementary dimensions. *Teachers College Record* 106, no. 1:87–95.

Dirks, G. 2007. Religion and public schooling at the Calgary Board of Education: A case study. Session 5-1 in *The Cooperation of Church and State Conference*. Video recording. Ottawa, ON: The Centre for Cultural Renewal.

Douglass, S. 2002. Teaching about religion. *Educational Leadership* 60, no. 2:32–36.

Dovre, P. 2007. From Aristotle to Angelou: Best practices in character education. *Education Next* 7, no. 2:38–45.

Edlin, R. 2000. *The cause of Christian education*. 3rd ed. Colorado Springs, CO: Association of Christian Schools International.

Edmunds, A., and G. Edmunds. 2008. *Special education in Canada*. Toronto: McGraw-Hill Ryerson.

Egan, K. 1983. *Education and psychology: Plato, Piaget, and scientific psychology*. New York: Teachers College Press.

———. 1986. *Teaching as story telling*. London, ON: Althouse.

———. 1997. *The educated mind: How cognitive tools shape our understanding*. Chicago: University of Chicago Press.

Evangelical Fellowship of Canada. 1996. *Diversity and faithfulness: Reflections for Christian teachers on plurality and pluralism in Canadian public schools.* Markham, ON: Evangelical Fellowship of Canada.

Evertson, C., E. Emmer, and M. Worsham. 2006. *Classroom management for elementary teachers.* 7th ed. Saddle River, NJ: Prentice-Hall.

Ferguson, S. 2005. How computers make our kids stupid. *Maclean's* (June 5): 24–30.

Fennema, J. 1977/1995. *Nurturing children in the Lord: A study guide for teachers on developing a biblical approach to discipline.* Sioux Center, IA: Dordt College Press.

Fenwick, T., and J. Parsons. 2000. *The art of evaluation: A handbook for educators and trainers.* Toronto: Thompson.

Fosnot, C. 2005. *Constructivism: Theory, perspectives and practice.* 2nd ed. New York: Teachers College Press.

Fritschy, H., and P. Reedyk. 1985. Work. A teacher resource unit in the *Look around!* series. Langley, BC: Society of Christian Schools in British Columbia.

Fuchs, T., and L. Woessmann. 2004. *Computers and student learning: Bivariate and multivariate evidence on the availability and use of computers at home and at school.* CESifo Working Paper No. 1321. Munich: CESifo.

Gardner, H. 1999. *Intelligence reframed: Multiple intelligences for the 21st century.* New York: Basic Books.

Garner, B. 2007. *Getting to "Got it!" Helping struggling students learn how to learn.* Alexandria, VA: Association for Supervision and Curriculum Development.

Ghosh, R., and A. Abdi. 2004. *Education and the politics of difference: Canadian perspectives.* Toronto, ON: Canadian Scholars' Press.

Giles, T., and A. Proudfoot. 1994. *Educational administration in Canada.* 5th ed. Calgary, AB: Detselig.

Goleman, D. 1995. *Emotional intelligence.* New York: Bantam.

Good, T., and J. Brophy. 2008. *Looking in classrooms.* 10th ed. Boston, MA: Allyn and Bacon.

Goudzwaard, B., M. Vander Vennen, and D. Van Heemst. 2007. *Hope in troubled times: A new vision for confronting global crises.* Grand Rapids, MI: Baker.

Graham, D. 2003. *Teaching redemptively: Bringing grace and truth into your classroom.* Colorado Springs: Purposeful Design.

Groome, T. 1980. *Christian religious education: Sharing our story and vision.* San Francisco, CA: HarperCollins.

———. 1998. *Educating for life: A spiritual vision for every teacher and parent.* New York: Crossroad.

Hargreaves, A., and D. Fink. 2006. *Sustainable leadership.* San Francisco, CA: Jossey-Bass.

Harlan, W. 2007. Formative classroom assessment in science and mathematics. In *Formative classroom assessment,* edited by J. McMillan. New York: Teachers College Press, 116–35.

Hatch, T. 1997. Getting specific about multiple intelligences. *Educational Leadership* 54, no. 6:26–29.

Haynes, C., and O. Thomas. 2001. *Finding common ground: A guide to religious liberty in public schools.* Nashville, TN: First Amendment Center. (Also available at http://www.mediastudies.org/templates/document.asp?documentID=3979.)

Herman, J., P. Aschbacher, and L. Winters. 1992. *A practical guide to alternative assessment.* Alexandria, VA: Association for Supervision and Curriculum Development.

Highet, G. 1950. *The art of teaching.* New York: Random House.

Howard, R., M. Berkowitz, and E. Schaeffer. 2004. Politics of character education. *Educational Policy* 18, no. 1:188–215.

Hunter, M. 1984. Knowing, teaching and supervising. In *Using what we know about teaching,* edited by P. Hosford. Alexandria, VA: Association for Supervision and Curriculum Development.

Jones, V., and L. Jones. 2007. *Comprehensive classroom management: Creating communities of support and solving problems.* 8th ed. Boston, MA: Allyn and Bacon.

Keefe, J. 1988. *Profiling and utilizing learning styles.* Reston, VA: National Association of Secondary School Principals.

Kolb, D. 1984. *Experiential learning: Experience as the source of learning and development.* Englewood Cliffs, NJ: Prentice-Hall.

Koole, R. 1996. *Humanities 8: A resource guide.* Langley, BC: Society of Christian Schools in British Columbia.

———. 2006. Teachers as colleagues: Problematic ideal or genuine reality? In *Educating toward wisdom,* edited by E. Brouwer and R. Koole. Langley, BC: Society of Christian School in British Columbia: 2.31–2.38 (in the "Community" section).

Lewin, L., and B. Shoemaker. 1998. *Great performances: Creating classroom-based assessment tasks.* Alexandria, VA: Association for Supervision and Curriculum Development.

Lewis, C. S. 1943. *The abolition of man.* New York: Macmillan. (Full text available at http://www.columbia.edu/cu/augustine/arch/lewis/abolition1.htm).

Lickona, T. 1991. *Educating for character: How our schools can teach respect and responsibility.* New York: Bantam.

Litke, C. 1996. When violence came to our rural school. *Educational Leadership* 54, no. 1:77–80.

Marzano, R., D. Pickering, and J. Pollock. 2001. *Classroom instruction that works: Research-based strategies for increasing student achievement.* Alexandria, VA: Association for Supervision and Curriculum Development.

McCarthy, B. 1996. *About Learning.* Barrington, IL: Excel.

———. 1997. A tale of four learners: 4MAT's learning styles. *Educational Leadership* 54, no. 6:46–51.

———. 2005. *Teaching around the 4MAT cycle.* Thousand Oaks, CA: Corwin Press.

McCarthy, B., and D. McCarthy. 2005. *Teaching around the 4MAT cycle: Designing instruction for diverse learners with diverse learning styles.* Thousand Oaks, CA: Corwin Press.

McLaren, B. 2004. *A generous orthodoxy.* Grand Rapids, MI: Zondervan.

McMillan, J., ed. 2007. *Formative classroom assessment: Theory into practice.* New York: Columbia Univ., Teachers College Press.

Middleton, J. R. 2005. *The liberating image: The* imago Dei *in Genesis 1.* Grand Rapids, MI: Brazos Press.

Molnar, A., ed. 1997. *The construction of children's character.* 96th Yearbook, Part 2. Chicago: National Society for the Study of Education.

Murray, H., E. Gillese, M. Lennon, P. Mercer, and M. Robinson. 1996. *Ethical principles in university teaching.* North York, ON: Society for Teaching and Learning in Higher Education.

Noddings, N. 1992. *The challenge to care in schools: An alternative approach to education.* New York: Columbia Univ., Teachers College Press.

Nord, W., and C. Haynes. 1998. *Taking religion seriously across the curriculum.* Alexandria, VA: Association for Supervision and Curriculum Development.

Oakes, J., and M. Lipton. 2003. *Teaching to change the world.* 2nd ed. New York: McGraw-Hill.

O'Connor, K. 2002. *How to grade for learning: Linking grades to standards.* 2nd ed. Thousand Oaks, CA: Corwin.

Oppenheimer, T. 2003. *The flickering mind: The false promise of technology in the classroom and how learning can be saved.* New York: Random House.

Ornstein, A. 2003. *Pushing the envelope: Critical issues in education.* Upper Saddle River, NJ: Merrill Prentice Hall.

Palmer, P. 1983. *To know as we are known: A spirituality of education.* San Francisco: Harper & Row.

———. 1999. Evoking the spirit in public education. *Educational Leadership* 56, no. 4:6–11.

Parkay, F., B. Hardcastle Stanford, J. Vaillancourt, and H. Stephens. 2008. *Becoming a teacher.* 3rd Canadian ed. Toronto: Pearson.

Parker, J. 1995. Effective stewardship: A model for teacher education programs in Christian liberal arts colleges. *Faculty Dialogue* 23:177–183.

Phillips, D., ed. 2000. *Constructivism in education: Opinions and second opinions on controversial issues.* Chicago, IL: National Society for the Study of Education.

Porath, M., and D. Matthews. 1997. Development in the social/emotional domain: Critical periods and educational facilitation. Unpublished paper presented at the Canadian Society for Studies in Education, June 12, 1997, St. John's, Newfoundland, Canada.

Postman, N. 1993. *Technopoly: The surrender of culture to technology.* New York: Vintage.

Pudlas, K. 1997. Exceptionality in a communal context. In *The crumbling walls of certainty: Towards a Christian critique of postmodernity and education,* ed. I. Lambert and S. Mitchell. Macquarie Centre, NSW, Australia: Centre for the Study of Australian Christianity.

———. 2007. Head and heart and hands: Necessary elements of inclusive praxis. *ICCTE Journal* 3, no. 1. From www.icctejournal.org. Retrieved December 24, 2007.

———. 2008. Head and heart and hands: Searching for inclusive education. Inaugural full-professor lecture, Trinity Western University. January 31, 2008.

Ridderbos, H. 1962. *The coming of the kingdom*. Phillipsburg, NJ: Presbyterian and Reformed Publishing.

Rosenshine, B., and R. Stevens. 1986. Teaching functions. In *Handbook of research on teaching*, edited by M. C. Wittrock. 3rd ed. New York: Macmillan.

Rothstein-Fisch, C., and E. Trumbull. 2008. *Managing diverse classrooms: How to build on students' cultural strengths*. Alexandria, VA: Association for Supervision and Curriculum Development.

Rubin, L. 1985. *Artistry in teaching*. New York: Random House.

Ryan, K., and K. Bohlin. 1999. *Building character in schools: Practical ways to bring moral instruction to life*. San Francisco, CA: Jossey-Bass.

Seerveld, C. 1980. *Rainbows for a fallen world*. Toronto, ON: Tuppence.

Sheets, R. 2005. *Diversity pedagogy: Examining the role of culture in the teaching-learning process*. Boston, MA: Allyn and Bacon.

Silver, H., R. Strong, and M. Perini. 2000. *So each may learn: Integrating learning styles and multiple intelligences*. Alexandria, VA: Association for Supervision and Curriculum Development.

Smalley, G., and J. Trent. 1990. *The blessing*. New York: Pocket Books.

Smith, D. 2001. The Bible and education: Ways of constructing the relationship. *Themelios* 26, no. 2:29–42.

Steensma, G., and H. Van Brummelen, eds. 1977. *Shaping school curriculum: A biblical view*. Terre Haute, IN: Signal.

Steffe, L., and J. Gale, eds. 1995. *Constructivism in education*. Hillsdale, NJ: Lawrence Erlbaum.

Stiggins, R. 1997. *Student-centered classroom assessment*. 2nd ed. Upper Saddle River, NJ: Merrill.

Stronks, G., and D. Blomberg, eds. 1993. *A vision with a task: Christian schooling for responsive discipleship*. Grand Rapids, MI: Baker.

Teichrieb, L. 2006. Learning from Japan. (unpublished sixth-grade curriculum unit. Langley, BC: Trinity Western University).

Todd, D. 2007. Seeking solid ground in a pluralistic world. *The Vancouver Sun*, November 17: D4.

Tom, A. 1984. *Teaching as a moral craft*. New York: Longman.

Tomlinson, C. 1999. *The differentiated classroom: Responding to the needs of all learners*. Alexandria, VA: Association for Supervision and Curriculum Development.

Van Brummelen, H. 1997. Curriculum development is dead—or is it? *Pro Rege* 26, no. 1:14–23.

———. 2002. *Steppingstones to curriculum: A biblical path*. Colorado Springs: Purposeful Design.

Van Brummelen, H., K. Franklin, M. Hilder. 2005. Creating space for personal meaning in schooling. *ICCTE Journal: Journal of the International Community of Christians in Teacher Education* 1, no. 1. http://www.icctejournal.org/ICCTEJournal/past-issues/volume-1-issue-1.

Van Brummelen, H., R. Koole, and K. Franklin. 2004. Transcending the commonplace: Spirituality in the curriculum. *The Journal of Educational Thought* 38, no. 3:237–54.

Van Dyk, J. 1986–1987. Teaching Christianly: What is it? *Christian Educators' Journal* 26, numbers 1–4.

———. 2000. *The craft of Christian teaching.* Sioux Center, IA: Dordt College Press.

Van Manen, M. 2002. *The tone of teaching.* 2nd ed. London, ON: Althouse.

Vanderhoek, J., ed. 1997. *Learning assistance and special education resource.* Langley, BC: Society of Christian Schools in British Columbia.

Walker, C., and E. Schmidt. 2004. *Smart tests: Teacher-made tests that help students learn.* Markham, ON: Pembroke.

Warnock, M. 1996. The neutral teacher. In *Philosophy of education: Introductory readings,* ed. W. Hare and J. Portelli. 2nd ed. Calgary, AB: Detselig Enterprises, 139–48.

Waterhouse, L. 2006. Multiple intelligences, the Mozart effect, and emotional intelligence: A critical review. *Educational Psychologist* 41, no. 4:207–25.

Webb, S. 2000. *Taking religion to school: Christian theology and secular education.* Grand Rapids, MI: Brazos Press.

Whitehead, A. 1929. *The aims of education and other essays.* New York: Free Press.

Willis, J. 2006. *Research-based strategies to ignite student learning: Insights from a neurologist and classroom teacher.* Alexandria, VA: Association for Supervision and Curriculum Development.

Willis, S. 1993. Learning through service. *Association for Supervision and Curriculum Development Update* 35, no. 6:1–8.

Wolterstorff, N. 1980. *Educating for responsible action.* Grand Rapids, MI: Eerdmans.

———. 2002. *Educating for life: Reflections on Christian teaching and learning.* Grand Rapids, MI: Baker.

Wright, A. 1998. *Spiritual pedagogy: A survey, critique and reconstruction of contemporary spiritual education in England and Wales.* Abingdon, UK: Culham College Institute.

Zwaagstra, M. 2008. Computers in the classroom: Technology overboard? *Frontier Backgrounder: Brief Analysis.* Winnipeg, MB: Frontier Centre for Public Policy.

Index